Cookbooks Worth Collecting

Cookbooks
Worth
Collecting

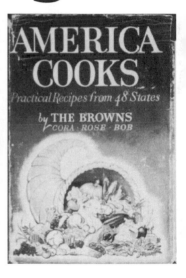

Mary Barile

WALLACE-HOMESTEAD BOOK COMPANY

Radnor, Pennsylvania

Designed by Adrianne Onderdonk Dudden
Manufactured in the United States of America

Library of Congress Cataloging In Publication Data
Barile, Mary.
    Cookbooks worth collecting : the history and lore of notable
cookbooks, with complete bibliographic listings and up-to-date
prices / Mary Barile.
        p.   cm.
    Includes bibliographical references and index.
    ISBN 0-87069-686-6 (pbk.)
    1. Cookery—Collectors and collecting.   2. Cookery—Bibliography.
I. Title.
TX642.B367   1993
641.5—dc20

                                                    93-31761
                                                    CIP

    1 2 3 4 5 6 7 8 9 0   2 1 0 9 8 7 6 5 4

Contents

Part Two: Bibliographic Listings with Prices

Acknowledgments

Obviously, this book would not have made it into any cook's library without the work of hundreds of dealers, collectors, historians, and others who over the years have prepared and issued important sources of research information. So, a tip of the toque to those who cherished cookbooks long before such books earned regard as valuable cultural resources.

For the hard-to-find photos of extremely rare and fragile books, thanks go to the Philadelphia Institute of Art, the American Antiquarian Society, and the Library of Congress photoduplication division. The holdings from personal collections were carefully photographed by Locust Grove Enterprises, Arkville, New York; thanks to Brian Sweeney for being so patient and meeting every deadline with time to spare.

Special thanks are also due to the American Library Association for suggestions and assistance in tracking down materials appropriate to the nonprofessional book lover; the Sluiter Agency, Margaretville, New York, for insurance information; Hofstra University for its excellent programs in antiques appraisals; Swann Galleries for auction information; Naomi Weiss and the Fairview Public Library, Margaretville, New York, for locating out-of-print and rare source materials; and the Culinary Institute of America for providing cookbook people with an excellent library and outstanding staff.

Thanks, also, to the two collectors who, although wishing to remain anonymous, allowed their ephemera collections and books to be used with a lavish hand.

And a final, heartfelt thank you must go to the following supporters, who cheerfully read, reread, commented on, and listened to everything from recipes for lima bean and bourbon cake to toad ointment: Margaret and Joseph Barile; Joan and Lou Toupin; Danny McGrath; Mary Woodman; and Betty Zirinsky.

Part One

The Collectible
Cookbook

1 | Getting Started

The Collector and the Cookbook

It always seems easy enough for someone to define what it is he or she collects—the words "mechanical banks," "stenciled chairs," "cookie cutters," and "cookbooks" all bring to mind identifiable, concrete items. But, of course, it is never that simple, since chairs come in many colors, cookie cutters come in many shapes, and cookbooks come in many subjects.

Cookbooks, probably more so than other categories of collectible books, have often been confined to the dusty shelves of used book dealers or jumble sale tables. Sometimes an unusual example from an earlier century will cause a flurry of action at an auction, particularly among serious collectors, but it is fairly uncommon for anyone to jump in and buy an American cookbook strictly for its social history or art design.

Most book buyers purchase a book because of the emotional response it elicits from the reader. A cookbook collector's favorite purchase is often-times a book bought because it was mother's standby or because the collector remembers fondly the cookies an aunt used to bake from a recipe found in the pages. This is not to say that cookbook collectors have failed to develop carefully selected, fine collections over the last century— Katherine Bitting, Esther Aresty, and Elizabeth Robins Pennell are only a few of the forward-thinking collectors whose libraries dispute that idea. But as a whole, cookbook collectors have been a quiet group, working on their own and then, like the above ladies or, more recently, Julia Child, Louis Szathmary, and James Beard, donating their now-important collections to libraries for scholarly use or plain enjoyment by thankful readers and browsers.

The value of these culinary books as sources of food, comfort, and plain good living was remarked upon in the *Belgian Relief Cookbook* (Figure 1-1), a fund-raising book published in 1915 in Pennsylvania. In this book, well-known celebrities shared their favorite recipes and their hopes for world peace, and also showed their strong support for cookbooks. Author Gene Stratton-Porter stated in the book that "There is nothing in life of which I am prouder than the ability to go into my kitchen and cook an appetizing, properly balanced meal." The producer David Belasco waxed as nostalgic as a Broadway romance, saying, "When heaven's last roll call is sounded, the best cooks of this earth should be given the choicest places. A good dinner eaten before seeing a good play makes the path of the dramatist smooth and rosy. Cooking is the foundation stone upon which the home life rests. I cherish some very tender memories of my dear mother making my favorite dishes." But it was Frances Starr who made a ringing defense of the cookbook which still holds true: "The Cook Book! Our most valuable literature! Men have done great things while starving, but not for long! Those who contribute to the wealth and progress of the world, whether in science, art or labor must be unconscious of the physical machine, and that is possible only through good health, and this is possible only through good cooking. As we are all not 'born' cooks, we can 'acquire' the art and gratefully thank Heaven for The Cook Book."

Fig. 1-1 Collectors fond of charity cookbooks should watch for a copy of the *Belgian Relief Cook Book,* issued in 1915 to aid victims of World War I. As with many other fund-raising cookbooks, the editors sought out celebrities for their recipes and thoughts, and readers will find selections from James Montgomery Flagg (of Uncle Sam fame) and novelist Jack London. The book itself was unusual; instead of the usual binding style, the pages flip up on two rings. The cover was designed to resemble the Belgian flag; this example shows wear but is still in good condition.

Why Collect Cookbooks?

People who love food often say that they read cookbooks the way other people read good novels, or that they use cookbooks as unique travel guides to unfamiliar culinary centers, from Tibet to Madagascar, Brooklyn to Seattle. But no matter how much someone loves cookbooks, it seems that cookbook collections form themselves, without benefit of human assistance. One day, a cook has several cookbooks on a single shelf; not long after, many shelves are needed to hold the accumulation.

One of the important benefits of assembling a cookbook library is getting a well-rounded perspective on a favorite subject. While an individual book states an individual viewpoint—for example, a method for making a stew or directions for turning out the perfect quiche—a collection of books brings together many ideas and in doing so offers an overview of a subject, along with theories and aspects that a reader might never have thought of had he or she read only a single book. One book containing suburban recipes from the 1960s might give the idea that all American women were white, played bridge, lived in upper-middle-class neighborhoods, and attended the same church. But twenty titles forming a collection from the same era could include cookbooks by African-American church groups, Jewish philanthropy organizations, single women, and people on a budget. Books in the style of how-to-feed-your-family-on-$2-a-day can provide balance and contrast to the kind of suburban mainstream cookbook mentioned earlier.

Putting together a cookbook collection can be an intriguing, fun-filled challenge that takes years of searching for, buying, and evaluating cookbooks. Skill, luck, study, and even serendipity all enter into the chase, which can bring together people from different backgrounds and widely varying tastes and make equals of the highest chef and the plainest cake salesclerk. But for collectors both new and old, for the experienced buyer and the novice, there are guidelines and definitions that need to be understood in order to create and maintain a cookbook collection which will not only provide enjoyment but will also bring a wider understanding to the study of America's culinary and social history.

Just what are cookbooks and why should they even be collected? How can a bunch of directions for making food change the way a collector looks at history? Since their earliest appearances in ancient days, cookbooks have provided people a place in which to record and share tastes and opinions. The books can be eccentric, nostalgic, instructive, and even erotic. In their simplest form, cookbooks consist of collections of recipes meant to guide the cook through the preparation of food. The recipe directions may be as simple as a line or two, or they may be very detailed and complete, with illustrations, say, for rolling out a pie dough or carving a fowl. The book may contain suggestions for serving dinner, for entertaining guests, for storing and preserving food, and even for first aid measures and etiquette, depending upon

Fig. 1-2 The advent of ladies' newspaper advice and home columns helped create an audience for cookbooks, a trend that has continued to the present. In this 1908 example, the recipes were not selected from the reading audience. The book itself was printed on inexpensive paper that has turned brittle with age, while the cover shows use and yellowing; however, the illustrations are vibrant, and the recipes ("Brunswick Stew is made from the large Southern gray squirrels") seem to indicate the wide variety of unusual foods available at city green markets and shops.

Fig. 1-3 Entertainment books like *Fairs & Fetes* can add depth to a cookbook collection, showing how food was used at various social occasions. The cover depicts two ladies enjoying a bowl of punch at a late summer's fair, while in the background a soda booth does a brisk business. Directions are given for organizing fairs based on such varied topics as dolls, *The House of Seven Gables,* peddlers, and Jack Frost's house. Many of these books focus on parties for children, and some of the old-fashioned amusements reflect the changes in both food and safety concerns; in the game of snapdragon, raisins were set alight with brandy, and the children were encouraged to snatch them out of the fire.

the era in which the book was published. Some cookbooks presented essay-style recipes that indicated a great deal about the author's taste and character. Other cookbooks were scientific views of food and diets. Handwritten cookbooks usually include notations from the owner and comments on the recipes, while charity or fund-raising cookbooks recorded an organization's membership and personal culinary tastes. Cookbooks from the eighteenth and nineteenth centuries are rare sources of information on everyday life in America, at a time when few people recorded what the middle-class woman was doing with her days. To read a cookbook from any era is to discover the varying philosophies that affected daily life: the trends, the fads, the development of scientific rules for healthy diets, even the religious beliefs that found their way into the story of American food. After all, the household was the source of family pride and the center of a woman's world; and a cookbook is one key to discovering how people ate, thought, behaved, and aspired.

When you collect cookbooks, you step back into the kitchens of the past. You get to peer over the shoulder of an eighteenth-century cook who is milking her cow into the bowl in which she will make a frothy syllabub. You stand beside a baker in the 1850s as she pummels her rye and injun bread into shape. You gain a sense of the bounty of America's larders in the 1890s, when barrels of oysters were stewed up for an election day dinner, and entire cows were roasted at a western shindig. As a collector, through the magic of photographs and illustrations, you can even sit down to dinner with people long gone, or learn how to properly cook for an engagement dinner or informal house party in the country. You have the unique capacity for exploring the daily lives of America's people—not the Vanderbilts or the Washingtons or the Astors, but the Smiths, the Browns, and the millions of other unrecorded women who had little attention paid to them, except in their roles as mothers, housewives, and cooks. Cookbooks are one of the few detailed sources available to collectors that chronicle everyday life and tastes from the seventeenth century to the present. These books are finally taking a well-deserved place as rich research sources. That so many early books have been preserved for use and study is due to the foresight of a few serious collectors and unnumbered cooks who cherished their libraries and, in doing so, maintained a direct link with our culinary past.

For the modern collector, the choice in cookbooks is so varied regarding the type of books and price range that the field remains one of the most accessible to the beginner. The selection of books on the market can range from carefully handwritten "receipt" books to elaborate picture cookbooks and landmarks in culinary history. The latter might include a 1796 edition of *American Cookery,* the first cookbook to consider American foods like johnnycakes, cranberries, and pumpkins—which could cost a collector several thousand dollars—or the *Tollhouse Cookbook* (Figure 1-4), which offered twentieth-century cooks the first recipe for chocolate chip cookies and can be found, with a little luck, for only a few dollars.

Collectors might concentrate on fund-raising or charity cookbooks with hometown offerings from Baptist churches, Mennonite groups, or famous contributors. Or a collector could build a library around books from a limited time period, like the 1890s; or books with certain types of illustrations (the pop art styles of the 1970s are interesting and still affordable); or books from

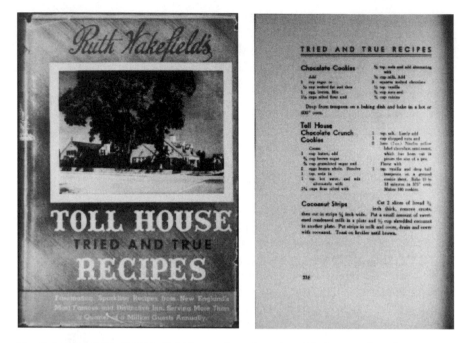

Fig. 1-4 Little did Ruth Wakefield know that when she added cut up chocolate chunks to a cookie dough she was creating a classic at the Toll House Inn. Her cookbook first appeared in 1936 without the cookie recipe, but by 1940 the Nestlé chocolate company had spread the cookie's fame far and wide and readers could find "Toll House Chocolate Crunch Cookies" on page 216 (modern bakers call them chocolate chip cookies). Although the dust jacket of the the copy pictured shows wear, this book is special because it was signed and dated by the author.

a particular era, like the Great Depression or World War II; or books which contain particular types of recipes, like cakes, cookies, or herbal teas. A chef who is interested in finding unusual recipes may collect cookbooks from exotic countries; a home cook who enjoys baking cakes may look for advertising leaflets from the 1950s; a food historian may decide to concentrate on charity cookbooks from African-American churches; an armchair travel buff may collect books that tell about a country's traditions as well as the food. The cookbook selections are virtually endless: cookbooks come in second next to the Bible in terms of number of books published. And the prices still range from under a dollar to perhaps several thousand dollars, putting the field of cookbook collecting in the unusual position of allowing beginners as well as advanced collectors a chance to assemble a collection which might become a valuable resource.

The books themselves may vary in style from a sophisticated essay on the new cuisines, to a down-homey, no-nonsense approach to making apple pie. We collect cookbooks for the information they provide about life and

Fig. 1-5 Louise Andrews Kent was a novelist who created the indomitable Mrs. Appleyard, a New England cook full of sly humor and great recipes ("Ladies are generally on a diet. They would faint at the sight of a baked potato but they can always eat cream"). Several books appeared in the Appleyard series, and all are eagerly sought after by collectors. This 1942 example has its colorful dust jacket intact.

food, as well as for the recipes, and even if a collector never puts a pot on the stove, he or she can enjoy cookbooks from a social or literary point of view.

Deciding What to Collect

Cookbook lovers should consider that a focused collection will not only increase the value of the books overall but will also provide a comprehensive view of a specific subject. There are several "styles" or collecting philosophies that you might want to think about before—or while—assembling a collection. Some people consider themselves to be "serious" collectors: they attend upscale book auctions, subscribe to cookbook catalogs, do extensive research on their holdings (including the preparation of bibliographies), and are in touch with other collectors the world over. Often these collectors seek to purchase only the best and sometimes the rarest cookbooks for their libraries, although they can take as much delight in a first edition book from the 1950s as in one from the 1780s. Other collectors collect on a more informal basis, picking up books at yard sales, at house auctions, or from other collectors, sometimes limiting their purchases to a certain price and under. A rare few buy for investment purposes, when money is no object and a $3,000 cookbook is looked upon as something as solid as a good stock or piece of furniture. There is no completely right or wrong way to collect; in fact, the best collector probably combines the various styles, looking for the best cookbook at the best available price with the hope that the collection will increase in value over the years—and all the while enjoying the delights that each book has to offer both the mind and the eye.

One debate that is often heard in the world of collecting—whether the focus is fine jewelry, prints, or cookbooks—revolves around whether a collection should be assembled for its value or for its interest. Some cookbook collectors argue that anyone who buys strictly for investment purposes is not a collector. According to these collectors, cookbooks should be collected above all for the joy they bring to the reader, as well as for the information they record about everyday domestic and culinary life; collectors, the argument goes, should buy only what they like and need, paying little attention to future book values, which could vary wildly or lead to a collection that is missing other, important elements just because they don't fit into the dollar value factor. While collecting for the joy of it is important, however, collectors would be foolish if they ignored the fact that a collection may increase in value; it's nothing to be ashamed of, and it needs to be thought about in the event a collection is to be sold, donated to a library, or passed along to heirs (see Chapter 7).

A well-rounded cookbook collection often includes selections of ephemera and cookbook-related materials, which can add a deeper dimension to a library. Since many early cookbooks did not come with color illustrations, the advertising leaflets and brochures of the late nineteenth and early twentieth centuries offer bright, if sometimes garish, views of what kitchens and food looked like at the time. Ephemera (a word meaning "things that are short-lived") refers here to paper collectibles that are related to cookbooks: advertising leaflets, recipe cards, cookbook leaflets, and even some menus, especially those commemorating special dinners or gatherings. As transient as ephemera was meant to be, it has found a audience both in and out of the world of collectible cookbooks, and collectors will, unfortunately, have to compete with non-cookbook people for these colorful selections of the printer's art.

The term "cookbook-related materials" is more difficult to define, although the books which appear under this heading may include those concerning the history of the kitchen or of cooking or of foods; etiquette and behavior books, which were heavily weighted toward the proper way to eat; seed catalogs, with their informative pictures of what recipe ingredients actually looked like; and books about houses or gardens, which often contain pertinent historical information about how a cook designed her workspace or planted her herbal borders and flower beds. The collector needs to be somewhat of a detective when locating these books since they may appear under listings for "etiquette," "domestic arts," "floriculture," "farming," and "medicine," but the search can be half the fun, and the result can be an extended library which helps the cookbooks come alive in their historic perspective.

Terms Used by Book Collectors

A beginning collector is not always a person with only a book or two; it can be someone with a thousand books who is not aware of booksellers' terminology, collection care, or the other sometimes abstruse trappings of collecting. Even the serious cookbook collector may feel uncomfortable talking about wraps, frontispieces, or book condition, no matter how well-versed he or she is in the history of food or printing. Don't let the terms of collecting frighten you from the field—book collecting takes discipline, perserverence, study, and luck. Add a little fun to the hunt for that favorite book, and you've got the ingredients for creating a culinary bibliophile. Just remember that cookbook collecting draws much of its vocabulary from the world of general book collecting, with a twist or two to keep things interesting, and that although definitions are helpful, they are usually open to interpretation by the experts.

Collectors will eventually be asked if they are interested in rare books, out-of-print books, scarce books, or antique books. "Rare" has been defined as "important, desirable and hard to get"; "out of print" means the book is no longer being printed by the publisher and generally refers to more recent or modern books; "antique" books are generally more than 100 years old; "scarce" books can be out-of-print or rare. Describing an old cookbook takes practice and care, and it is still pretty much a subjective art. An "edition" refers to the printing of a book from one setup of type; a different edition occurs when the type is reset or changes are made in the text or design or actual printing method.

First editions are generally held to be the first appearance of a book in print, but first editions are not easy to identify or even to define accurately. The first printing of a book is called the first issue of the first edition, and there are no hard-and-fast rules for determining whether a book is the first edition. Publishers, especially modern ones, sometimes note on the copyright page the edition and the number of books in print. Other publishers indicate that a book is a later edition, thus eliminating the possibility of its being a first. Still other companies show an edition by a series of letters or numbers, which, unfortunately, have varied with the individual publishers' methods through the years.

Some nineteenth-century cookbooks contain introductions in which the author says that due to the popularity of an earlier book, a new edition was required. In other words, it is often simpler for a collector to look for clues that a book is a later edition than to try to prove that the book is a first edition. Often, the determination can only be made by researching the publishing history of the book and comparing the book with a known first edition. A first edition of Fannie Farmer's *Boston Cooking-School Cookbook* may bring fifty times what a much later edition will command. Beginning collectors need to understand that a famous title on a book does not by itself guarantee worth; it only provides a way of identifying the item more easily. A general rule of thumb for collectors, however, is that the earliest edition of a book is more valuable than later editions.

Why should an edition make such a difference to a collector? Why have entire books been written about first editions, and why do certain collectors turn their culinary noses up at anything less than a "first?" For some collectors, the thrill of a first edition is simply the thrill of holding a book that existed at the same time as its author. When they read Miss Eliza Leslie's words in *Miss Leslie's New Cookery Book*—"I hope those who consult this book will find themselves at no loss, whether required to prepare sumptuous viands 'for company' or to furnish a daily supply of nice dishes for an excellent family table or plain, yet wholesome and palatable food where economy is very expedient"—collectors of first editions of the book may well feel that they are getting a firsthand taste of antebellum American food. In many cookbooks, particularly those by popular authors long gone, like Fannie Farmer and Irma Rombauer, later editors (or, sometimes, plagiarists) changed the recipes, illustrations, and descriptive material in order to update the recipes or add a "modernizing" touch; this resulted in text that bears little resemblance to the *original*. So a first edition brings the reader back to the point where the cookbook really reflected the spirit and style of the times, when new theories, ideas, and products—from Graham crackers to microwaves—made their appearance.

Over the years, some book publishers noticed that certain cookbooks kept on selling and that some important research materials and books were out of print and unavailable to scholars or serious collectors; thus, the publishers issued reprints. These have proven a blessing to the world of cookbooks. Finally, rare cookbooks like Amelia Simmons's *American Cookery* or "a Boston housekeeper's" *The Cook's Own Book* are available to cooks and culinary historians for a few dollars, instead of a few hundred or more. But again, the collector, and particularly the beginner, should realize that while a reproduction of a cookbook, like those in the Cookery Americana series from Louis Szathmary, is important, a reproduction does not have the same value as an original. The nineteenth-century edition of *The Cook's Own Book* (Figure 1-6) may command several hundred dollars on the market; the twentieth-century reproduction may cost $20 or less. Obviously, the book that brings a sense of history to a collection is the earlier one; the book for reference or daily use is the later edition. Reprints can provide a fascinating window into the tastes of the past without the need of buying a book in poor condition at a high price or of using a rare, fragile book more than is necessary. "Limited editions" are usually cookbooks that have had a restricted number printed; sometimes the books are numbered and signed, or have a certain type of binding or illustrations.

Condition is another problem in book collecting, and particularly with cookbooks. Since cookbooks belonged in the kitchen, the books were prone to accidents and environmental problems not faced by other paper collectibles. Flour, grease, water, sugar, batter—all could stain cookbooks, and at the same time increase the chance of vermin and insect damage. Cookbooks

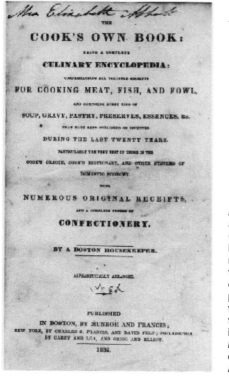

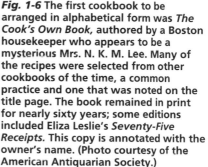

Fig. 1-6 The first cookbook to be arranged in alphabetical form was *The Cook's Own Book,* authored by a Boston housekeeper who appears to be a mysterious Mrs. N. K. M. Lee. Many of the recipes were selected from other cookbooks of the time, a common practice and one that was noted on the title page. The book remained in print for nearly sixty years; some editions included Eliza Leslie's *Seventy-Five Receipts.* This copy is annotated with the owner's name. (Photo courtesy of the American Antiquarian Society.)

were meant to be used and enjoyed. A cookbook's unique function as' a reference book for the kitchen rather than the library presents a special challenge to the collector.

Book dealers and buyers use specific terms to define the condition of their books, although these terms are subjective and open to interpretation by buyer and seller alike. "Mint" is used to describe a book that is just as it was when it was newly printed: no pencil or ink marks, no bookplates, a dust jacket in perfect condition, no price tags or markings, crisp pages, an uncracked spine, and even a clean smell. Unfortunately, the older the cookbook, the smaller the chance of finding a copy in mint condition (unless by chance some books were warehoused and forgotten by the publisher). "Fine" condition implies little wear, with the book looking nearly brand new. "Very good" books may show slight wear to the dust jacket (the separate paper covering), but the pages, permanent cover, and spine must be clean and without obvious signs of use. "Good" is the condition that describes many collectible cookbooks: there are indications that the book has been used, but the pages and cover are intact, the illustrations are present, but the dust jacket may be worn or not present at all. The majority of used and old books listed in catalogs are usually described as being in good condition.

Books that do not achieve one of the previously listed ratings fall into one of several other condition categories. "Fair" alerts the buyer to the fact that the book has been used and shows the use. Although the book is complete, there may be repaired pages or slight tears or folds, the cover may appear worn, the dust jacket may be in tatters or missing, and the edges of the cover may be "bumped" (slightly dented). There is nothing wrong with owning or buying a book in fair condition, but you should not expect to pay top dollar for the book unless it is a rare example. "Poor" is easy to recognize: the book has torn or loose or missing pages, writing in the margins, chipped page edges or torn corners (where someone dog-eared the page), cooking stains, and perhaps even a squashed insect or two inside. A book in poor condition may also be described as a "reading copy." That is all the book is good for—reading or reference. It usually has the complete text, but it may not be considered a strong addition to your library or even a book that will increase in value over the years. "Disbound" indicates a complete book that needs to be rebound; if the cost of the book is low enough and if the book is of value to the buyer, having it rebound will make it usable once again. A book that is described as "ex-library," that is, one which has been deaccessioned from a public or private library, must be described as such, and the book may have a library stamp, card pockets, dog-eared pages, or a heavy library binding. This is a book to buy if you don't think you'll ever find another copy of the cookbook, but it is usually not aesthetically attractive or in good condition.

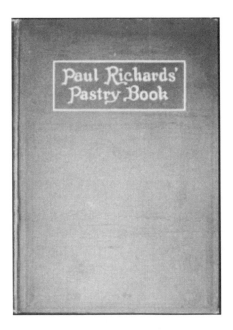

Fig. 1-7 The Hotel Monthly Press specialized in books for the cooking trade and offered a wide range of titles, including *The Lunch Room, The Bell-Boy's Guide,* and *Paul Richards' Pastry Book* (1907). Paul Richards was, according to the book, "one of the most skillful all around bakers, pastry cooks and confectioners in America." The series offers modern collectors a look behind the scenes at the workings of hotels, tearooms, and other public food centers at the turn of the century. This example is in fair condition, with bumps to the four corners and slight waterstains at the top edge of the cover.

Fig. 1-8 For people in our modern society used to enjoying ice cream at home or sampling dozens of flavors at the shopping mall stand, *The American Soda Book* is an introduction to the art of ice cream and soda fountain treats unknown today. Starting in 1863, various editions of the book were issued by the American Soda Fountain Company of Boston. The text contained detailed directions for setting up and running a soda fountain, while black-and-white illustrations depicted the elaborate marble dispensaries and equipment used by soda jerks to create more than 1,000 different desserts and beverages. The book's cover shows what appears to be a leaded lampshade above soda dispensers. With loose interior pages and a bumped cover, the book pictured is in poor condition, but it represents an important source for collectors interested in ice cream and social refreshments.

Fig. 1-9 A cookbook collector sometimes has to decide whether the book he or she is considering for purchase is a reprint of an earlier publication. In the case of *Blue Ribbon Recipes: County Fair Winners,* the book is a reprint offered in 1968 by the Cookbook Collectors Library of the Favorite Recipes Press, a company that brought out-of-print cookbooks back onto the market. The colorful cover is not a dust jacket—the design was printed directly onto the hardcover itself. Reprints are valuable since they offer the collector a chance to obtain books that would ordinarily be too expensive or difficult to locate. However, since the books are rarely reprinted from the original photos and type, they can lose a lot when it comes to clarity in photos and text. (Note that this book has nothing to do with *The State Fair Blue Ribbon Cook Book.*)

Always try to buy a book in the best condition you can find or afford. But if you need a book to fill a gap in your collection, or if a book is so scarce that it rarely comes on the market in any condition, don't hesitate to buy it just because its condition does not meet your standards; you can trade or buy up to a better example at a later time. One fortunate fact about cookbooks: few, if any, American cookbooks have been faked or altered for profit (such as having missing pages added from another copy), so the collector does not have to worry about deciding whether a book is an original or a fake. What a beginner should be aware of is whether the book is a reproduction (fairly easy to notice) or a later edition being sold as a first (a little more tricky), but after becoming familiar with the types of cookbooks you are collecting, even these identifications will be easy to make.

Reading and Interpreting Catalogs

Many of the terms used in describing cookbooks have to do with the physical parts of the book, and reading a dealer's or auction catalog can take some practice. The "binding" is the outside covering of the book; it can consist of leather (sometimes called "calf"), cloth, or heavy paper. A catalog or booklist will note when a cover has become detached from the binding, or if it has been taped back into place or repaired in any way. "Wrappers" are heavy paper covers, sometimes decorated or colorfully printed; some dealers use the term "card covers." "Dust jackets" are used to protect bindings; the jackets often receive heavy wear and are torn or soiled, so a cookbook with a good dust jacket may command a higher price. The "spine" of the book, also referred to as the "backbone," serves to hold the covers to the book; it may also be stamped with the book's title and author's name or embossed with a design. "Perfect bound" refers to a book in which the pages have been glued to the binding, as opposed to being sewn together in groups of pages called "signatures"; unfortunately, perfect bound cookbooks defy their names and often fall apart if forced to lie flat. Sometimes the term "saddle-stitching" is used to refer to books that were sewn together in the center; it may also describe books that have been stapled together in the center. Cookbooks also use "comb binding," the plastic or wire spirals that were (and still are) popular with charity and fund-raising cookbooks. Some early comb bindings have become brittle with age, and the "teeth" have broken or bent.

"Inner hinge" refers to the section of the book where the covers are joined to the book; many times, a hinge has "cracked," a term which describes the slitting of the paper (the "endpaper") along the hinge's length. This may weaken the book, and cause the condition rating to drop from good to fair (or less). The outside "joint," where the cover joins the spine, may also split or crack, a problem that can require rebinding. When a book dealer indicates that a copy is "tight," he or she refers to the fact that the hinges and bindings are strong and the pages have not loosened. An "endpaper" attaches the inside cover to the book's body and may be decorated or plain; a "free endpaper" is a blank sheet that is not pasted to the book. Cookbooks also appear in manuscript (handwritten) form, which can be abbreviated "ms."

Illustrations in cookbooks vary with their age. Earlier books boasted engravings (Paul Revere did one on carving fowl); later books offered photographs or colored illustrations, and, if the book itself was not illustrated, there were sometimes advertisements which contained line drawings of everything from stoves to cherry pitters. Illustrations and advertisements should be noted in a book's description. In the case of charity cookbooks, the word "signed" in a catalog description indicates that recipes bear the names of the contributors, and "signed" recipes can include those from famous cooks, like First Lady Eleanor Roosevelt, as well as from the everyday family cook.

"Waterstains" may be used to describe damage that occurred as a result of a book's getting wet or damp—perhaps the cook spilled a cup of water on the pages, or the book was stored in a basement (which can also mean mold problems.) Slight waterstains to a cover may not affect a book's value

Fig. 1-10 The White House and its inhabitants always interested the average American, and the "first kitchen" received its due attention as well. First Ladies were often asked to submit recipes to charity cookbooks, and chefs who served in the White House authored cookbooks of their own. The Kennedys were known for the French elegance of their table, while Lyndon Johnson emphasized his Texas roots with huge barbecues. Caterer Walter Jetton penned his history of barbecues and the favorite recipes of LBJ in 1965. Not all books first appeared in hardcover; some titles appeared only in a paperback edition, which may make it difficult to locate a book in good condition. This example was signed by the author.

significantly, but the pages, text, and illustrations should never have damage of this type, which can cause warping, rotting, and distortion of the book. Also included in a damage description may be the word "foxing," denoting a rusty stain on a book's pages caused by chemical reactions (iron salts within the paper fibers actually rust and cause the distinctive reddish coloring). Correction of foxing is expensive and time-consuming, and it needs to be handled by an expert. Sometimes with older cookbooks, particularly those from the nineteenth century or earlier, it is nearly impossible to find an example that does not suffer from foxing because of the type of paper used in the book. If there are limited foxing marks and the rest of the cookbook is in generally good condition, a collector may be wise purchase it, especially if he or she is unsure about locating a better example. However, the foxing may continue to develop, especially if improper storage conditions exist.

Other damage that may be described includes general staining (with cookbooks, this is sometimes from cooking ingredients), wormholes, tape repairs (which do even more damage to a book than the original problem), and loosened or missing covers. The latter often occurs with charity cookbooks or advertising samples from the nineteenth century, a time when the covers were stapled in place or the cover paper or "stock" itself was flimsy. The spine of the book may also show wear at the top or bottom (sometimes described as "missing an inch of spine" or "torn spine") because the user pulled the book from the shelf by grabbing it by the spine edges.

Different dealers use various ways of describing a book in a catalog or booklist. Some note the basics only, such as the title, author, publisher, date, and price, while others offer more complete information, including edition, number of pages, type of binding, a comment on the book, recipe examples, and detailed condition descriptions. If the book belonged to a celebrity, or the author herself, or if the book was signed by the author, this will be noted and, depending upon the author, will probably increase the price of the book. If the ownership of a cookbook is described (for example, "originally from the library of Mrs. Famous Author, dated 1815; consigned for sale by her son") this is known as the book's "provenance," or history.

Cookbook dealers may also cite from several bibliographies about cookbooks, so a description might contain a notation like "Lowenstein 771," or "Not in Bitting." The Lowenstein bibliography lists books chronologically and by number, so a reader can look up the book numbered 771. In the second example, the book did not appear in *The Gastronomic Bibliography*, by Katherine Bitting; thus, "not in Bitting." The bibliographies used in preparing the catalog are usually listed, in order that a potential buyer may check the publishing history of the book more fully. It is unfortunate that many of these bibliographies are out of print and are costly when they do turn up on the market, but a library can usually obtain copies at a user's request. If you are serious about collecting, then assembling a reference library along with your cookbook library makes sense, but if you are collecting inexpensive books for

Fig. 1-11 One baking cookbook that turns up frequently is *All About Home Baking,* first issued in 1933 by General Foods. The book sold for 25¢ and was filled with detailed photographs of baked goods in all stages of production. The example pictured was found in very good condition and even contained the original order blank so that the baker could order more copies for her friends.

the fun of it, you may decide to spend your money on cookbooks instead. (A list of cookbook bibliographies appears in the Bibliography at the end of this book.)

When dealers use the traditional method of noting the size (or "format") of a book, the measurements can be confusing, based as they were on the old printing methods of folding a large sheet of paper in order to create a series of smaller pages. The following height sizes are *approximate,* as the measurements can vary by an inch or more (the abbreviation is noted in parenthesis): sextodecimo (16mo), 5 inches; duodecimo (12mo), 6 to 7 inches (the size of a paperback novel); octavo (8vo), 8 to 9 inches, the size of a common hardcover novel; quarto (4to), 11 to 12 inches; folio (F), up to 18 inches or larger (sometimes called "coffee table books").

The catalogs that you receive from dealers are themselves valuable price and history resources. Many dealers who issue catalogs take the time to research the material so collectors can refer to the listings over and over again for bibliographic information and price history. If you are trying to evaluate your own collection, catalogs will give you an idea of what some people are paying for specific books or what the replacement value of a book is (what you would have to pay in order to replace a book in your collection).

How to Use This Book

As the interest in collectible cookbooks grows, so does the need for information which considers the books as more than plain recipe collections. Today, a collector can assemble a cookbook library for hundreds of dollars or hundreds of thousands of dollars; unlike many collectibles, the cookbook field still has good buys and excellent prospects for collection development. Is there a chance that a collector may stumble upon a rare eighteenth-century book at a yard sale? Yes. Are general book dealers as well-versed in cookbooks as they are in other American publications? Not as well as they should be, so prices can vary widely from one bookstore to the next. The joy of cookbooks is that there are so many already published, and so many more to come, that nearly anyone can become a collector without having to remortgage the house.

This book provides an introduction to cookbooks through their history, art, and recipes, and it is hoped that both the advanced book collector and the novice will be able to satisfy their interest in the following chapters. This book is also intended for use as a price guide, and since price listings, be they for wicker, postcards, or quilts, seem to inflame the passions of collectors everywhere, some points of explanation are perhaps required.

Assigning value to any collectible item is akin to stepping into a hornet's nest of dealers, collectors, and other price guide authors who disagree with you, only to leave the nest and discover that there are just as many readers who *agree* with your evaluations. *Cookbooks Worth Collecting* is a guide and just that: it offers a suggested value for a book based on the current book market and on personal experience. As a whole, cookbook values have not settled into well-defined categories like those used for Depression glass or Tiffany lamps, nor have the books attained standard prices in different areas of the country, even when evaluated by the same "level" of collectors or dealers. The prices found in this book reflect prices 1) offered by cookbook and related subject dealers across the United States; 2) paid at auction; and 3) found during visits to hundreds of book dealers, shops, and antiquarian book shows in the United States. It is important to understand that these prices, for the most part, indicate the experiences of people who are familiar with cookbooks, not those of general antiques dealers or bookshops where the proprietor's interest may lie in the literary, rather than the culinary, field. The prices are also based on the author's experience as a collector, dealer, and writer in the antiquarian cookbook field.

Any cookbook value is more than a specific number. It also contains such widely diverse and sometimes subjective considerations as whether the buyer is purchasing a cookbook printed in her town in 1920 (because the book was produced locally, the collector might spend more for it than would a collector in another part of the country); whether the buyer is on a budget; whether the book contains information or artwork that a particular buyer is desperate to own; whether the book is common on the market or is decidedly rare or very popular; and even whether one collector's evaluation of "good" condition is another collector's "poor" condition. Of course, some cookbook and ephemera prices have become more or less settled, as is the case with a first edition *Betty Crocker Cookbook,* which is not usually sold for under $30, or with good nineteenth-century examples of any cookbook, which rarely appear for less than $75.

Cookbook buyers need to use common sense when it comes to weighing the fairness of a price: if you see several copies of *What Cooks in Suburbia* for $15 in a variety of catalogs and then spot the book for $45 at a book fair, you may decide that the book has been overpriced (then again, the dealer may be using a specific price source, so ask!). Will a collector be able to find books for less than the prices listed here? Of course, and he or she will also find that some books are just not to be had for less than twice the price listed. Just remember that condition and value are subjective, no matter which price guide you use. The books noted in the pricing section of this book include a few entries which are infrequently found on the market; they are listed to give some sense of their rarity. Still, the majority of books, leaflets, and other ephemera discussed and listed herein are accessible to the collector of generally modest means. The author also believes that, with the exception of items in exceedingly poor condition, all culinary collectibles have an intrinsic value, whether it is based on monetary or historic considerations. Gone are the days in the antiques world when smaller items were junked at auction or in a shop. Today, the value of the past, even the smallest piece, is finally recognized, whether it comes in the form of a single horn button from 1830, a postcard from Saratoga Springs dated 1896, or a four-page leaflet from 1914 showing how to use a breadmaker.

While it would be impossible to list all cookbooks and pamphlets, the attempt has been made to offer a selection that represents a wide view of what is available on the market and to encourage collectors to assess their books and other holdings with a more critical, if loving, eye.

2 〔 Early Cookbooks
From Ancient Rome to Colonial America

The Very First Cookbooks

Since the earliest period of white settlement in America, cookbooks have been treasured sources of family history, recipes, medical concoctions, and other information important to daily living. The books were carefully handed down from mother to daughters and sometimes to daughters-in-law, until generations had enjoyed the wisdom, common sense, and humor found in the cookery books' pages. American cookbooks can be said to have had their culinary start in the late eighteenth century, but knowing a bit about their ancient sources can add to the enjoyment of collecting and reading these first American cookbooks.

Over the centuries, cookbooks have been second in popularity only to the Bible, according to sales, and it seems that as humans developed a desire for something other than chunks of fire-seared greasy meat or fermented grains, the cookbook developed right along with human tastebuds. Social scientists and food historians have not yet found the "first" cookbook, since the Egyptians, Greeks, and Romans all were known to have recipe collections complete with directions for preparing everything from beer to flamingos, but a "book" in Yale University's Babylonian collection may well lead the race. There, clay tablets dating from before 1500 B.C. hold recipes that were etched in cuneiform. The tablets indicate that food preparation in ancient Iraq of the period included techniques such as braising, boiling, and roasting, and the foods were prepared with a sophisticated taste for seasoning and flavoring.

Because men were usually the head cooks in wealthy houses of the ancients, men wrote the cookbooks (the first known cookbook written by a woman did not appear until 1598), but the audiences for the books were not those from average homes. Recipe collections in ancient Rome and Greece were written for the upper classes, for the men and women who had their own cooks and who could afford the exotic, rare ingredients called for by the writers. In addition to the expense of the food itself was added the cost of maintaining a good cook on the premises: cooks were skilled culinary artists, held in esteem by their employers or their owners. Indeed, Roman cooks were rewarded for their imagination and culinary skills and might be invited in to drink with the dinner guests after a particularly special celebration; in Greece, cooks were allowed to copyright special recipes and to receive royalties from recipe sales. One philosopher recorded that a good cook was worth the same amount of money spent on a public triumph for a returning hero. Those women allowed in ancient kitchens were usually slaves with a special talent for preparing a particular food, but religious and social taboos could prevent women from participating fully in the cooking and food management of the house.

Both the Greeks and Romans dined on elaborately prepared foods served in sophisticated menus, yet while references to early cookbooks and works of gastronomy may be found, except for a single culinary work, the cookbooks of these early times did not survive. This unique exception, *De Re Coquinaria,* or *The Art of Cooking,* is believed to have been authored during the first century by one Marcus Gavius Apicius, and it is considered the earliest extant cookbook from the western world. It is probably the longest in-print cookbook as well, with editions and selections appearing for nearly 1500 years, and reprints still available. Even Queen Anne of England owned a copy in 1705; the publication of that edition was paid for by well-known men of the day, including Isaac Newton.

The Art of Cooking was a varied selection of recipes. It included classic dishes like lamb stew, which would not be out of place on today's table, as well as some distinctly odd dishes, like brain sausage, which only the adventurous modern diner might try. The recipes contained ingredients and directions for preparation of the dishes, but translators of the work have agreed that a modern cook would need to understand the quirks of Roman language, measurements, and agriculture, and would have to have the ability to recognize later editorial additions, in order to prepare many of the original dishes. Some of the ingredients, like the fish sauce "liquamen" and certain spice mixtures and sweet sauces, have been lost to history, resulting in the need to guess at Roman tastes.

Scholars still debate the exact identity of Apicius, since there were several men of that name who lived during the appropriate time. Was he the author of the work or only the compiler of the recipes? Was he a gourmand who had the recipe collection named in his honor by another writer? Was his name merely a pseudonym for another writer? Translators of his book may despair of ever knowing exactly which parts, if any, he actually wrote; like the Bible,

The Art of Cooking was added to and embellished through the centuries with new recipes and new foods. Regardless of who Apicius really was, the work attributed to him affected cooking for centuries, as European kitchens learned and copied Roman ways with food, such as the lavish use of spices and sauces and the spectacle of foods prepared to fool the eye as well as the tongue. (The story of Apicius does not end with his cookbook. Legend relates that upon discovering that he did not have enough money left in his estate in order to dine properly, he hosted a large banquet for his friends and then poisoned himself after the meal.)

Through the long centuries of the Dark Ages and early Middle Ages, society swayed under the combined blows of barbarian invasions, bubonic plague, and the loss of the steadying hand of a central Roman government. During that time, the emphasis was on trying to preserve a hold on life and to keep together a social order, no matter how simple. Some manuscript recipe collections are known to have been made, but even those were based on what was recognized as the Apician methods. The wealthy tended to follow older food traditions rather than institute new ones, and they were still interested in maintaining a well-stocked and tempting kitchen.

Food of the period was chopped and pounded into shape and was heavily spiced, for some very plain reasons. With cold storage generally unavailable most of the year, meats, dairy, and prepared foods spoiled, so heavy use of herbs and spices helped to disguise the taste and smell of rotten dinners. People still used their hands and teeth as their main dining implements (the fork didn't appear in cookbooks until 1570), so food needed to be soft enough to be pulled apart with fingers or chewed easily with bad teeth, resulting in many chopped and mashed dinners. It was not unusual to read recipes calling for coloring the food with natural berry and vegetable dyes, in order to add impact to the bland-looking dishes, or for shaping the foods in molds, then garnishing them with jellies and other decorations. Some foods were made to resemble others, or to hold surprises: pastry "eggs" filled with roasted birds, and "flames" created from plums and pomegranates were only two of the techniques used by inventive cooks. Outside the manor houses, the peasants made do with simple brown bread, locally caught fish, boiled and salted meat, and stews flavored with homegrown herbs; the more fortunate would perhaps have a taste of honey if a bee tree could be located. Meanwhile, the well-to-do feasted on imported delicacies, including citrus fruits, sturgeon, and exotic Italian cheeses.

As the abbeys, villages, and towns attempted to struggle back to a civilized order, France helped to lead the way to a new cuisine in the last quarter of the fourteenth century, when Guillaume Tirel (or Taillevent, as he was known) wrote *Le Viandier de Guillaume dit Taillevent,* a book which gained fame as the first cookbook of the Middle Ages. Taillevent was a chef in the royal French courts, and his coat of arms included a cozy grouping of small cauldrons and a sharpening blade. His recipes ranged from stews and purees and custards flavored with pounded almonds, to peacocks served with their heads gilded in gold and their tails arranged in full glory. Within the book's pages, cooks could find recipes for many sauces, vegetables, and even sops, a forerunner of modern soups, and the kitchens of the well-to-do did their best to copy the tastes of the castle and manor house.

Across the sea in England, *The Forme of Cury* (The Art of Cooking) was written around the year 1390, and this book lays claim to being the first cookbook to be written in English. The author's name is forgotten, although some historians believe him to have been a master chef at the court of King Richard II, at whose behest the book was written. The recipes called for a wide variety of foods, and royal dining was not dull. Crane, goose, chicken, pork, salmon, eel, garlic, mushrooms, turnips, apples, strawberries, grapes, wines, marzipan, and cheesecake all appeared in recipes and, presumably, in the dining hall. There is even a recipe for a "salat" dressed carefully and simply with vinegar, oil, and salt. But while the recipes in *The Forme of Cury* told the cook what ingredients to use and offered general preparation guidelines, there were few accurate measurements and the assumption was that the cook could read or at least have the recipes passed along by someone who could.

One reason that only the very wealthy could afford cookbooks is found in the history of early book production: in the days before printing presses, books had to be carefully copied out by a clerk's hand, and in many cases, the clerk was monk or member of a religious order. Cookbook history would probably have been set back several hundred years had it not been for the work done in monkish scriptoriums. One of the most beautiful Renaissance cookbooks (and the first to be printed on a press in later editions) appeared in 1474 and had the effect of turning the culinary world upside down. Titled *De Honesta Voluptate* (Of Honest Indulgence; see Figure 2-1), the book is thought to be the work of two men: Platina, a philosopher who became a Vatican librarian, and Martino, a cook in the house of a papal treasurer. The recipes, especially those for meat and fish sauces, were sophisticated and elegant and were accompanied by essays on correct behavior, etiquette, and good living, a combination of information that cookbooks would continue to contain for centuries. Platina's work was so well received that a joke of the period said there were more buyers for his book than for Plato's, a foreshadowing of the popularity cookbooks were destined to entertain in the coming centuries.

Throughout the Renaissance period, cookbooks called for rich flavorings and excesses in service. Huge "set pieces" were actually made of food and shaped like everything from vases of flowers to gods and godesses, a holdover from the Roman style of service. One set piece, shaped like a pie, actually held a group of musicians, while another released the famous "four and twenty blackbirds." The guilds of bakers, confectioners, pastrymen, and others would prepare huge floats for royal pageants and parades, highlighting their culinary skills with doughs, sugar, and fruits formed into sailing ships

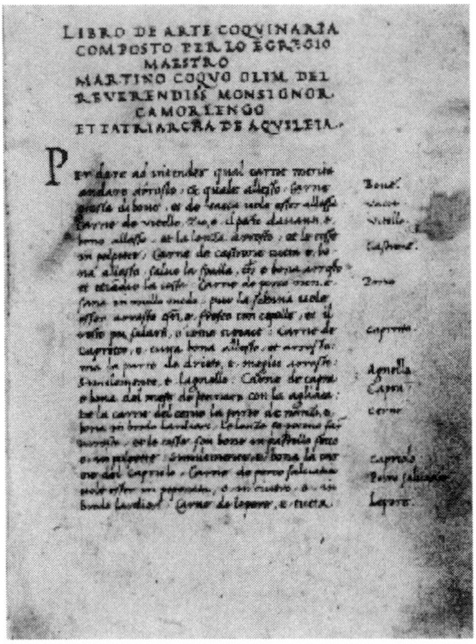
LIBRO DE ARTE COQVINARIA
COMPOSTO PER LO EGREGIO
MAESTRO
MARTINO COQVO OLIM DEL
REVERENDISS MONSIGNOR
CAMORLENGO
ET PATRIARCHA DE AQVILEIA

Fig. 2-1 **This page is from the Martino manuscript, in the collection of the Library of Congress, which may have been used by Platina in writing *De Honesta Voluptate.* The manuscript page shown here is from the mid-sixteenth century and may have been owned by Platina himself. The text discusses the ways in which a cook should determine which meats should be boiled and which should be roasted. (Photo courtesy of the Library of Congress.)**

and figures from classical myths. The Renaissance was also the time when marriages among royal and politically connected families helped to spread Italian, French, and Dutch fashions and styles across Europe and to begin the trend of sharing tastes and foods between countries.

Early English Cooks and Cookbooks

Women had been writing family cookbooks for generations, though much of their work still remains to be analyzed and organized by historians. The majority of women from the upper and middle classes who kept their own manuscript cookbooks did not have the recipes published; rather, they passed down their knowledge and experience to family members over the generations. Included in many of these collections were recipes for soups, meats, and cakes, as well as those for mixing cough cures, concocting inks, and making sweetmeats for children. The books were important repositories of the changes in foods that took place from the late Renaissance through the Georgian periods. New foods were being introduced from the New World, and the time of exploration which shaped the new maps also reset the dining table. Food was still roasted and boiled in open fireplaces, but it was not colored and shaped into odd forms. Tea became a popular beverage, improved supplies of sugar had an impact upon the types of baked goods found on the family table, and vegetables were slowly entering the cook's repertoire, although many cookbook writers continued to offer the thought that undercooked vegetables were poisonous. Men may have continued to rule the royal kitchens, but women began to make their mark on the food world through personal family cookbooks.

The material covered in early cookbooks extended far beyond the kitchen doorway; books published today still display the influence of their culinary ancestors. The arts of food and medicine, alchemy and science were never really that far apart, for a cook might also be familiar with the mysteries of yeast and wine, a chemist would know the best way to compound and administer antidotes to poisons (necessary in the days of the de' Medicis and their cooks), and a mother and wife would be expected to understand cures and palliations for fever, childbirth, and injuries. Directions for all of these mixtures appeared in cookbooks, along with instructions for brewing dyes, extracting flavorings, and curing all manner of illnesses. Readers could also seek information about etiquette, food service, child care, and even religion.

The do-it-yourself cookbook sections may have had their roots in the ancient medical writings of the Greeks, the Chinese, and the Arabs, who believed that the four elements of fire, air, earth, and water matched the bodily humors of blood, bile, black bile, and phlegm. In theory, a healthy balance was obtained by eating or avoiding particular foods, and over time certain foods gained a reputation for preventing or curing illness. There was also a belief in the use of herbs and plants for healing, as well as the following of an ancient theory, the "doctrine of signatures," which said that plants cured what they physically resembled. Thus, a root that resembled a leg might be used in a tea to soothe varicose veins, or walnuts might be served to help someone's memory, as the nutmeats recalled the brain. Regardless of which theory a cook adhered to, many of the concoctions, which might include toads, snakes, and other oddities in the ingredients, sounded awful and tasted worse. But sometimes the mixtures worked, and these successful traditions were handed down, to eventually appear in household cookbooks.

Although cookbooks written by men did much to reinforce the idea that it was proper for women of all social classes to spend their lives in the service of family, by the time the eighteenth century was underway, the "frail" sex had begun to take both recipes and pen in hand. Several changes, albeit slow ones, led to the writing of cookbooks by women. First, the middle class had started to develop and, with it, the desire of many women to copy the styles and social mores of the noble "great houses" and the food that came out of the wealthy kitchens. Second, anti-French sentiment led some women to write about good, healthy English cooking and to avoid what they believed was extravagant French cuisine. (In fairness to French cooks, however, some of the recipes attributed to them in English cookbooks had little to do with the chef's original intention, having passed through many mutations on their way into written recipes.) Third, more women were literate, had money to spend on books (which were becoming more affordable), and were eager to try out the "new" cookery they were reading about in popular novels and daily city newspapers. Eighteenth-century townswomen had a strong advantage over their country sisters: instead of having a large fireplace for cooking, townhouse kitchens were being introduced to the latest in kitchen technology, the Rumford stove, which made food preparation faster, easier, and safer.

One forward-looking English cookbook writer was Mary Kettilby, who in 1714 self-published *A Collection of Above Three Hundred Receipts in Cookery, Physick and Surgery for the use of All Good Wives, Tender Mothers and Careful Nurses.* Her recipes included directions for pharmaceutical mixtures, which were as important to a woman's domestic knowledge as knowing how to fry an egg. Kettilby's book indicated that the recipes had been gathered from other housewives, possibly making this one of the earliest contributed cookbooks. (Although cookbooks would eventually prove to be excellent sellers, it was not until nearly sixty years later, in 1773, that writer Elizabeth Raffald was able to sell a publisher the rights to her book *The Experienced English House-Keeper* for a large cash consideration.)

One of the next woman-authored cookbooks to appear came from Eliza Smith in 1727; her work, *The Compleat Housewife* (Figure 2-2), had the self-assurance to attack English attitudes toward food in general and women cooks in particular:

> What you will find in the following Sheets, are Directions for generally for dressing after the best, most natural and wholesome Manner, such Provisions as are the Product of our own Country; and in such a Manner as is most

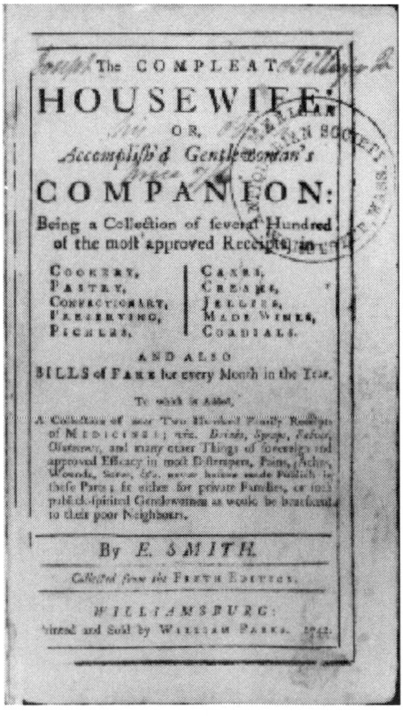

Fig. 2-2 Eliza Smith's *The Compleat Housewife* had its first American printing in 1742 at the shop of William Parks, in Williamsburg, Virginia. The book, while not adjusted to the needs of American kitchens, became the first cookery best-seller in the New World. Note that the title page indicates that recipes are included for both food and medicinal mixtures and suggests that a gentlewoman can use the medicines "as would be beneficent to their poor Neighbours." Only a few copies of the 1742 edition are known to exist. (Photo courtesy of the American Antiquarian Society.)

agreeable to English Palates . . . these Receipts are all suitable to English Constitutions, and English Palates, wholesome, toothsome, all practicable and easy to be performed; here are those proper for a frugal, and also for a sumptuous Table; and if rightly observed, will prevent the spoiling of many a good Dish of Meat, the Waste of many good Materials, the Vexation that frequently attends such Mismanagements, and the Curses not unfrequently bestowed on Cooks, with the usual Reflection, that whereas God sends good Meat, the Devil sends Cooks.

Smith's recipes were easy to understand, and they ran the gamut from instructions on how to pot eels and pickle mushrooms to how to make orange chips crisp and prepare medical compounds. The fact that Mrs. Smith had worked as a cook in various upper-class houses for more than three decades also meant that in addition to her culinary skills, she had developed the common sense necessary to winnow out the pretentious from the plain. (It also shows that by this time, while men might still have been chefs to royalty, women were now well accepted as cooks in the most discriminating houses.) There is no doubt that Mrs. Smith took pride in her skills and in her work history (she noted, "I have been constantly employed in fashionable and noble Families"), but she also realized that "fantastical messes," as she called some French dishes, had little place in a gentlewoman's home. She did, however, maintain a listing of carving terms which contain directions for lifting a swan, breaking a deer, and splating a pike, indicating that while not all gentlewomen might be faced with a crane in their kitchen, it was still important to understand the niceties of preparing English game in the proper manner. Housewives who mastered these problems but who were stumped by the intricacies of serving food properly could also breathe a sigh of relief, since the book contained foldout diagrams for placing the serving dishes on the table in artistic ways. (Smith's book also holds pride of place as the first cookbook to be printed in the American colonies; William Parks of Williamsburg, Virginia, published and sold the work in 1742.)

Twenty years after the appearance of Smith's well-known work, a woman named Hannah Glasse published in 1747 what would become a standard kitchen reference for more than a half-century. Glasse wrote *The Art of Cookery Made Plain and Easy,* in her words, "to instruct the lower sort," and she indeed directed her work to everyday cooks and those who hired them. Even in the mid-eighteenth century, few women of upper-middle-class culture or high social standing, in Europe or the colonies, did their own cooking. Servants were inexpensive to hire, and in America, African slaves proved to be excellent, skilled cooks, and would remain as valued kitchen workers for nearly two centuries. The woman of the house would see that the foods were purchased or processed and carefully stored; each day she would help to plan the menu, distribute the ingredients for meals, and, if necessary, read the recipes to the cooks. Her daughters were taught to run a household, especially the kitchen and larder, but feminine skills meant knowing how to cook but not necessarily doing it if you could afford someone else to do it for you. One edition of Glasse's book contained the following verse, which highlighted the importance of hired cooks: "The Fair, who's Wise and oft consults our Book, And thence directions gives her Prudent Cook, With Choicest viands, has her Table Crown'd, And Health, with Frugal Ellegance is found."

The recipes in Glass's cookbook were detailed and focused on English specialties: roasts, loins, simple sauces, potted fish, preserved fruits. In the spirit of cookbook writers past and present, Glasse lifted many recipes from earlier collections. Herself the object of early bibliographic and historic mystery (some researchers insisted that she didn't exist or that her name was in reality the nom de plume of a male writer), she was also the object of cookbook folklore, which insisted that she told cooks to "first catch your hare" (she didn't.) She did, however, become the focus of the famous Samuel Johnson's ire at a dinner party. Johnson believed that a cookbook should be based on philosophical principles, and he decided to write such a book. During a discussion of Glasse's work, he noted that "women can spin very well; but they cannot make a good book of Cookery." Johnson never produced a cookbook, philosophical or otherwise, while Hannah sold out many editions.

Cookbooks in the Colonies

It was an unfortunate condition, but during the first two centuries of settlement, American cookbooks were in short supply. For homemakers in the American colonies, printed cookbooks were a luxury which could only be obtained from the homeland; often, a woman preferred to use her treasured family recipes as a guide through times of uncertainty, illness, and want. Perhaps the loneliness of a new home in a new world was eased by reading a mother's recipe and seeing the familiar handwriting describe the baking of a Queen's Cake. Or maybe the fear of childbirth was soothed when a recipe told how to brew a drink that would ease the pain. Cookery books, imported or homemade, represented more than recipes to colonial women: they were important links with home and sometimes the only sources available for domestic and medical information. English manuscript cookbooks were carefully carried across the Atlantic by the new immigrants. Dutch housewives in New Amsterdam referred to copies of *De Verstandige Kock* (The Sensible Cook), part of a household/how-to book first printed in old Amsterdam. Even Martha Washington treasured a manuscript collection of recipes that had been passed down through her first husband's family over several generations.

Until after the American Revolution, cooks in the colonies could read only reprints of cookbooks previously published in Europe, complete with recipes based on impractical tastes and outdated or unavailable ingredients. Although some English cookbooks were imported and sold at bookshops, few were actually printed here (Eliza Smith's cookbook printed by William Parks

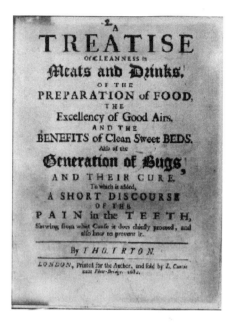

Fig. 2-3 Thomas Tryon's theories of health and cleanliness were read by no less a personage than Benjamin Franklin, who, however, did not follow Tryon's later suggestions for a vegetarian lifestyle. This page from a 1682 edition shows how closely cookbooks and medical matters have been related over the centuries. (Photo courtesy of the Library of Congress.)

was the exception). The books and their recipes weren't a problem when they called for stewing a rabbit—New World rabbits stewed just as well as Old World coneys did—but the recipes did present roadblocks to good cookery when the fine white sugar and flour called for by recipe writers were in short supply. And what were cooks to do with new foods like cranberries, maple syrup, pumpkins, and corn, or oysters the size of dinner plates, sturgeons the size of cows, and eels as thick as an arm? The earliest settlers were fortunate indeed when Native American cooks took pity on them and taught the preparation of wild turkey and popcorn (Native American cookery was not written down but was passed along through oral traditions), but later cooks had to make do by trial and error, substituting ingredients that did not always work in the old recipes and developing new dishes which would someday become known as regional American cuisine.

That "someday" arrived in 1796 at Hartford, Connecticut, when a lady named Amelia Simmons published *American Cookery: or the art of dressing Viands, Fish, Poultry and Vegetables, and the best modes of making Pastes, Puffs, Pies, Tarts, Puddings, Custards and Preserves and all kinds of Cakes from the imperial Plumb to the plain Cake. Adapted to this country, and all grades of Life* (see Figure 2-4). Little is known about the author, and most of our information must be inferred from her work. Readers of Simmons's book discovered that Amelia was "an American orphan" who believed that "the orphan, tho' left to the care of virtuous guardians, will find it essentially necessary to have an opinion and determi-

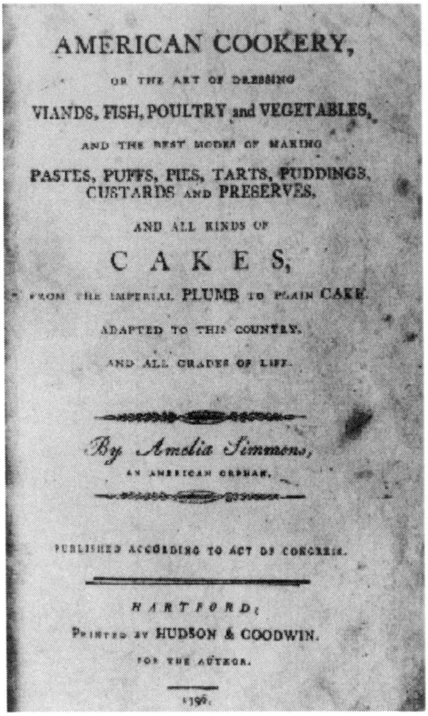

Fig. 2-4 *American Cookery,* by Amelia Simmons, was a "first" in several ways: it was the first cookbook to consider American ingredients like pumpkins; it was the first self-published American cookbook; and it was the first cookbook written by an American woman. The illustration shows the edition printed in Hartford, Connecticut, although others were issued in Vermont, New Hampshire, and New York. Some of the editions had Simmons's name on the title page; others had only the words "an American Orphan." Many plagiarized editions were made through the years as well, confusing the collecting issue even more. (Photo courtesy of the American Antiquarian Society.)

nation of her own." She must have been a good cook and baker, perhaps trained in the home of her guardians. She had enough education to realize that her work had value, enough business acumen to pursue the project, and enough perceptiveness to realize that America's cooks had little reference material to draw on. Simmons took a no-nonsense approach to the domestic arts, telling readers how certain vegetables are cultivated, how certain meats are cooked, even how to keep boys out of trouble (let them raise English beans). Her directions were detailed; the sections "To dress a turtle (and) To Dress a Calve's Head. Turtle fashion" are nearly 2½ pages in length, and this in a book of under 50 pages.

While some of the recipes seem relatively up-to-date, others provide links to cooking of the past, calling for an unusual combination of ingredients. Take, for example, "A Sea Pie," an elaborate main dish in the spirit of medieval kitchens:

> Four pound of flour, one and half pound of butter rolled into paste, wet with cold water, line the pot therewith, lay in split pigeons, turkey pies, veal, mutton or birds, with slices of pork, salt and pepper and dust on flour, doing thus till the pot is full of your ingredients expended, add three pints water, cover tight with paste and stew moderately two and half hours.

Clearly, the recipe serves a large company, a hint that perhaps Simmons was used to cooking for entertainments like political meetings, which called for a large number of servings.

Simmons also appears to have been an experienced gardener, offering suggestions for raising crops like melons, asparagus, and peas, and she held definite ideas about garlic ("Tho used by the French, [garlic is] better adapted to the uses of medicine than cookery"). She was a finicky cook, and warned, "In dressing all sorts of kitchen garden herbs, take care they are clean washed; that there be no small snails, or caterpillars between the leaves; and that all the coarse outer leaves, and the tops that have received any injury by the weather, be taken off. . . ." Simmons also used a clever method to keep parsley fresh through the cold months, a precursor of the modern interest in fresh herbs, as well as food styling:

> Parsley . . . may be dryed for winter use; tho' a method which I have experienced is much better—In September I dig my roots, procure an old thin stave dry cask, bore holes an inch diameter in every stave, 6 inches asunder round the cask, and up to the top—take first a half bushel of rich garden mold and put into the cask, then run the roots through the staves, leaving the branches outside, press the earth tight about the root within, and thus continue . . . till the cask is full; it being filled, run an iron bar thro' the center of the dirt in the cask and fill with water, let stand on the south and east side of a building till frosty at night, then remove it . . . where during the winter, I clip with my scissars the fresh parsley, which my neighbors or myself have occasion for. . . . Its . . . a pleasurably tasted herb, and much used in garnishing viands.

Although she borrowed recipes from other cookbooks of the period, Simmons may be forgiven this common practice because of what she offered to the new American cooking. She is thought to be the first writer to indicate, in recipes for cookies and soft gingerbread, the use of pearl ash, an early form of baking powder. She was also the first cookbook author to call a small, crisp sweet a "cooky" (from the Dutch *koekje;* other cookbooks referred to them as "little cakes") and the first to record the recipes for "pumpkin" pie, Indian pudding, "cramberry" tart, and Indian slapjacks. Simmons described dishes that made New England one of the first regional areas to have a recognized cuisine. Collectors should note that *American Cookery* is rare in any edition (and expensive, with some copies bringing several thousand dollars), and it also represents several "firsts" in the United States publishing field: the first cookbook by an American woman and the first cookbook that was self-published by an American.

For all of Simmons's innovations, the book itself is a small, unprepossessing volume, but one which was also the focus of some publishing intrigue. In a later edition of *American Cookery,* Simmons notes that "not having an education sufficient to prepare the work for the press, the person that was employed by her, and entrusted with the receipts, to prepare them for publication (with a design to impose on her, and injure the sale of the book) did omit several articles very essential in some of the receipts and placed others in their stead, which were highly injurious to them, without her consent. . . ." Cookbook historians can only guess as to the motivation behind this treachery: did the "person" hope to publish his (or her) own book and thus sabotage the Simmons work, or was there jealousy among local cooks? Regardless of this editorial interference, the book continued to be printed, in editions both authorized and plagarized, for almost thirty-five years, and did more than its share of promoting American food and regional specialties.

Decoding Old Cookbooks

Collectors and readers of the earliest American cookbooks, whether the books were imported or native, printed or written, will certainly discover that the recipes can be difficult to understand and nearly impossible to "translate" correctly from page to table without a lot of detective work and quite a number of unsuccessful cooking attempts. Few cookbooks of the colonial and early Federal periods make sense to anyone but an eighteenth-century cook, and even historical societies that are active in reproducing "antique" food admit that the food is an approximation of the past, not a recreation. Two of the most common problems arise when a reader tries to understand the printing and writing styles of the era: due to typesetting traditions, shaped "f" letters were used to represent the long "s" sound (so "goose" appears to

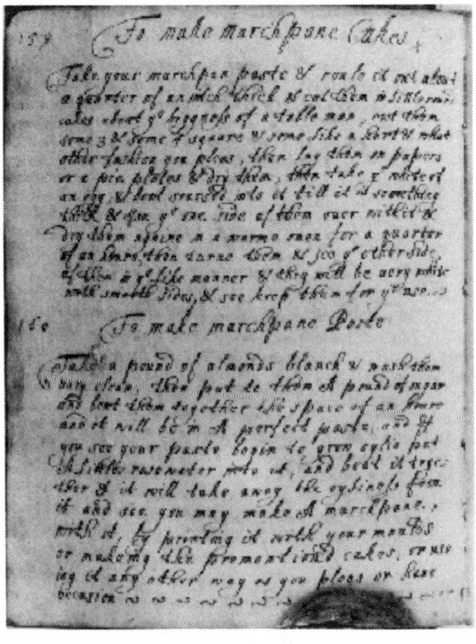

Fig. 2-5 Manuscript cookbooks were treasured by housewives and handed down through families for generations. This page is from a cookbook that once belonged to Martha Washington, but the recipes in it date from at least the sixteenth century. The recipes shown here are for "marchpane cakes" and "machpane paste," a still-popular almond and sugar mixture that was a favorite with families of Martha Washington's time who were lucky enough to be able to afford to make it. (Photo courtesy of The Historical Society of Pennsylvania.)

Fig. 2-6 Handwritten receipt or recipe books are joys for the collector, since the books offer a direct link to the cook of times past. The book on the left in the illustration came from Spittle Falls, New York, and is from around 1882; the one on the right is from the same era but an unknown place and contains recipes in German as well as in English. Both books were written by at least two different cooks, and the recipes seem to span many years and emphasize desserts and sweets. Some of the dishes have also received special notations, like "good" and "delectable." Neither book shown is in anything better than fair condition, but their immediacy and charm are unmatched by commercially published cookbooks.

be "goofe," and "taste" becomes "tafte"), while some letters, including I, J, and E, may be easily mistaken for others. Handwritten recipe (or, in the older terms, "receipt" or even "rule") books, offer their own charming headaches, as the reader struggles to decode the florid writing, strange abbreviations, and unconventional spellings ("pompian," "pumpkin," "punkion," or "punken"; "sillibub," "sulebubbles," or "syllabub") common to the period and apparently different for each cookbook author.

Collecting old cookbooks while having little understanding of the recipes, the flavors, and the methods of food preparation places does little justice to the books and eras they represent, so owners of cookbooks from the seventeenth to the early nineteenth centuries should take the time and the interest to study the recipes in order to decipher the cooking information, even if the dishes are never prepared. First, try to read the recipe straight through, developing a sense of what it is the cook is talking about (it's smart to write the recipe down as you work); then try to fill in the words that are unclear or missing. Say the sentence with the missing word aloud, or copy the unclear writing, to help you get a feel for a problematic phrase. You can also track down an elusive ingredient or mysterious action by comparing the recipe to one in an existing book with modern spelling. If you manage to decode a word that doesn't make sense to your twentieth-century cooking beliefs, you may need to dig into some books on antique cookery and food history—after all, you may not be able to recognize whether "syllabub" is actually a word unless you first know that it was a beverage and/or dessert. Also remember that some words were shortened, abbreviated, or badly misspelled and that you may have to just guess as to their correct meanings.

Measurements from the seventeenth and eighteenth centuries are also problematic for a collector and user of old cookbooks (you don't have to own the originals; reprints provide the same headaches!). The fortunate reader/cook will be faced with recipes and ingredients lists that call for weighed amounts, like pounds, pints, and quarts, but oftentimes the recipes called for measurements like a wineglass, a gill, a spoonful, butter as big as a hen's egg, and so on. This is fine if you are only trying to read the recipes, although you will still not be able to imagine the taste, but it is quite a challenge if you plan to actually use them. Recipes, like musical scores, are open to interpretation by cook, reader, and diner alike. Adding to the challenge of providing delectable fare from old cookbooks is the fact that foods and tastes have changed and that some recipes were recorded after the fact (as in the case of Victorian ladies writing down from memory their colonial grandmama's recipe for Bath buns). It is difficult to recreate exactly the old recipes, and what we arrive at are approximations of the dishes from centuries ago. (See "Measurements from Old Cookbooks," in the back of this book, for some assistance.)

In addition to understanding outdated measurements, collectors need to be wary about antique terms like "doughspur" (a pie crimping device) and "bladder" (used for sealing jars or pots). "Spiders" were not hearthside creatures, but rather footed pans which stood above the coals. And "jacks" weren't servants, but mechanisms used to turn food on a spit over the fire. The foods themselves must also be interpreted, sometimes through their preparation steps instead of through their names (for example, Simmons's "pumpkin pudding" was actually a pie, as a careful reading of the recipe will show).

Jumbled together any which way, the ingredients lists are also difficult to read, since they are not usually presented separately from the cooking directions or in the proper order of use. The directions themselves might consist of a terse order to "bake like a custard," or "bake somewhat more than other tarts." Other challenges come from dishes that include somewhat unsavory terms like "hack," "rend," and "tear." At this point in culinary time, cooking was treated as an art, rather than a science, so that recipes were meant as a sort of mental outline—it was assumed that the cook knew how to mix up a pie paste (pastry for the pie shells), how to light a fire in the fireplace with the proper wood for the required heat (slow and steady, or hot and "bright"), and how to time her dish for the best cooking results (some cooks suggested singing a hymn or reciting a prayer as a sort of timing device).

Another problem with understanding older American cookbooks is the necessity of placing them in context in the kitchens of the period. The seventeenth- and eighteenth-century kitchens were hot, dangerous places, and accidents there accounted for a large number of womens' deaths in colonial America. Huge fireplaces held long cross or lug poles, from which hung the pots and cooking utensils. Several small fires burned on the hearth, allowing the cook to prepare a variety of dishes at once, while the bake oven might have been built into the wall of the fireplace, alongside, or even outside in certain regions. The ovens were heated with coals, then the hot ashes were scraped out and the shaped bread doughs, pies, and bean pots were placed inside to cook. (Baked beans were an excellent Sabbath meal, since they allowed the housewife to start the baking on Saturday night and avoid cooking on the day of rest.)

Some cooking implements called for in the older cookbooks are still found today, but while Dutch ovens, frying pans, skillets, and even trivets were and are popular cooking tools, a cookbook collector still needs to research such items as "hoops" (cake pans), horsehair sieves (sifters), and "salamanders" (browning irons). Sometimes the cookbook provides its own hints to the use of the item, as when a cook is directed to use a hot iron or poker to heat a drink before serving; even if you didn't know beforehand what a toddy iron was, the directions are usually clear as to what is needed, and a suitable modern substitute can be used. Other times, however, the reader must understand the recipe first. In Amelia Simmons's directions for hoe cake, she tells the cook to "bake before the fire." What the modern cookbook reader might not know is that hoe cakes were often baked on slabs of wood or planks (or even the flat side of hoe), which were propped before the hot coals. But as none of this is evident in the recipe, the reader is at the mercy of his or her knowledge of cooking and history. Cooking and preparation terms have changed, so that "rubbing together sugar and flour" means "cutting in" to modern pastry cooks, and it would take a modern reader some time to realize that pies were stored for weeks or months in a pie safe or on a cool shelf. So when a recipe for minced pies directs the cook to remove the top crust; spoon out, heat, and replace the filling; and then heat the crust separately and serve, it demonstrates that while very early cookbooks are fascinating to collect, they also require the careful and interested reader to become historian, domestic scientist, and detective before he or she can become a cook.

3 | The New America
Nineteenth-Century Cookbooks

After the success of *American Cookery,* homemakers and cooks would never again lack for books telling them how to prepare the perfect biscuit; indeed, before the country's centennial year of 1876, more than 1,000 cookbooks and pamphlets would be printed in the United States. *Finding* a recipe would not be a problem, even in the earliest decades of the nineteenth century; however, there were problems in trying to discover recipes that actually worked. Although copyright laws were in existence by 1790, enforcing the laws was something that the new federal government was often unable, or unwilling, to do. Recipes and even entire books were plagiarized and republished under other names in other states; in fact, several women had the Simmons work reprinted, some offering changes and some presenting the exact original as their own (but at least none of these "authors" had the gall to claim to be an orphan as well!). Bibliographers have been able to chart such plagiarism by keeping track of the errors that appeared in the Simmons text and then appeared, subsequently, in the plagiarized editions. Unfortunately, the stolen recipes also resulted in at least one generation of cooks faced with some unworkable directions.

But along with the unauthorized reprints, new, singular works were being offered to the public as well. The nineteenth century was a time of expansion, of national pride, of a rising middle class, and of awareness that food preparation was not a hodgepodge of guesswork but rather part of something that would come to be called "domestic science." Women were on the receiving end of new technology like iron cookstoves, eggbeaters, and methods for canning and food preservation, and these home cooks had available to them a new understanding of the hows and whys of nutrition. New, mass-produced, factory-made kitchen tools, like bread dough mixers and metal whisks, lightened the housewife's normal drudgery just a little bit, and cookbooks began to reflect and encourage all of these changes in the kitchen and dining room. Cooking schools run by women, for women, became popular for ladies of all social levels, and women's magazines like *Godey's* and *Scribner's* began to spread the new gospels of household management, healthy cooking, and domestic science to the thousands of housewives who were, much like their modern sisters, still looking for something different to serve for tonight's dinner.

The nineteenth century was also the first time in the history of American society when women authors dominated the cookbook world. Several were "female novelists" who turned to the new field of cookbook and domestic writing; others wrote cookbooks in order to inform women about their duty to their families and the need to do things right; and still others wrote in response to the need of women who were forced to live frugal, careful lives in reduced or even impoverished circumstances. Cookbooks came from the north and south, from professional instructors and plain good cooks. The trends that were taken up by cookbooks of the nineteenth century included cleanliness, careful use of food, healthy cooking, temperance, common sense, and dislike of European (particularly French) melanges. Collectors will discover that these books reflected the huge upheavals occurring in society along with the attitudes of the women who were living through the problems and advances of the era.

Early American Cookbooks and Authors

The first distinctly southern cookbook, *The Virginia House-Wife* (Figure 3-1), appeared in 1824 and was written by Mrs. Mary Randolph. In her introduction Randolph noted with unconcealed directness that "management is an art that may be acquired by every woman of good sense and tolerable memory." And certainly, Mrs. Randolph knew the ins and outs of management. Cousin by marriage to Thomas Jefferson, Mary and her husband, David Meade Randolph, lived the earlier part of their marriage in well-to-do circumstances, but a change in their political and personal fortunes forced them to move to Richmond, where Mary opened a boardinghouse. She became so well known for her cooking that in 1800, after a slave revolt had been thwarted, it was discovered that the leader had ordered Mary spared, in order that she might become his cook.

The Virginia House-Wife was well received and reflected the rich sophistication of southern fare, from old-fashioned, homely dishes, like buckwheat cakes and jumbals (cookies), to African, East and West Indian, Spanish, French, and Italian offerings, including gumbo, curry, and vermicelli. Randolph's recipes were written in paragraph form, with the ingredients set in among the method, but the directions were clear and easy to follow. For

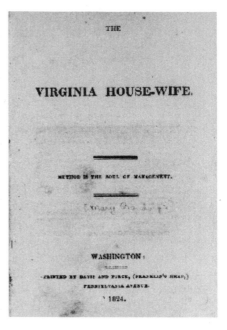

Fig. 3-1 When Mary Randolph wrote *The Virginia House-Wife* she was already a well-respected hostess and cook. She was a relation of Thomas Jefferson, and her sophisticated recipes included French and African dishes, along with newer delights like ice cream. The simple title page reflects her no-nonsense cooking style. (Photo courtesy of the American Antiquarian Society.)

eggs and tomatoes, she directs: "Peel the skins from a dozen large tomatos, put four ounces of butter in a frying pan, add some salt, pepper, and a little chopped onion; fry them a few minutes, add the tomatos, and chop them while frying, when nearly done, break in six eggs, stir them quickly and serve them up." In addition to this being a quick, tasty, one-dish meal which any housewife would appreciate, the recipe shows southern cooks had accepted the tomato as a tasty food, while cooks in other parts of the country still believed the berry needed to be boiled for hours in order to make it safe and edible.

There were also regional specialties in her selections, showing that foods were recognized as being characteristic to specific areas. Mary Randolph lists recipes for catfish soup ("an excellent dish for those who have not imbibed a needless prejudice against those delicious fish," although she warns the cook to use fish "caught in deep water"), potato pumpkin (a pumpkin stuffed and baked), and cocoa nut ice cream ("When ice creams are not put into shapes, they should always be served in glasses with handles"). The recipes also contain selections like sippet pudding and sea pie, throwbacks to dishes of the Middle Ages. Mrs. Randolph's book found a ready audience for her simple and elegant dishes, with *The Virginia House-Wife* going through more than a dozen printings and lasting in popularity until the Civil War created separations along both political and culinary lines.

Cookbooks underwent an important change when the popular novelist, Eliza Leslie, turned her hand to writing about food. In 1828 her slim volume,

Seventy-Five Receipts for Pastry, Cakes and Sweetmeats By A Lady of Philadelphia, appeared for sale in printers' shops. Leslie's work was easy to follow, clear in its directions and distinctly American, an important attribute in the ambitious and proud young republic. In *Seventy-Five Receipts,* Leslie boasted that the recipes "are drawn up in a style so plain and minute, as to be perfectly intelligible to servants, and persons of the most moderate capacity. All the ingredients, with their proper quantities, are enumerated in a list at the head of each receipt, a plan which will greatly facilitate the business of procuring and preparing the requisite article." Whether Leslie was the first cookbook writer to organize her recipes in this manner is uncertain; but she was one of the earliest American writers to do so, and to recognize the importance of making a cookbook easy to use for all levels of cooks. Her method of recipe writing was not to become an accepted standard for nearly a century.

In the spirit of Amelia Simmons, Leslie offered a mixture of dishes, with older recipes, like cheesecake and plum pudding, served up alongside newer and distinctly American sweets like sweet potato pudding, Boston pudding, Lafayette gingerbread, and apees. The last two named desserts indicated a trend that would continue in cookbooks until the present: foods named after famous people, with presidents and entertainers being particular favorites. The gingerbread was immortalized when George Washington's mother prepared it for the French hero in 1784; apees were cookies believed to have been made by a noted Philadelphia cook, Ann Page, who pressed her initials into the dough before baking. (Cookbook collectors should consider that they can sometimes place books within a certain time period by identifying the important society or political figures in recipe titles.)

After the success of *Seventy-Five Receipts,* Leslie went on to produce other influential cookbooks, including *Miss Leslie's New Cookery Book* (1857), a large collection of 652 pages and more than 1,000 tested recipes, ranging from fried chicken and southern veal stew to the more continental Italian pork and West Indian fried bananas. Miss Leslie was an excellent food writer, one of the first of her kind. Her writings were clear and opinionated, and she was sensible enough to see the problems that could occur when English cookery books were sold on an American market: "There is frequently much difficulty in following directions in English and French Cookery Books, not only from their want of explicitness, but from the difference in the fuel, fire-places, and cooking utensils generally used in Europe and America; and many of the European receipts are so complicated and laborious, that our female cooks are afraid to undertake the arduous task of making any thing from them."

Cookbooks had finally become personal statements of *American* cooks and their culinary styles and were no longer solely compilations of European recipes that might, or might not, work (although badly written cookbooks were never eliminated from the market altogether). One of Leslie's strengths as a recipe writer lay in the fact that she never hesitated to tell the cook what she thought. For Maryland biscuits (a beaten biscuit), after she explained the mixing of the dough, Leslie tartly directed the cook as follows:

> Divide the dough into several pieces, and knead and pound each piece separately. This must go on for two or three hours, continually kneading and pounding, otherwise it will be hard, tough and indigestible. . . . This is the most laborious of cakes, and also the most unwholesome, even when made in the best manner. We do not recommend it; but there is no accounting for tastes. Children should not eat these biscuits—nor grown persons either, if they can get any other sort of bread.

Leslie's work also showed that cookbooks were beginning to be accepted by publishers as possible money-makers, whether the publisher actually paid for the book or merely acted as sales agent. Leslie's savvy publisher noted in one preface that all the recipes were tested by the author and that none of the recipes appeared in her earlier books, two selling points still in use in modern cookbooks. He did sound a bit like P. T. Barnum when he claimed that Miss Leslie had produced "the most complete Cook Book in the world," but he was only echoing the national spirit: America was going to be bigger and better than any place else on earth, and cookbooks reflected this attitude—well into the next century.

While a new generation of American women dominated the cookbook market, this period also saw the first publication of a household guide and cookbook written by an African American. Robert Roberts was the butler and manager in the household of a Mr. Christopher Gore of Boston. In 1827, Roberts published *The House Servant's Directory Including 100 Useful Recipes* (Figure 3-2). (It was noted in the book that Mr. Gore purchased six dollars' worth of the volume.) Roberts was a well-spoken, educated man, who desired that his book would assist readers in learning the disparate and technical skills needed to serve as a house servant in an upper class family. His suggestions were full of common sense and an awareness of the methods that would be publicized by domestic scientists in the next several decades. "To taste any thing in perfection, the tongue must be moistened or the substance applied to it contain moisture, the nervous papillae which constitute this sense are roused to still more lively sensibility by salt, sugar, aromatics, &c. If the palate becomes dull by repeated tasting, one of the best ways of refreshing it, is to masticate an apple or to wash your mouth well with milk."

Although Roberts does give detailed directions for running a wealthy household, discussing such skills as trimming lamps, brushing hats, and serving tea, his book is not a cookbook; in fact, he is unusual because he credits many of his recipes and suggestions to *The Cook's Oracle* by William Kitchiner, popular with both European and American readers. African-American cookbook writers rarely appeared in print until the twentieth century, and

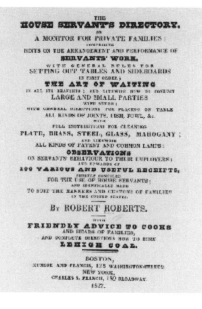

Fig. 3-2 In 1827, Robert Roberts was the first African American to publish a household guide. His graceful prose, humor, and thorough knowledge of management indicated that Roberts was an educated and respected professional. Like many household guides, *The House Servant's Directory* contained recipes, essays, and instructions for running an upper-class home, along with directions for heating by "cleaner" Lehigh, or anthracite, coal. (Photo courtesy of the American Antiquarian Society.)

if they did, they were usually depicted by white authors as mammy or Uncle Rastus characters who could fry chicken or whip up a light-as-air shortbread. Cookbooks from the post-Civil War era would sometimes offer memories in pseudo-slave dialects of family cooks and their dishes. The truth was that African-American cooks had spent nearly two centuries as slaves, blending southern, African, and Caribbean flavors into a unique cuisine that would eventually be credited with equaling the finest European dishes.

The year 1829 saw the debut of another well-known novelist turned cookbook author, Lydia Maria Francis Child. Her work, *The American Frugal Housewife, Dedicated to those Who are Not Ashamed of Economy,* would become a standard in American kitchens for several years, although her later essays condemning slavery and her belief in the education of that "class of Americans called Africans" resulted in her fall from popularity with certain readers. Lydia Child was an independent woman, who noted in the book's introduction that frugality was a virtue and that "the writer has no apology to offer for this cheap little book of economical hints, except her deep conviction that such a book is needed. In this case, renown is out of the question and ridicule is a matter of indifference." Child also offered a backhanded swipe at an English cookbook which, although sharing nearly the same name, was "so little fitted to the wants of this country" that she was "able to extract but little."

Child was to become a champion of frugality and of the idea that while a woman might face hardships in life, with religion and proper cooking she could get over the difficulties with her spirit intact. Throughout the book,

Child encouraged thrift ("Raspberry shrub mixed with water is a pure, delicious drink for summer; and in a country where raspberries are abundant, it is good economy to make it answer instead of Port. . . .") and included recipes that were already considered part of the good-old-days of the colonies only a short time after Amelia Simmons noted them as regional specialties (Child: "Old-fashioned election cake is made of four pounds of flour. . . ."). Still, corn bread, Indian pudding, and baked beans were offered as stolid standbys ("Baked beans are a very simple dish, yet few cook them well"), and Child's ultimate compliment of "good" is applied to whortleberry pie, loaf cake, and beer, although she does note that beer can be made from spruce, molasses, boxberry, fever-bush, sweet fern, and even horseradish, making beer a "healthy diet-drink" rather than an alcoholic tempter.

Child's book, like *The House Servant's Directory,* was actually a household guide, of which cooking was an important, but not the sole, part. These guides offered much more than instructions to the bride or help for a housewife in search of recipes: they gave a view into the changes that were occurring rapidly in a woman's social position. Along with hints on how to select household goods and which plants were suitable for a dining room, the books contained short essays on moral behavior, uplifting thoughts, and suggestions for getting through the dark days of life. Other household books, like *Household Gems* or *Collier's Encyclopedia of Social and Commercial Information,* had extensive recipe sections presented along with chapters on selecting a mate, building a house, writing well, parlor games, riddles, and conundrums.

By this time, cookbooks had moved from being recipe collections read solely by cooks to publications having the capability of reaching tens of thousands of women and spreading the latest social gospel through the words of the author. (While a good cook, Child was also something of a kill-joy; her book had a section on "Travelling and Amusements" [the hidden costs to be found in these occupations], and a depressing essay on "How to Endure Poverty.") The cookbooks were sources of social and religious commentary, and they provided an acceptable (at least more acceptable than novels) way for a woman to learn about the changes taking place outside of her kitchen. No longer were women expected to tolerate dirty, dangerous cooking and food preparation areas; reformists were taking up the ladle and stirring the pot in the cause of kitchens.

Cookbook authors in the mid-nineteenth century began to offer the reader advice on diets, family health, and food preparation, all with the aim of improving the lot of women. Several of the major cookbooks published during these years include works by women who supported women's rights, women's education, abolition, and temperance. The books were no longer directed solely towards the upper classes, or to the lady with domestic help, but to middle-class women and women in lower circumstances. Reformation was in the air, and temperance, antislavery, and health concerns were debated at public meetings, in the papers, and in columns of women's magazines.

The Women's Christian Temperance Union and other female groups against vice began to attack local saloons and the unfortunate imbibers caught inside. Books like the *Temperance Cook Book* appeared as early as 1841, part of an unsuccessful attempt to regulate the alcoholic intake of America. Writers like Catharine Beecher (sister of Harriet Beecher Stowe) included in their household guides chapters on nonalcoholic temperance beverages, giving recipes for effervescing jelly drinks, sham champagne, boy's coffee, delicious milk lemonade, and other concoctions. In her *Domestic Receipt Book* (1846), Beecher noted that there were three classes of temperance people: those who would not touch intoxicating liquors on any account, those who would not use it in food (to avoid the appearance of evil), and those who believed it was fine to use alcoholic beverages in cooking (she listed herself in agreement with the cooks).

Regardless of the writers' explicit beliefs on particular issues, most cookbooks placed the welfare of the family's moral behavior squarely on the shoulders of the wife and mother and tried to guide her along a path that would curtail a husband's need for the wineshop. A Mrs. Cornelius noted in 1867 "instances of worthy merchants and mechanics whose . . . hopes are chilled by the total failure of the wife in her sphere of duty; and who seek solace under their disappointment in the wine-party. . . ." Cookbooks were more than recipe collections: they were now uplifting tracts that were consulted daily and relied upon by women across the country.

At the same time women were working to overcome the evils of alcohol, doctors and health faddists were turning their studies toward the needs of the human body, and health foods made their first appearances on the market and in the cookbooks. One self-styled doctor of dietetics, Sylvester Graham, believed that whole wheat flour used in bread, coupled with a vegetarian lifestyle based on quotes from the Bible would produce a healthy diet. Graham, although pompous and self-assured, advocated ideas that are still in use, including personal cleanliness, diets light in fats and sugar, and the intake of whole grain foods to avoid the loss of vitamins from food processing.

Christianity was also brought into the kitchen during this time, when women might be directed by someone like Lydia Child, who advised "that a thorough, religious, useful education is the best security against misfortune, disgrace and poverty. . . . A mind full of piety and knowledge is always rich [and] it yields a perpetual dividend of happiness." Religion was tied up with raising a family, so it was not surprising to find that cookbooks were starting to place an emphasis on family life, health, and organization in the American home, as well as on recipes. Of course, "religion" in the mid-1800s almost always meant a form of Christianity, and "American" meant those with a white, Anglo-Saxon Protestant background, at least in cookbook publishing, but collectors should be aware that there were nineteenth-century publications that also considered German, Swedish, Jewish, and other ethnic cooking, both in the native languages and in English.

Women like Sarah Josepha Hale, author of "Mary Had a Little Lamb" and editor of the influential magazine *Godey's Lady's Book,* urged housewives to consider their work as "home administration." Hale went against the more liberal writers, including Catharine Beecher, and declared that women ought to turn their talents to their personal lives. She supported education for women but did not believe that women should become involved in politics. Hale stated in 1853 in *The New Household Receipt Book,*

> Would that those of my sex who are urging onward, into the industrial pursuits, and other professions appropriate for men, might turn their attention to improvements in domestic economy. . . . The really great woman never undervalues her own sphere. . . . Personal appearance is important; the art of beautifying a home is important; . . . more important than all is a knowledge of the best means of preserving or restoring health. . . . I have sought to give variety in the (cookery) receipts, so as to suit different conditions and constitutions. When one set of ingredients cannot be obtained, a substitute may be at hand. . . ."

The recipes also typify middle-class problems with food, with suggestions for ascertaining the quality of nutmegs, for example, and ideas on how to preserve eggs, how to concoct a substitute for cream in coffee, and how to brew walnut tea, which "subdued nausea and vomiting" (a common problem in the days before refrigeration).

"Practical" was the watchword of Catharine Beecher, who penned *A Treatise on Domestic Economy* in 1841, and later, *Miss Beecher's Domestic Receipt Book,* published in 1846. Her focus was on encouraging women to run a kitchen as a scientist would run a laboratory, the end result being well-organized and clean preparation space, efficient use of time, and healthy cooking. She was ahead of many other dietary writers in her dislike of lard and animal fats in cooking, noting "The most injurious food, of any in common use, is the animal oils, and articles cooked with them. . . . The most common modes of preparing unhealthful food, is by frying food, and by furnishing bread that is heavy or sour, or so newly baked as to become clammy and indigestible when chewed. . . . A housekeeper that will always keep a supply of sweet, light bread on her table, and avoid oily dishes, oily cooking and condiments will double the chances of good health for her family." Beecher was also concerned, as were many cookbook authors of the early domestic science days, with organizing time, so that while she provided many recipes for the cook, she also offered much in the way of advice, including suggestions for managing domestic help.

By the nineteenth century, women were required to run establishments and households or even huge plantations, raise children, tend to the sick and the elderly, provide for poorer neighbors, cater to a husband, and ensure a moral atmosphere in the home, all the while fulfilling the ideal of a mother who was a kind, guiding light and mistress of a perfectly maintained and quietly run household. Cookbooks helped a woman navigate the difficult waters of home life, providing all manner of advice, encouragement, and education. Domestic workers were an integral part of a smoothly running home's machinery, and if a woman could afford a cook or household maid, she was expected to hire one. Cookbook collectors will find that many books contain directions for employing, training, and dealing with domestics. Modern collectors of nineteenth-century cookbooks will discover essays with titles like "Suggestions in Regard to Hired Service," "Words of Comfort for a Discouraged Housekeeper," and "Friendly Counsel for Domestics."

Cookbooks provide one of the few views into the usually harsh daily world of domestics, many of whom were characterized in chapters as Irish or American country girls who needed to be taught the proper ways of a home, and who would be lazy, tyrannical, or clumsy by turns. In *The Young Housekeeper's Friend,* Mrs. Cornelius was sympathetic to the plight of domestics, and noted that for waiting maids, "It seems as if her employers had forgotten that she is made of flesh and blood, and is therefore capable of having an aching head and weary limbs. . . . If the unfortunate being is a homeless, motherless little girl, or a friendless foreigner, so much the worse. By a little consideration on the part of the lady or ladies, of a family, such hard requisitions might be avoided without any real sacrifice of comfort."

Things changed but little over the next few decades, for in *The National Cook Book* (1896), by Marion Harland and her daughter, Christine Terhune Herrick, the authors note that a down-at-the-heel state of affairs in the kitchen is "not always the fault of the mistress. Often it happens that she has

Fig. 3-3 Marion Harland authored many cookbooks, among them *Cookery for Beginners* (1893). This cookbook was directed toward beginning housekeepers who perhaps did not have the guiding influence of a mother. The book emphasizes the correct baking of bread, the use of leftovers, simple dessert making, and proper roasting and preparation of meat ("It is a common fallacy to believe that this branch of the culinary art is uninteresting drudgery, fit only for the hands of the very plain hired cook"). Not all cooks could attend class, so the availability of cookbooks like this probably helped many new marriages.

provided all the essentials, and the carelessness of her servants has brought about the dearth and disorder." The recipes in many cookbooks also hinted at the need for household help, even in more modest homes. When biscuits had to be beaten for half an hour or syllabub whipped for the same period of time, and when cookbooks suggested dinner menus of seven or eight or twelve courses for a dozen people, then domestic help was indicated, whether it was permanent or hired just for the day. Household books attempted to help the housewife in all her endeavors, and even Catharine Beecher noted that unless a woman learned her trade properly, friends and neighbors would wonder why she couldn't cope even with the help of one, two, or three domestics.

A New Sense of Economy and Precision

Cookbooks suffered little during the period of the Civil War; in fact, one of the most popular types of cookbooks received a boost from the fund-raising efforts of relief agencies and ladies' clubs (see Chapter 4). Both northern and southern cookbooks of the time continued to be printed with only slight interruptions, and the authors and publishers used the economic problems of the country to increase their sales. As life on the great plantations was reduced to a simple search for survival, and as many northern kitchens suffered the loss of the breadwinner, the housewife needed help in making certain that her family would have at least simple food on the table. Cookbooks began to offer ways of economizing, including among their pages directions for turning brown sugar into white, patching and recutting clothing, and running smaller households; for some southern women, it was a new experience entering a kitchen and trying to make a meal without the help of slaves.

Even though Eliza Leslie separated her ingredients listings from the cooking directions, as a rule, cookbooks of the nineteenth century presented "paragraph style" recipes, with the ingredients and methods combined in a single narrative. Although this offered the author a chatty way to present cookery directions combined with personal thoughts on just about everything from shopping to French tastes, paragraph recipes required more attention from the cook, who had to read the entire recipe and pick out the necessary ingredients—or search for ingredients as she cooked, a sure path to kitchen disorganization. Catharine Beecher's cookbook is a curious mixture of paragraph recipes and two-step recipes (ingredients and method listed separately), and Marion Harland's *Common Sense in the Household* (1872) arrived at the technique of offering cooking recipes, like soups and gravies, in paragraph form, and baking recipes, like cakes and breads, in two-step form. Even Mary Lincoln, cooking instructor at the Boston Cooking School and author of *Mrs. Lincoln's Boston Cook Book* (1883; subtitled "What To Do and What Not To Do In Cooking"), had an eccentric method of writing recipes: some contain ingredients listings and directions, while others have the ingredients in the directions but set apart in italics. Her recipe for Brown Bread Brewis is typical: "Break *one pint* of *dry brown bread* and *half a cup* of *stale white bread* into inch pieces. Put a *tablespoon* of *butter* in a large frying pan, and when it is melted, but not brown, add the bread and cover with *one pint* or more of *milk.* Let it simmer, stirring occasionally to keep it from sticking, until the bread is soft and the milk absorbed. Salt to taste." (This recipe also points out one of the treats of collecting cookbooks: the fact that a modern collector can discover medieval dishes, like brewis, in use more than 500 years or so after they first appeared in recipe form.)

Cookbooks experienced a kind of revolution in the late 1800s as a result of work done by Fannie Merritt Farmer, an instructor at the Boston Cooking School. Fannie suffered ill health as a young woman, but her interest in cooking eventually resulted in her becoming first a student and then the director of the Boston Cooking School. While her fame could be based solely on her clear writing and inventive recipes, like Harvard salad and coffee ice cream served in cantaloupe, Fannie is best known as the developer and promoter of a cooking system based on level measurements. As a practitioner of domestic science, she raised careful measurements and testing of recipes to an art. "Correct measurements are absolutely necessary to insure the best results. Good judgment, with experience, has taught some to measure by sight; but the majority need definite guides," this unique cooking instructor

Fig. 3-4 Collectors who are fans of Fannie Farmer should look for copies of both *The Boston Cooking-School Magazine* and the later version retitled *American Cookery.* The magazines are filled with recipes, photos, and advertisements for the "latest" in kitchen items, including stoves, home cooking classes, and utensils, (like the "chic copper whistling egg cooker" or the "krusty korn kob moulds"). This example, from 1936, is in very good to fine condition, showing little wear and even retaining a crisp, new feel.

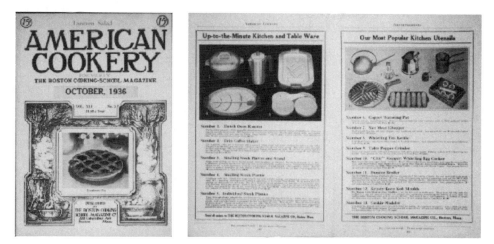

Fig. 3-5 The Up-To-Date Waitress (1906, 1929) **was written by Janet McKenzie Hill, an editor of** *The Boston Cooking-School Magazine.* **The book contains black-and-white photos demonstrating such important skills as serving celery club-house style, carving a meat pie properly (just follow the lines), and selecting toast racks. The book encourages the waitress to raise her work to the level of other female occupations, including stenography, teaching, dressmaking, and millinery.**

wrote. "To measure a cupful, put in the ingredient by spoonfuls or from a scoop, round slightly and level with a case knife, care being taken not to shake the cup." With such specific, consistent directions, cookbook users could be guaranteed that the recipe was workable and tested under conditions that could be repeated at home. Gone were the vague quantities of "butter the size of a hazelnut," "a wineglass of milk," or "a spoonful of flour."

Even though she was the director of the school, Farmer's *The Boston Cooking-School Cook Book* (1896) was a personal gamble: according to her agreement with the original publishers, she paid for the book's publication while the company acted simply as the sales outlet. Farmer was also placed in the uncomfortable position of updating the school's text, which was originally written by Mrs. Lincoln, a formidable woman who was still alive and teaching and who still claimed many readers and fans. A general rewrite was performed, and the main difference between the two women and their styles is illustrated in the opening chapter. Mrs. Lincoln took the highhanded thought that "all civilized nations cook their food, to improve its taste and digestibility. The degree of civilization is often measured by the cuisine." Fanny was more down-to-earth, noting that "progress in civilization has been accompanied by progress in cookery."

Cookbook collectors and others interested in culinary history will discover in the *The Boston Cooking-School Cook Book* a treasure chest of how-to information that unravels antique kitchen arcana like how to adjust a cooking-stove, how to tell the difference between coal types (nut, coke, or hard coal), and the proper way to select, use, and prepare coffee. To date, millions of copies of the Fannie Farmer book and its revised versions have sold to generations of pleased cooks, who do their share in adding to the progress of civilization.

The success of Fannie Farmer as an innovator was continued by many other food writers until the end of the century. Juliet Corson founded the New York Cooking School in 1876 and was well-known for self-publishing a leaflet called *Fifteen Cent Dinners for Workingmen's Families*, which provided information on purchasing and preparing good, nourishing foods within a limited budget. Her publication showed that reformers concerned with the living conditions of the poor, the disadvantaged, and the newly immigrated were gaining ground in the cookbook arena and would strongly influence American cookery and cookbooks into the twentieth century. (Eventually, the immigrant situation resulted in the development of settlement houses, places where women could go to learn the ways of their new home and where cooking was an important topic in classes.) Cookbooks, however, were still not a sure sell with book publishers, and many authors were forced to underwrite the costs of their own books or to accept advertising in order to pay for the printing.

Sarah Tyson Rorer was a cooking teacher in Philadelphia, but early in her career she mastered the art of product promotion, a skill that would serve her well in the many commercial endorsements and cookbooks she produced over the years (Figure 3-6). Her recipes were thorough and wide-ranging,

Fig. 3-6 Mrs. Sarah Tyson Rorer was famous for her product endorsements and the large number of articles and publications she wrote. This booklet from 1900 begins with a letter of recommendation for Cottolene, a shortening that was packed in attractive tin pails. Rorer was not alone in praising the product: a letter also appears in the book from Ogden Doremus, "professor of chemistry, toxicology and medical jurisprudence at Bellevue Hospital Medical College," obviously a man whose word was intended to put the wary Cottolene customer at ease. The booklet pictured is in fair condition, with some cover stains and fading on the inner pages; the cover reflects the popularity of Art Nouveau design.

covering the likes and tastes of many classes: "[Raccoons, skunks and opossums] are eaten by many people, but as I have had no experience in cooking the above animals, I will merely state that they may be cooked in all the ways that rabbits are, and served the same." Rorer's book, *The Philadelphia Cook Book* (1886), contained recipes for Moravian sugar cakes, schmier-kase (cottage cheese), and planked shad, recipes that reflect her Pennsylvania surroundings. She also presented a chapter on leftovers called "What To Save And How To Use It," reflecting the skills of the thrifty cook, and a detailed listing of utensils she deemed necessary to a well-furnished kitchen, including an asparagus boiler, a boned-turkey mold, a Boston brown-bread mold, and items made by some of "her" companies, including a Dover egg beater, a Ridgway refrigerator, and an Enterprise food chopper. Cookbooks would continue to list the names of famous contributors, including cooks and instructors, counting on the homey appeal and trust that such people projected to the readers.

Many cookbooks published near the turn of the century emphasized thrift, still placing careful household management squarely on the shoulders of the wife. But while some books preached the virtues of careful living and insisted upon the all-knowing wisdom of the husband, a few cookbooks offered a sly sense of humor and a new awareness of the value of domestic skills. In a cookbook essay by Christine Terhune Herrick, she tells the tale of a wife (named Woman of Small Means) who served a luncheon for three at a total cost of 90¢. After the husband belittles her numbers by indicating that she did not take into account the skill of the cook and the cost of the waitress, the reply puts the man squarely in his place: "'Oh, those don't count,' replied the Woman of Small Means, calmly. 'They never allow for the salary of the *chef* in the fashionable 50¢ luncheons and dinners.' And the Man of the House, sad, surprised, astounded by the sovereign strength of woman's logic, said no more."

The Men of the Kitchen

Since the beginning of "professional" cookery in ancient times, men were the visible representatives of the culinary arts and the titular heads of the kitchen, often eclipsing women cooks who, as slaves specializing in particular dishes like sweets and desserts, obviously knew what they were doing. That men were chefs and women were cooks was a separation caused by a variety of social factors, not the least being the fact that women had little chance to act as independent beings unless they were wealthy, eccentric, or both.

It took until the nineteenth century for women to secure their places in the kitchen and to create a new "domestic science," but the food snobs among the wealthy and upwardly mobile still turned to Europe searching for male guidance through the Gilded Age kitchens of the 1880s and 1890s. Chefs were sometimes sent undercover to Europe, there to learn coveted recipes which were then smuggled back to America. Even though world expositions and fairs displayed the fruits (and vegetables!) of American progress, food from Europe was still considered by those in the know to be the epitome of modern taste. So while cookbooks by Fannie Farmer pleased one section of the cooking populace, other books, including those by male authors, were to become best-sellers with the trendsetters and aspiring chefs across the United States.

One of the most popular of these books was *The Cook's Guide and Housekeeper's & Butler's Assistant: A Practical Treatise on English and Foreign Cookery In All Its Branches,* by Charles Elmé Francatelli, student of the great French chef Carême. Francatelli was also chief cook to Queen Victoria, which guaranteed him a place in the upper-class hearts of the American gentry. His cookbook, which was read widely in the United States, gave backhanded acknowledgments to American food (presumably some of the foreign cookery in the title) and included recipes like "Wild Fowl, American Fashion," which indicated that the fowl was to be prepared according to general directions and served "with the addition of some black-currant jelly." No fruit pies, no buckwheat cakes (even though they were popularized in London by the American artist James Macneill Whistler), and no mention of the wealth of regional foods found in the old colonies. He also claimed that the book was for the middle classes, and yet the book carried page after page of dishes with inflated titles like "rice a la Soeur Nightingale," "snipe pudding a l'epicurean," "baron of hare, German fashion," and recipes for anything European, including Albert biscuits, Victoria biscuits, and biscuits Venetian, Swedish, Italian, Russian and Sicilian. Collectors can still find this book in one of several editions, and, although not an American publication, it provides an indication of how little regard European kitchens had for American cuisine.

In the United States, male chefs with an eye toward the newly wealthy upper and upper-middle classes were also writing cookbooks. Examples include Charles Ranhofer's *The Epicurean* (Figure 3-7) and Alessandro Filippini's *The Table: How To Buy Food, How To Cook It, And How To Serve It,* both published in 1889. Ranhofer and Filippini had been chefs at Delmonico's in New York, a restaurant which was famous for its lush foods, elaborate menus, and social cachet. Ranhofer's huge compendium covered everything from table and food service to meals, both American and foreign. Collectors value the book for its unique vision of the kitchen in America during the Gilded Age and for its wealth of illustrations, which include detailed—and decidedly bizarre—food presentations resembling the great dishes of ancient banquets, which, when considered in light of the gargantuan appetites of an expanding America, seem oddly suitable for the times. The book also contains detailed menus from famous dinners served at Delmonico's, including some given for royalty.

In strong contrast to the cookbook of Francatelli, Filippini's book sang the praises of American food, noting the wealth of the midwestern meat markets

Fig. 3-7 Charles Ranhofer's huge work, *The Epicurean*, was a complete course of study in the art of preparing and serving fine foods; first issued in 1895, it was reissued in 1916 and 1920. With nearly 1,200 pages and hundreds of detailed illustrations, the book is an important source for menus, food preparation, service techniques, and recipes of the nineteenth century. The pictured illustration of a table set for dinner only hints at the wealth of material found in the volume. Collectors should watch for any edition; all tend to be costly when found in good condition.

and the new refrigerator cars that were changing the quality of the meat found on the American dinner tables. In fact, he proclaims, "These 'gourmands' [American epicures] have, with the aid of the excellent resources of the American market and the encouragement given to the culinary art of the period, brought the modern American table to virtual perfection. This is saying a great deal, inasmuch as the famed restaurants of London, Paris, and Vienna have ever claimed a reputation and an ascendancy over others that seemed to form a part of history itself." It is interesting to see that whereas Francatelli relegated American waterfowl to a secondary category, behind European gamebirds, Fillippini notes, "No game is more highly prized or more eagerly sought after in Europe than our American canvas-back ducks, grouse and wild turkeys." And while he bows to the European mode with recipe names like "minced veal á la Catalan," he also offers chapters on muskmelons, watermelons, strawberry shortcake, buckwheat pancakes, and pumpkin pie. These authors apparently expected that chefs and, of course, women cooks, were willing and able to produce some of the more elaborate dishes—acknowledgement, perhaps, of the effect that cooking schools, cookbooks and domestic science were having on the cookbook psyche.

Cookbooks Respond to Technology

Readers of cookbooks will discover that while technology was moving along in the nineteenth century, it didn't necessarily make life all that much simpler for the cook. Safer, yes, but as far as simplicity went, that was still open to debate. Cookbooks reflected changes in the kitchen, including the use of cast iron cooking stoves, new foodstuffs (like baking powder and "automatic," or self-rising, flour), and canning jars, but the books still tended to straddle the worlds of the old and the new kitchen, since not all women could be expected to catch up with the future so quickly. Cookery and household books were more necessary than ever, since they provided guidance through the byways and details of the new technology.

Iron cookstoves that burned either wood or coal came on the market in the 1840s, but many cooks grappled with open fireplaces until the Civil War. As late as 1857, *Miss Leslie's New Cookery Book* tendered explicit directions for heating brick ovens (fireplace wall ovens), including an old method for checking temperature: "For baking bread, the floor of the oven should look red, and a little flour thrown in should burn brown immediately." Even *The Young Housekeeper's Friend,* published in 1864, stated that although "stoves and cooking-ranges have so generally taken the place of brick ovens, that the following directions . . . will seldom be of use now. . . . Yet, as they may sometimes be needed, they are suffered to remain." Those fortunate enough to own a range needed to practice with the baffles and doors in order to get the hang of the new cooking method, but help could be obtained from the stove companies themselves. One of the most famous cast-iron stoves was produced by the Home Comfort Stove Company. Established in 1864, the factory produced ranges that were still in use more than fifty years later, as attested to by letters printed in the company's advertising cookbook. The *Home Comfort Cook Book* (Figure 3-8) also contained illustrations of the stove through the years, including the addition of such useful items as a water reservoir, a drying shelf, teapot brackets, and a square oven. But although the stoves made cooking simpler in some respects, even the earliest and simplest iron units required much care. "There are many ways of cleaning a stove," wrote Sarah Josepha Hale in 1857, "but if the ornamental parts be neglected, rust will soon disfigure the entire surface and lead to incalculable trouble. Emery dust, moistened into a paste with sweet oil, should be kept in a little jar; this should be applied . . . up and down, never crossways, until marks or burns disappear. A dry leather should then remove the oil and a polish should afterwards be given with putty powder on a dry clean leather."

The nineteenth century is sometimes viewed by people as a time of cooking that was heavy with lard, short on taste, and dull in the extreme. It would be difficult to dispute this view if it weren't for cookbooks, which show a richness in flavors and a wide availability of ingredients that is sometimes

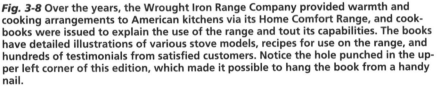

Fig. 3-8 Over the years, the Wrought Iron Range Company provided warmth and cooking arrangements to American kitchens via its Home Comfort Range, and cookbooks were issued to explain the use of the range and tout its capabilities. The books have detailed illustrations of various stove models, recipes for use on the range, and hundreds of testimonials from satisfied customers. Notice the hole punched in the upper left corner of this edition, which made it possible to hang the book from a handy nail.

ignored by casual readers. Spices, exotic fruits, vegetables, game, seafood, shellfish, and chocolate were all stocked on grocery shelves. A cookbook of 1876 noted that

> the amount of game and fish which our great country and extent of sea-coast give us, the variety of climate from Florida to Maine, from San Francisco to Boston, which the remarkable net-work of our railway communication allows us to enjoy, all this makes the American market in any great city almost fabulously profuse. Then our steamships bring us fresh artichokes from Algiers in mid-winter, and figs from the Mediterranean, while the remarkable climate of California gives us four crops of delicate fruits a year.

The author then went on to list two dozen different fish and thirty kinds of game birds found in a private club's kitchen on a single day!

Baking powder was a revolutionary substance that changed the way Americans prepared foods. Although the properties of pearl ash as a leavening agent were understood in the eighteenth century, it was not until the 1860s that commercial baking powder made its appearance on the American market. Homemade mixtures could give food an off color and off taste, but the commercial powders were carefully measured in order to ensure that

Fig. 3-9 Baking powder changed the way Americans dined, but some powders were accused of being adulterated with harmful chemicals, and the resulting "baking powder wars" resulted in advertising that touted a product's purity and safety. Royal Baking Powder Co. printed letters saying the product was "healthful and free from every deleterious substance. . . ." The 1906 booklet warned, "Do not buy alum baking powders under any circumstances," and it of course told cooks to demand Royal Baking Powder at their shops. The collector of kitchenware will appreciate the illustrations of baking pans and equipment. Note the wear to the cover edges; although the booklet is complete, there is interior wear and brittle edges, making it a poor copy.

baked goods would rise evenly and in a timely manner. Manufacturers had to overcome the home baker's dislike of chemicals and her distrust of purchased foods, which were sometimes heavily adulterated by unscrupulous grocery suppliers, so many advertising cookbooks noted that the powder was absolutely harmless, leaving no "Rochelle salts, tartaric acid, alum, lime or ammonia" in the foods. By the 1880s, cookbooks were showing that women had learned well the new chemistry, as recipes for layer cakes, lightning cakes, and upside-down cakes proliferated.

A new advance in publishing that affected the design and look of cookbooks in the nineteenth century concerned illustrations. Printing had advanced over the years to include engravings (for which a picture was cut onto a block and inked onto paper) and chromolithography (a method of printing elaborate color designs). By the last quarter of the nineteenth century, changes in printing and photographic techniques made it affordable for

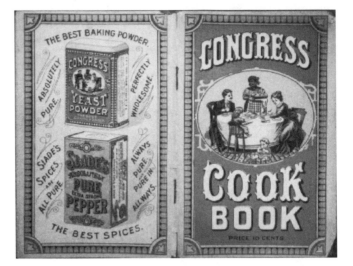

Fig. 3-10 The *Congress Cook Book* was published in 1899, at a time when worries over tainted baking powder were attracting the cooking public's attention. This colorful example shows the emphasis placed on purity and wholesomeness. In fact, the company even called its product "yeast powder," perhaps in an attempt to distance its product from the poor reputation of baking powder.

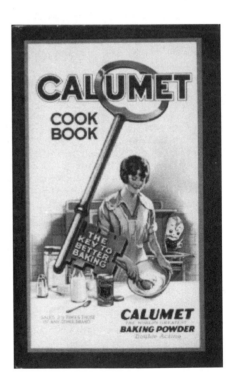

Fig. 3-11 As late as the 1920s, baking powder companies were still competing with each other through endorsements and certificates of merit. Calumet also offered the thought that it was "never touched by human hands" during its production at the sanitary factory facilities. The cartoon child who advertised Calumet (shown here peeking out from behind the stove) was one of many—from the Gold Dust Twins to the Jell-O Girl and the Campbell's Kids—who became the mascots of companies and helped to build product recognition.

cookbook publishers to offer illustrations along with the text, including pictures of kitchenware and advertisements for related goods; collectors of cookbooks and kitchenware find the material a wellspring of information on what the well-dressed kitchen looked like during the period. The early nineteenth-century cookbooks contained only a few illustrations, some of which were copied from book to book, including a popular series of pigs, cows, and sheep with the different cuts of meat neatly outlined on each animal. Simple line drawings were also used to show kitchen furniture and utensils and to introduce the housewife to new additions in the kitchen cabinet. *Miss Beecher's Household Receipt Book* shows everything from tin bakers and a footman (a warming grate), which indicated that fireplaces were still common in 1847, to balances (for weighing out ingredients, an important part of the new domestic science), fish and preserving kettles, apple corers, and saucepans. The section also contains directions for building a refrigerator from a barrel filled with ice. But by 1878, in *Practical Cooking and Dinner Giving,* author Mary Henderson was able to describe (and have illustrated) several dozen serving pieces probably not found in the average kitchen: for example, "the fish stand—fried smelts are hung by catching them to the sharp points of the stand. The intervening places are filled with parsley or leaves and the whole served in the form of a pyramid."

In addition to the text, advertisements began to appear, especially in books published in the 1890s, like *The Table.* Cookbooks became important vehicles of advertising for all types of goods, allowing modern collectors a look into the commercial world of late-nineteenth-century restaurants, booksellers, and food purveyors. Many cookbooks of the time also contained nonillustrated listings of novels and recently published books by the same company and, of course, by the same author. So while a reader of Miss Leslie's cookery book might discover that *The Pirate's Son, A Sea Novel of Great Interest* had just been released for 25¢, she would also be told, in great detail, "what the editors of the leading newspapers say" about Miss Leslie's work— and would, it was hoped, purchase the book at once. But the award for self-promotion might be reserved for Catharine Beecher, whose *Receipt Book* contained a 23-page insert informing readers about the recently published (1864) edition of *A Treatise on Domestic Economy!* Both the editors and the author were smart marketers, since Miss Beecher would refer readers of one book to recipes or directions in another of her books, ensuring increased sales of her works.

Cooks desirous of learning the proper way of carving up a cod's head or an entire pig could turn to the drawings in cookbooks like *The American Practical Cookery Book,* which borrowed several of its how-to illustrations from earlier works. The book also contained pictures of fruits and berries in the section on preserves, so it may indicate that cooks had a difficult time telling one berry from the next. Other books displayed cuts of meat (buying and identifying meat seemed to be a particular problem of nineteenth-century cooks), various jellied or iced desserts, and decorated cakes. Without the help of photography, which did not become common in cookbooks until the early twentieth century, the cook was left to interpret small, odd-looking pictures of food and try to duplicate them in the finished product she eventually brought to the table. And, of course, the artwork sometimes depicted food items that either were far beyond the capabilities of the cook for whom the book was meant or represented dishes that were impractical or impossible to duplicate in a home kitchen.

Food Styling

Cookbook collectors can also find while browsing through old cookbooks that the theories of serving food have changed over the centuries. Each era had its own method of placing and removing (or not removing) the food from the table; meals could last several hours, while banquets could go on for several days. In the medieval period, meals might contain three or more courses, with a dozen dishes or more offered in each course. Some early manuscript cookbooks show bare tables with only a few serving utensils, while others depict courtly meals with many dishes.

By the time of the Renaissance, the upper class and royal English were still dining higgedly-piggedly, with sweets, meats, dessert wines, and fish served in one course, then seafood and cakes for the second course. Eighteenth-century cookbooks, including Eliza Smith's, offered detailed "maps" of how to set a table with the proper course. A supper's first serving might consist of carp, a "ragoo," Scotch collops (slices of meat), tarts of all sorts, veal, pigeons with artichokes, and "very small chickens." Smith also offered a "bill of fare for every season of the year," a guide to monthly dinners that were served in first and second courses. Of course, the fact that these elaborate meals were listed in a cookbook does not mean that anyone actually prepared them on a regular basis (no more so than do modern cookbooks indicate what we actually eat). At the very least, however, cookbooks helped to preserve the theory of dining, something that was rarely recorded outside of royal records.

Most eighteenth-century and early nineteenth-century American dinners were being served "à la francaise," meaning diners helped themselves from the serving plates set nearby; unfortunately for the diners, they often missed dishes placed at the other end of the table. Not until the 1800s did a Russian prince popularize service "à la russe," meaning the diner is served from a platter offered by a servant or, as in today's family dining, passed around the table. In *Practical Cooking and Dinner Giving,* Mrs. Henderson noted one reason for the "new" serving style's popularity:

> It is very simple to prepare a dinner served a la Russe, as it matters little how many courses there may be. If it were necessary to prepare many dishes, and to have them all hot, and in perfection at the same minute, and then be obliged to serve them nearly all together, the task might be considered rather formidable and confusing. But with one or two assistants, and with time between each course to prepare the succeeding one, after a very little practice it becomes a mere amusement.

Some cookbooks, especially those of the last quarter of the nineteenth century, include sections on how to set a table and serve food elegantly. *The Successful Housekeeper* (written in 1882, by M. W. Ellsworth and F. B. Dickerson) even provided the young wife with a how-to guide for creating the perfect dining room, including selecting wainscoting, using rich colors like crimson and olive; choosing mirrors, rugs, sideboard, lamps, curtains, and screens; and maintaining a clean fireplace. The serving chapter notes:

> It is quite impossible for the average female mind to confront unmoved the delightful possibilities today afforded by the service of a dinner table. . . . The now universal dinner a la Russe, with its airy hints, suggestions, innuendoes of ministry of the coarser needs of human nature, has limited each course to the one dish offered at a time, with its companion sauce or vegetable. Giving a dinner party in days gone by meant a good deal of hard work for the housewife. . . . It meant hours of seclusion in a pantry with curls tucked up under a pastry cap, and dress obscured by a gingham apron, weighing, measuring, egg-beating, almond blanching, icing, garnishing, seasoning, tasting and invariably gossiping! . . . The march of civilization and modern degeneracy have materially lessened the labors of dinner-giving in the present. . . .

Although mean-spirited in its nostalgia for the labor of the "good old days," this passage indicates that women who were able to afford household help could now also expect to enjoy the social entertainments of middle-class life, after they prepared dinner.

By the turn of the century, some cookbooks began to show the change which occurred as families like the Astors, Goulds, and Vanderbilts helped to create a market for cookbooks that would help home cooks copy the upscale foods and cooking methods of the wealthy. Elegant service and elaborate food preparation had replaced the earlier calls for plain domesticity, and, in fact, the anti-French sentiments found in earlier cookbooks had given way to the use of utensils like the bain marie, the French vegetable cutter, and silver scallop shells for serving food "en coquille" for lunch or dinner. Even middle-class families abandoned the simple, commonsense approach to food and dining, although they used silverplate instead of silver, and gaudy carnival glass instead of Tiffany. The standard cookbooks still sold well, but pretentious guides to the high life began to appear. However, in one such book, *The Art of Entertaining,* a guide to social niceties (1892, M. Sherwood), the following realistic warning appeared: "There would be no sense in telling a young American housekeeper to learn to make sauces and to cook like a French chef, for it is a profession requiring years of study and great natural taste and aptitude. . . . As well tell a young lady that she could suddenly be inspired with a knowledge of the art of war or navigation. . . ." Many American cookbooks had come full circle, back to their preoccupation with European food.

Tips for Collecting Nineteenth-Century Cookbooks

Collectors can still locate nineteenth-century cookbooks, although those in good condition by popular authors such as Beecher, Hale, and Farmer can command $125 or more. When you are considering buying a particular book, check to see whether the frontispiece, engravings, and other illustrations are all intact. Many of the books from this period received extensive use, and they may have loose or missing pages, torn hinges and spines, stains, and other marks of wear; such books should be priced accordingly. Cookbook covers were usually plain, with embossed titles in solid color inks or gold lettering, although some books published near the turn of the twentieth century had more elaborate treatments, including printed cover designs. Illustrations were usually simple in the early part of the 1800s; and throughout the century, pictures were usually line drawings offering a vague idea of the way food was supposed to look when prepared correctly. Some cookbooks contained engravings—and later, photos—of the author, along with a facsimile of her autograph. Few cookbooks, if any, were issued with dust jackets; collectors would be very fortunate indeed to come across a nineteenth-century cookbook still in a protective wrapping of that kind.

For those collectors who enjoy recreating meals of a particular historic period, there are many nineteenth-century cookbooks that contain daily menus for the year. These were meant as guides for confused housewives or the newly married woman who had not the slightest idea as to what she should serve at Sunday breakfast, Thursday supper, or Christmas dinner. One of the most interesting menu lists appears in *Practical Housekeeping*, published by the Buckeye Publishing Company of Minneapolis in 1883. There, 365 bills of fare from January through December show not only the foods of the middle class (breakfast, October 1: broiled steak, flannel cakes, fried potatoes) but also offer glimpses into meals for the holidays, including Easter, Thanksgiving, and Christmas, which were celebrated at home. Recreating such a Thanksgiving dinner might tax even the modern cook, since the cookbook lists nearly two dozen dishes for the meal; not surprisingly, readers may also discover that leftover turkey occupied the dinner plates for a few post-Thanksgiving meals.

In addition to looking for cookbooks with an American slant, collectors may also enjoy seeking out cookbooks that had not yet been adapted to the wants and needs of American kitchens, even decades after Amelia Simmons had attempted to solve the problem. Many European cookbooks were sold in the United States, and examples of French, German, and English books can convey the roots of American cooking, as well as offering a look at the ancestors of foods still enjoyed today. Some of the most overlooked buys for collectors include household management books—one-volume guides like *Gems of the Household*—which cover many unusual and often forgotten pieces of household and kitchen-related lore, including mixing inks, preparing dyes, and decocting medical mixtures. They arc often oversized books, and some covers have elaborate printing, while the interior text contains charming examples of the printer's and illustrator's art. Farm guides are another cookbook-related item; besides containing directions for planting a kitchen garden or veterinary how-tos, they have canning and other standard farm recipes as well. Both types of books are not always shelved or listed with cookbooks; look for them in the agriculture or encyclopedia sections of bookshops or catalogs.

4 ❘ Funds from Food

Charity and Fund-raising Cookbooks

What Is a Charity Cookbook?

It has been nearly 150 years since what the cookbook collectors call "charities" were first used to raise money for worthy causes, and since then, tens of thousands of the books have been published, to the delight of collectors and the despair of bibliographers. Down through the generations, America's reputation for good home cooking was stirred, whipped, chopped, and folded into successful cookbooks that supported everything from homes for friendless women and aged Hebrews to orphan asylums, garden clubs, women's colleges, and reading groups. The enjoyment of these books was immediate and went beyond simple culinary enjoyment: the purchaser of a book had the satisfaction of helping a fund find money for an important cause. Also, she could read what her neighbors were cooking, compare her own cooking skills with local cooks, and learn which advertisers supported (or failed to support) the community.

The cookbooks could be described in one word—bountiful—because the contributors gave time, money, recipes, and, most important, a part of their lives. Although men provided recipes and advertising dollars to untold numbers of cookbook committees, it was the women who used these books to share their talents and to support some part of their world at a time when charity cookbooks were one of the few ways in which nonprofessional female authors could shine and unemployed housewives or spinsters could gain financial aid for something very dear to their hearts. There were snippets of poetry, essays on local history, household hints, personal reflections, quotations, and prayers strewn among the recipes, making the books tasty ragouts

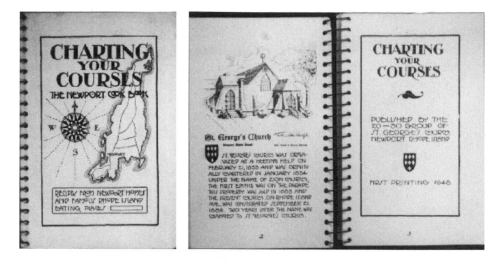

Fig. 4-1 *Charting Your Courses* was a charity cookbook that took advantage of the cachet that Rhode Island had as home to the wealthy and well-known. Simply printed in black ink on off-white paper, the design and type styles were as interesting as the recipes. The book was issued with a spiral wire binding and contains line drawings of historic sites and text on their histories. Each recipe appeared in the handwriting of the contributor, and each was signed. The editors unwittingly made things easy for collectors, noting on the title page that this 1948 printing was the first to reach the public.

of American style, filled with the cherished old and the daring new, in food and social thought.

It is ironic that these once inexpensive and overlooked books are now eagerly sought after as source material by social scientists, culinary historians, and even those who are interested in the history of type design and small-town publishing. For the modern charity cookbook collector, there is still a great deal of delight to be discovered in this unusual aspect of cookbook collecting. The fact is that charity cookbooks still tend to be the most charming cookbooks on the market, with a personal, singular flavor that is often missing from other books. The voices of women generations gone speak out with their humor, their knowledge, their religious fervor, their hopes. And for collectors on a somewhat limited budget, "charities" can offer an easy and interesting entry into the cookbook world.

Collectors and booksellers refer to charity cookbooks in a variety of ways: the various terms used are "charities," "fund-raisers," "contributed cookbooks," and "church cookbooks." Sometimes the books are called "regionals" because of emphasis on an insular area (like Key West, Florida or Anchorage, Alaska) and the local foods, but the term "regionals" can also be used to encompass commercially published cookbooks as well. Charities had many variations on a basic theme, but basic it was: recipes were gathered, usually from a limited, specific group like a ladies' club, then printed in book form and sold to raise funds for a special cause. The idea of people contributing recipes to a cookbook was not new; some English cookbooks from the eighteenth century indicated that the author had collected recipes from friends and family, but it took American cooks to turn the idea into a money-maker for charities. Although charity cookbooks have been compiled in England and Canada, especially during the two world wars, the books never matched the intensity of use found in the United States.

The Variety of Charity Cookbooks

Collectors disagree over which was actually the "first" charity cookbook printed in the United States. Some argue for temperance cookbooks of the 1840s, which contained recipes collected from cooks other than the author and were sold to raise money for the fight against the widespread use of intoxicating beverages. Other cookbook historians point out that Alexis Soyer, humanitarian, writer, and, not the least, chef to Queen Victoria, wrote a cookbook used during the Crimean War (Figure 4-2). The book was eventually

Fig. 4-2 Alexis Soyer was a French dandy, an inventor, an author, and a chef, who also helped to change the way in which the military fed its soldiers during the Crimean War. *A Shilling Cookery for The People* was first published in 1855 and sold 10,000 copies on its first day in the shops; the copy shown here was one of the 260,000 that sold by 1857. (Photo courtesy of the Library of Congress.)

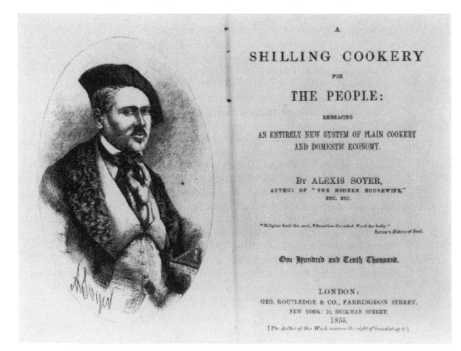

reprinted in New York in 1861 by a service organization, with the apparent goal of raising funds to be used in assisting destitute or bereaved family members through the hard times brought on by the Civil War. Margaret Cook, author of the bibliography *America's Charitable Cooks,* believed that the first cookbook used to raise funds appeared in Philadelphia in 1864. Written by Maria J. Moss, *A Poetical Cook Book* offered rhymed recipes and was dedicated to the Sanitary Fair of 1864 (a forerunner of the Red Cross fairs in later years).

It seems unlikely that this question of firsts will be settled soon, since Cook noted that of the more than 2,300 charitable cookbooks published between the years 1861 and 1915, nearly 75 percent of the books were known only in the form of a single copy tucked away in a small town, private, or university library across the United States. (That many more unique copies wait to be discovered or recognized for their importance in the history of cookbooks is likely, and this offers collectors the unusual chance to discover a new addition to the cookbook field.) But as far as American charity cookbooks are concerned, it was the Civil War that proved the worth of such books and encouraged a popular type of publication that has continued to be popular right into the present.

Charity cookbooks furnish the reader with a chance to step back into small-town America and gather around the table with great-great-grandmother. The books were compilations of favorite recipes, philosophies, and household hints, to which were added a twist of humor and an ounce of business sense. The production of the books settled into a routine early on in their history and has remained much the same into the present. Usually, a

Fig. 4-3 Cookbooks like this example from Salem, Massachusetts, showed the pride of the contributors, who reached back into history to highlight their food traditions. But they borrowed liberally from other cookbooks; in this book the editors note that they used recipes from *The Compleate Cook's Guide, The Frugal Housewife,* and others, and they sprinkled the text with quotes from authors like Byron, Shakespeare, and Herrick.

Fig. 4-4 Wolf & Dessauer, a department store in Fort Wayne, Indiana, sponsored *The Tried and Proved O.K. Recipe Book* in 1914, combining the style of a fund-raising cookbook with canny advertising. Recipes were gathered from "Fort Wayne and vicinity housewives," although contributor names like Mrs. Churchman, Aunty Drudge, Miss Farmer, and Fannie Merritt most likely sprung from someone's imagination. The book is a treasure trove of local advertising, for products from lanterns and nutcrackers to curly birch bedroom furniture, and the illustrations, of such things as dresses for the "stylish stout" woman, offer a look at middle-class needs at the turn of the century.

group of women formed a cookbook committee and various duties were assigned, including collecting and presenting recipes; selling advertising to local businesses; arranging for printing; publicity; and, finally, sales and marketing. The book titles ranged from the straightforward *(The Robert E. Lee United Daughters of the Confederacy Cookbook)* and the baldly honest *(The Tried and Proved O.K. Recipe Book* or *How to Keep a Husband)* to the cute *(At Home on the Range)* and the sophisticated *(Fashions in Beverly Hills)*. Sometimes the editors or compilers of a book received special mention; more likely, the introduction was self-effacing, as in this example from the 1883 edition of the *First Dutch Reformed Cook Book* of Pompton Plains, New Jersey:

> The ladies make no apology in presenting to their friends this little collection of recipes, as it is intended principally for each other's benefit. It has been hastily gathered, but we believe there will be found in it something of the

ancient hospitality, the spirit of the hearth-log and crane, for which our venerable homes have become proverbial. . . . The names and initials attached to many of (the recipes) will disclose the fact that we have enjoyed the cooperation of ladies from beyond our immediate community, for whose assistance, and that of all who in various ways have aided us, we offer our cordial thanks.

One book even contained an ode entitled "To A Cook Book," which told the book:

> You'll be welcome where you go.
> All the housewives you will know.
> Happy brides you will befriend,
> And to matrons, knowledge lend.

This was also an important, if sometimes unacknowledged, part of the charity cookbooks' job: the sharing of recipes and the passing along of kitchen knowledge across the generations.

Some books, like *Fashions in Beverly Hills* (Figure 4-5), the 1930 project of a woman's club, added a twist to marketing: instead of having a famous chef write the introduction to the book or borrowing recipes from other publications, the compilers would gather recipes from famous people. Early in this century, First Ladies were the prime target of charity cookbook compilers, with Mrs. Theodore Roosevelt, Mrs. Calvin Coolidge, Mrs. Herbert Hoover, and Mrs. Eleanor Roosevelt the favorite among recipe contributors. Well-known cookbook authors were also good for a recipe or two or a comment of encouragement, as in this note from Marion Harland in 1877 to the ladies of one church committee: "Please convey my acknowledgments for the Presbyterian Cook Book to the compilers. I have examined it carefully, and take pleasure in pronouncing the recipes it contains, as a whole, practical, economical, and good. . . . I shall make use of the work in my own family, having a sort of passion for trying new recipes that promise well. . . ."

Collectors should watch for the names of famous people from film, stage, and literary arenas as well, particularly in cookbooks from artists' colonies, like Bucks County, Pennsylvania, or Woodstock, New York; film production centers, including Hollywood; and even social centers, including Palm Beach, Florida, and Newport, Rhode Island. In the Beverly Hills book, the introduction was written by Will Rogers, and recipes were donated by screen idols, most of whom probably never saw a kitchen, including Ramon Novarro (guacamole), Joan Crawford (salad), Constance Bennett (Spanish chicken), and Farina, from the "Our Gang" series (pumpkin pie). *Bucks the Artists' County Cooks* book (Figure 4-7) contains a signed recipe from, among others, Pearl S. Buck, and *The Belgian Relief Cook Book* contains the names of artist James Montgomery Flagg and novelist Gene Stratton Porter. Of course, if a compiler couldn't find anyone famous to donate a dish or two, she

Fig. 4-5 Although most cookbooks with signed recipes were produced by small-town ladies' organizations, others had the punch of celebrity behind them; such a one was *Fashions in Foods in Beverly Hills* (1930), from the Beverly Hills Woman's Club. With an introduction by Will Rogers, the book capitalized on American's interest in the movie business and contained recipes from Fannie Brice, Dolores Del Rio, and Norma Talmadge (who offered something called an East India Squab Nest, with curry powder, cocoanut, raisins, pineapple, banana, onion, garlic, and squab). Not surprisingly, the ads were directed toward upper-class ladies of leisure—few middle-class wives had a chance to stay at the Los Angeles Biltmore or rent a limousine with a uniformed chauffeur. But with few exceptions, the recipes were down-to-earth and affordable, and for a reader smitten with Hollywood and the silver screen, the cookbook was an introduction to the personal tastes of the stars.

could always fall back on namesake recipe standbys like Martha Washington's Mother's light fruit cake or the Prince of Wales cake, which, if not actually personal recipes, at least had the cachet of personality. Sometimes a recipe was listed as "anonymous" or signed "contributed" or "selected," which indicated that the dish was borrowed from another publication in order to add more dimension to the recipes included in the book. (Incidentally, recipe names sometimes changed as the recipes moved from book to book. For example, the title "Better Than Sex" chocolate cake in one northern cookbook is changed to "Better Than Heaven" cake in a more conservative cookbook from a southern Baptist congregation.)

Although the earliest charity cookbooks had their origins in the eastern United States, the books gradually moved west and south, picking up many regional specialties along the way, including unusual ingredients and cooking methods. Cookbooks from Massachusetts and New York had recipes for maple chiffon cake, lump maple sugar cookies, and maple buns, while

Fig. **4-6** Even politicians have to eat, and their wives (or husbands) need recipes. The Congressional Club, until only recently made up of the wives and daughters of members of Congress, the Cabinet, and the Supreme Court, presented its first fund-raising cookbook in 1927 and then went through several style changes (the 1945 edition was presented in the handwritten style found in many fund-raisers). This example is from 1965 and contains a foreword by Mrs. Lyndon Johnson; some of the most interesting reading in the book comes not from the recipes, which are extensive, but from the section about protocol and precedence in Washington. The book was presented by a member of Congress to one of his constituents and contains a calling card with his signature.

Fig. **4-7** Artists' cookbooks have long been popular fund-raisers, and *Bucks the Artists' County Cooks,* issued in 1950, was one of the best. Sponsored by the Woman's Auxiliary of Trinity Chapel, Solebury, the ladies explained in their introduction that "this is a cookbook sufficiently attractive to display on your library table, practical enough to be at home in your kitchen." The Bucks County region was home to many writers, painters, and theater people, and the book has recipes reflecting this population, like this rhymed recipe for oysters-on-a-stick from Anne Matthews (the original Stella Dallas) and dishes from novelist Pearl S. Buck and Mrs. Oscar Hammerstein.

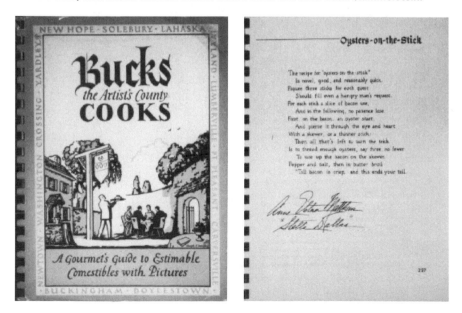

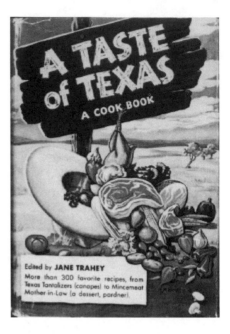

Fig. 4-8 Interest in American regional foods began in the eighteenth century with Amelia Simmons, and cookbooks have continued to reflect that interest. Many of the best regional cookbooks came from community groups, like the Junior League, but local pride could also prove to be profitable to commercial publishers as well. *A Taste of Texas* was issued by the folks at Neiman-Marcus, that upper-class emporium, in 1949, after customers from around the world requested a Texas cookbook. The recipes came from all over the state and are signed by the contributors. Collectors should note that the modern folk story of the $100 cake and recipe (where the diner asked for the recipe and was then billed $100 by the restaurant) is recorded in this cookbook.

Fig. 4-9 One of the best-selling fund-raising cookbooks of all time, *River Road Recipes* was first printed in 1959 and is still available, with more than one million copies in print. The road referred to in the title ran from Baton Rouge to New Orleans, and the recipes in the book encompass Spanish, French, Creole, Cajun, African, and American dishes. The simple presentation of the book offers a stark contrast to many of the elaborate Junior League productions of recent years.

southern books had such specialties as Confederate daughter's pudding and Southern egg-nog ("For some reason, it requires a Southern woman to make it," noted one contributor). Maine cooks might offer lobster soup or hickory nut cake, while midwestern farm wives would present dozens of treasured

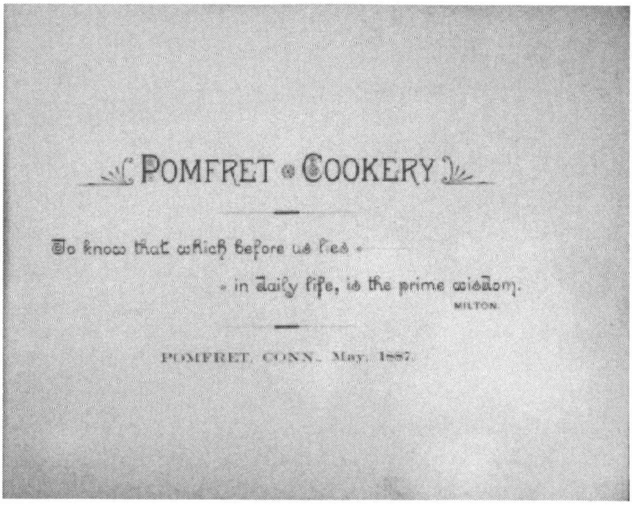

Fig. 4-10 The women of Pomfret, Connecticut, offered this book in 1887 to raise money for church beautifying and repair needs. The recipes are simply presented and include many old-fashioned dishes, like Indian puffs, corn bread, bannocks, common apple pie, and salt fish in cream. The book is an unusual size (7¾″ × 5¾″) and is a graceful example of a rural, small-town cookbook. The title page (shown in the illustration) offers a quote from Milton, displaying a touch of sophistication.

secrets for preparing beef and veal, and California cooks compiled dishes that included dates, chilis, and Spanish-influenced seasonings. What makes these books important to both collectors and historians is that at a time when many commercial publishers were beginning to believe that food started and ended with bland, controlled, cooking-school recipes, the richness of regional dishes was being carefully preserved for future cooks to enjoy within the pages of the charities.

Collectors will discover when browsing through the pages of charity cookbooks that many recipes left a lot to be desired in the way of description, with terse ingredient listings and even terser directions, like this one from 1920: "Mamma's Muffins: To one teacup of sweet milk sift flour to make a batter, beat well, teaspoon salt, teaspoon baking powder, one egg, lard. Excellent." Although Fannie Farmer was making headway with her assault on unscientific cooking, charity cookbooks remained firmly old-fashioned in their use of outdated measurements, like gills or "butter the size of a walnut," well into the twentieth century. In fact, it wasn't unusual to find saleratus (a leavening agent made from potassium or sodium bicarbonate) called for instead of baking powder, more than a century after the latter had appeared in Amelia Simmons's *American Cookery*. But even the cooks knew they created problems for the cookbook readers. A recipe for "exactness" from a 1926 Pennsylvania Grange cookbook made fun of the compilers' eternal problem of getting a recipe in accurate form for use in the book:

Like old Aunt Milly, when asked if she was willing to give her recipe for a nice cake, she replied: "Why certainly. It's just as easy as nothing to make it. I just take as much flour as I think I'll need and quite a little dab o' butter and a pinch or two o' creamy tartar, an' sev'ral eggs, if they're plenty, an' less if they ain't, an' mebbe a mite of salt an' stir 'em until I git tired, an' bake it in an averidge oven until I think it's done. That's all there is to it."

While the recipes or the region represented might be the means of attracting a collector to charity cookbooks, much more than food is found within these sometimes fragile pages. Contributors often signed their recipes by initial or by full name, providing a look into a town or church's makeup of married ladies, young women, and spinsters. By the 1940s, some of the books, including classics like *Out of Vermont Kitchens* (Figure 4-11) and *Bucks the Artists' County Cooks,* contained recipes written, illustrated, and signed by the contributors, making for interesting browsing as well as cooking. One of the enjoyable aspects of collecting charity cookbooks is in discovering the handwritten comments that sometimes appear next to the recipes: "try," "good," "awful," and rating stars seemed to be the easiest ways of noting which recipes to make again and which to avoid for the family's dinner. At least one cookbook contained the notation that "this recipe received a prize of fifty dollars in 1923" (given to the contributor's mother). Others stated with pride things like "Wisconsin pioneer pie was my mother's invention" and "Mother's sponge cake won the $50 prize." Obviously, mothers were important players in teaching cooking and eventually were rewarded for their efforts by appearing in their daughters' cookbooks.

Fig. 4-11 Fund-raising cookbooks often continued on their mission for years, as was the case with *Out of Vermont Kitchens.* Collectors look for the first edition, issued by the Trinity Mission and Women's Service League in 1939, although many other editions followed. The recipes were handwritten and illustrated by the contributors; in the case of the directions for corn cake, shown here, the recipe was also a rhyme. A look at the advertising, which was done in the same handwritten style, shows the variety of goods and services offered in a small country town half a century ago.

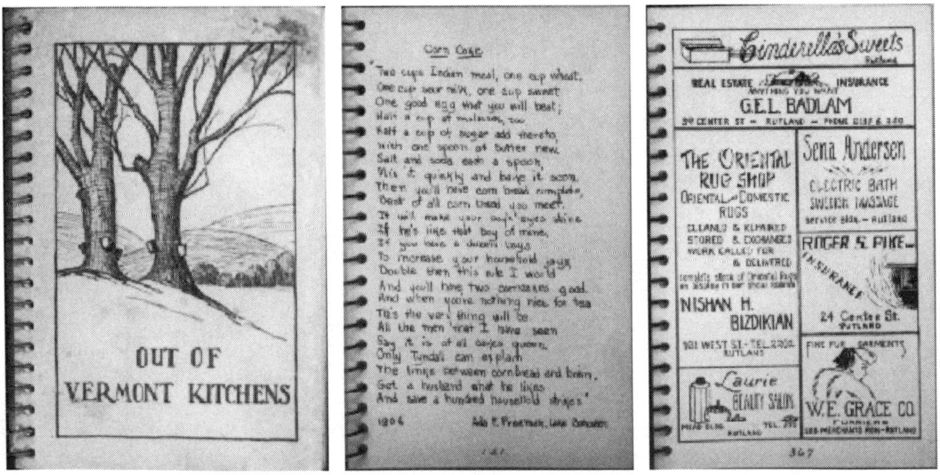

Cookbooks compiled by churches and synagogues can provide a look into religions other than those of the area majority. The relatively uncommon Jewish cookbooks from the early 1900s contain recipes for Passover dishes and advertisements from businesses that catered to the special needs of a Jewish community, with ads for such places as the Prince George Baths and such companies as Goodman & Sons, who produced "matzoths" and potato flour. Jewish charity cookbooks began to enter the mainstream after World War II and the creation of Israel, when women's groups like Hadassah started to expand from local to international fund-raising. Catholic cookbooks had dishes that included Lenten soup and Friday fish meals, while Lutheran and Baptist books often embraced temperance values and eliminated all types of liquor from recipes, substituting fruit juices and herbal teas.

One recipe that turns up in many church cookbooks is Scripture Cake, a rich fruitcake flavored with honey. The trick to making the cake lay in the fact that the ingredients for the recipe were given cryptically, with the clues consisting of quotes from the Bible: ½ cup Judges 5:25 (usually butter), 2 Jeremiah 17:11 (eggs), and so on. A cook could interpret the recipe in her own way, but she always followed Solomon's advice for making a good boy (Proverbs 23:14 "beat well"). Unusual cookbook examples are sometimes found around places where groups like the Shakers, the Amish, and the Mennonites resided; even if the religious group did not produce a book, its influence often spread into the surrounding communities, which were proud

Fig. 4-12 This church cookbook from Hyde Park, Vermont (1912), used an unusual textured paper for its cover. As was the case with many charity cookbooks, it was printed by a local newspaper company, The News and Citizen Press. Since it is the enlarged edition, the editors added a section for new contributors, who gave recipes for traditional dishes, like salmon, peas, and white sauce, along with new tastes, like "hygienic doughnuts" (they were dipped in water to remove the fat). Even at this late date, recipes in this book are still referred to as "receipts."

to offer snowball cakes from the West Pittsfield Shakers or poppy seed dressing from a Texas Mennonite.

Recipe names are another unusual sidelight to consider when collecting charity cookbooks; unlike the standard cookbooks from large publishing houses, charity cookbooks were in most cases written by and for amateur cooks. Many of the recipe titles were straightforward, such as Cousin Fanny's crullers, rice muffins, fruit punch, clam fritters, while others offered a bit of poetry in the dining room. Who would not want to try "husband's favorite sour milk raisin pie," "harlequin cake" with ribbons of lemon jelly, or "watermelon cake," colored and spotted with raisins to look like the summer fruit? And snow flake cake, berry snow, and snow jelly could help recall the cooling winds of winter when served at a summer luncheon. Names such as aristocratic cake, honey comb pudding, Lookout Mountain griddle cakes, Black Hill cake, and pompadour pudding are intriguing, to say the least, as are names like sawdust pudding, a pretty dropped egg, brambles, and no name cookies. Sometimes names got helplessly tangled as they were "translated" from cook to cook: for example, "jumbaltaya" was a version of the Cajun dish, jambalaya, while "mustard gingerbread" was a misunderstanding of muster day gingerbread, once made in New England on days when the local militia mustered out and practiced its military skills.

In addition to regional dishes, many local books contained recipes and directions for dishes from colonial days that were no longer recorded in mainstream cookbooks. Once the cookbooks began to gain strong acceptance in the 1870s, ladies searched their family recipe books and their mothers' and grandmothers' memories for dishes that would preserve the past. America's centennial also encouraged the interest in "old-tyme" foods and beverages, and many of the human sources consulted for charity cookbooks were themselves not far removed from the colonial and early republic eras. A 1909 Dutch cookbook had recipes for waffles, souse, appel koek, and buhling (a buckwheat and cornmeal cake that was baked, cut in slices, and fried). The *Centennial Cook Book* (1913) from New Bedford, Massachusetts, contained recipes for Indian pudding (complete with a suggestion that only Rhode Island cornmeal be used, a tradition still strong in New England), winter blueberry pudding, and baked corn and beans. And *The Virginia Cookery Book* (1921) offers fried green tomatoes, baked Smithfield ham, and chess pie. Within these cookbook pages, collectors can follow the story of American cooking from the days of the open hearth to the microwave, from the distinct regionality of the country's food to the "blandinization" of the American palate.

At the end of the nineteenth century, when the era of immigration was at its peak, and into the 1930s, ethnic groups asserted their awareness of food history, with recipes for family favorites from the old country included among the new "standards" of the United States. Croation cookies, Italian polenta, Hungarian paprikas, and dishes like pickled herring salad and matzoh fritters from Jewish communities began to appear in cookbooks, but many standard recipes were also offered in conjunction with these ethnic dishes to encourage buyers for a cookbook outside of an organization's limits. Ethnic recipes were usually passed down through families, and in many instances their appearance in charity cookbooks was the first time they had been in print; thus, the cookbooks did their share in preserving some food traditions.

Charity cookbooks began to take on a poignant tone during the upheaval of the world wars, when fund-raising was carried out through publications like *Russian Cook Book for American Homes* (1942), *Practical Italian Recipes for American Kitchens* (1918), *Allied Cookery—British, Belgian, French, Italian, Russian* (1916; see Figure 4-13), and *Old and New British Recipes* (1940). The books all served one purpose, clearly described in *Allied Cookery:* "To help in the supply of seeds, farm implements, and other simple but essential means of enabling these suffering people to regain by their own efforts the necessaries of life, the compilers offer to the public this book on Cookery."

Unfortunately, charity cookbooks did not always live up to their names, and they sometimes reflected the prejudices and fears of small communities toward the new and the different. Collectors will stumble upon recipes named using ethnic slurs, like wop salad (tomatoes and lettuce) and nigger toes (cookies); the bulk of the offenses were against African Americans, who could

Fig. 4-13 Although the cookbook pictured shows wear and the title (*Allied Cookery*) has faded, the colors are still bright, and the interior of the book is sharp, making it a good copy. Authors Grace Clergue Harrison and Gertrude Clergue collected recipes from England, France, Italy, Belgium, and Russia and produced the book to raise funds for the war sufferers in the devastated districts of France. There are introductions in French and English, with one writer noting that his recipe for rum omelette ("take a dipper full of rum and insert an omelette in it") was not accepted.

not shake the Aunt Jemima image of the kindly old mammy for more than a century after the Civil War. Into the 1930s both northern and southern cookbooks often contained memories of valued family retainers and slaves, and their recipes for such dishes as terrapin and oyster stew. If the cook was acknowledged, he or she was usually identified according to his or her position in a family's home: for example, "John Erwin, a negro cook" or, in the case of Irishwoman Mary Black, "cook for 40 years to the Weekes family." Often, the recipes were offered in a style of writing that was supposed to resemble the cooks' accented speech.

African-American charity cookbooks began to gain importance in the 1950s, when church groups published family recipes from parishoners. It is sometimes difficult to recognize these books, since photographs were not commonly used and the organizations that offered the books usually limited sales to their own communities.

Charity cookbooks, however, did not necessarily dwell on the lost days of history. While some recipes were culled from the past, many of the included recipes reflected the daily foods of everyday people, the foods that people actually ate at church suppers, barbecues, and picnics. The women who contributed recipes were aware that people they knew would use the recipes and judge them (and the contributor) and the success of the dish. Until the 1950s, at least, recipes tended to be either simple, plain, and foolproof or else company-worthy and well-tested; after that time, dishes began to appear that had been "discovered" in magazine food columns or contest booklets, or that were meant to impress the reader, rather than to actually taste good. So while recipes like Mrs. Woodson Waddy's quick layer cake, Grandma's crullers, and Mrs. Upjohn's fruit cake nearly cry out their tested pedigrees, later dishes, like caviar flowers, potato chip casserole, and braised celery with meat glaze, make the reader wonder if anyone ever really tasted these dishes or even cared if they worked.

Throughout their long history, charity cookbooks have been repositories of the latest cooking fads, so that even today, readers can trace the movement of recipes from the ladies' magazines, food contests, and newspapers into the kitchens of small towns. For example, in the nineteenth century, Saratoga Springs was an important resort area and home to trendsetting restaurants, one of which invented the Saratoga chip, an early potato chip. By the 1880s, recipes for the snack began to turn up in charity cookbooks far distant from the Spa City. Health trends, which included Graham flour, resulted in the charity books offering Graham breakfast rolls, breads, and biscuits in the hope that some women would cook healthier meals for their families. As canned foods made their entrance onto the market, ensuring that the cook and baker would always have items like greengage plums, pineapple, and condensed soups on the kitchen shelf all year long, recipes were collected for pineapple fluff, Roman Holiday casserole, and ambrosia, that ubiquitous mixture of pineapple, mandarin oranges, marshmallows, and coconut. Even the

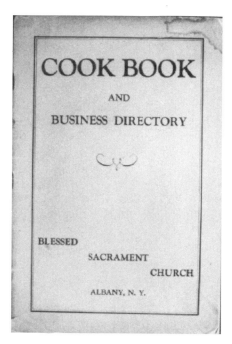

Fig. 4-14 Not all charity cookbooks aimed at being personal as far as recipes were concerned. Even those that are impersonal can offer collectors some unusual reading. The *Cook Book and Business Directory* from the Blessed Sacrament Church in Albany, New York, did not gather signed recipes, but it did assemble a lot of advertising from local businesspeople, including Joe's Bookshop and Library and the Zwack & Sons Funeral Service (which offered "an unchallenged reputation for attention to detail"). The book contains a bizarre chapter on "Cosmopolitan Recipes" with such nonurban offerings as New England gingerbread, New York hot cross buns, and Mississippi pecan muffins.

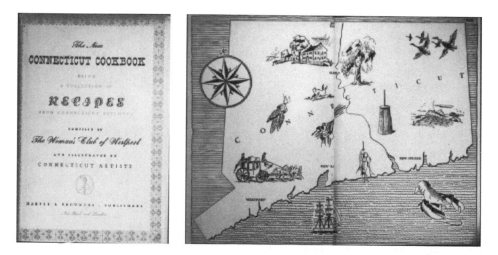

Fig. 4-15 Not all charity cookbooks began as softcover, do-it-yourself publications; in the case of *The Connecticut Cookbook and The New Connecticut Cookbook,* the ladies of The Woman's Club of Westport had the support of Harper & Brothers Publishers. The first edition of the book was issued in 1944 and contained illustrations by neighborhood artists, along with traditional recipes from local kitchens and dishes adapted for wartime cooking. In the later edition of 1947, the artwork changed, the inside cover gained a map of the state, and there were many new recipes (and no wartime versions). Both books make interesting additions to collections, but collectors should be aware that only the "new" version notes that it is a first edition.

Pillsbury Bake-Off contributed to charity cookbooks, as "tunnel of fudge" cakes began to appear not long after the recipe took a grand prize in the contest.

Until the mid-twentieth century, it seemed that most contributors to community or charity cookbooks enjoyed offering recipes made from scratch. Then the desire for more leisure time and the availability and improved quality of cake mixes and other convenience foods resulted in some unusual, if not downright bizarre, concoctions, like lime gingerale salad, chocolate cake with canned baked beans, and salmon loaf made with condensed mushroom soup, then topped with crushed potato chips.

If there was one thing charity cookbooks did exceedingly well, it was to offer advice and guidance to the housewife on her journey through domestic life. Recipes weren't enough; in the spirit of the old family books that had extended wisdom across generations, "charities" made certain that women everywhere knew the secrets to running a successful household. With titles such as "A Few Practical Hints" or "Items of Interest and Value," these short guides prefigured the hints from Heloise by seventy years and more. Like the recipes, the household hints were a way in which the traditions of domestic history could be transmitted across the generations. Part folklore, part science, part common sense, many hints a century old are still in use. Suggestions encompassed the medical ("To stop hiccoughs, put a few drops of good cider vinegar on a lump of sugar and dissolve in the mouth"), the practical ("To wash windows, wring a clean chamois out of hot water. Rub the windows thoroughly and they will need no drying"), and the esoteric ("Javelle water is an antidote for iron rust"). Cooking timetables were also provided, some several pages in length, detailing the proper guidelines for preparing food. Modern collectors of antique recipes are often surprised to see recommended boiling times of 2 hours for carrots and 1 hour for asparagus, string beans, and spinach, although some cookbooks did note that the younger and fresher the vegetable, the less time it might need in the pot—perhaps only 40 minutes or so!

Eventually charity cookbooks became more than simple money-makers content to raise $100 for the church; the books were big business, not only for the organizations (some of which have earned millions of dollars over the years) but for printing companies as well. By the mid-1950s, several printing firms offered organizations package deals: the women would collect and organize the recipes, and the company would publish them in book form. The organizations did not have to prepay either; they could sell advertising or sell the book during a grace period and then pay the company. And if the organization didn't have enough time to do even this, it could purchase ready-made books (one had a cookie theme, another contained household hints, and so on), have its name imprinted on the cover, and then sell away. Ironically, charity cookbooks, which had once been charming, individualistic recipe collections, began to look alike: stock covers and subject dividers, simple ads with little decoration, and even preprinted sections on how to choose the proper baking pan, select the best cooking temperature, or maintain the healthiest weight—all of which replaced the quirky look of the earlier books. But even these newer fund-raisers preserved a good part of America's cooking history if not its best tastes, and they deserve to be collected, if only for that fact.

As collectors will discover, "Junior League" is nearly synonymous with fund-raising cookbooks, and with good reason; since the publication of *Charleston Receipts,* offered by the Junior League of Charleston, South Carolina, in 1950, millions of these books have helped to raise funds in support of community programs. But the cookbooks have come a long way from the early spiral-bound versions with line drawings; modern copies are often elaborate confections of full-color illustrations, easel-style covers, and sophisticated, appealing recipes. The books show professional panache (some even offer preparation times and food value tables for each recipe), and many are treasured by collectors, both for the book designs and for the fresh look at American cuisine and regional cookery. But try as they might, they are still not the homey, slim cookbooks of the past. And collectors should be aware that many of these Junior League books go through several printings and remain in print for many years. As with other cookbooks, a first edition, with its own voice, mistakes, and recipe selections intact, is usually the most interesting of the lot.

Fig. 4-16 Cookbooks were also printed with the aim of raising funds for an organization rather than for a charitable cause, and historical sites and associations produced a variety of excellent collectibles. *The Plimouth Colony Cook Book,* issued by the Plymouth Antiquarian society in 1957, contains recipes borrowed from older, local cookbooks, for dishes like Burlington love knots, muster gingerbread, and toad in the hole, an English dish. This softcover cookbook has charming silhouette illustrations throughout.

Advertisements

One alluring aspect of collecting community cookbooks, especially those examples printed from the 1880s to the 1930s, is contained in the advertisements that appear throughout the books. The name of the person who came up with the idea of selling ad space to pay for printing is not recorded, but English cookbooks from the 1700s sometimes had "subscribers," people who paid for the book before it was printed, thus underwriting publishing costs for an author of moderate means. It may be said that without the support of local advertisers, the history of charity cookbooks would have been very short, and much less interesting. That the cookbook editors were aware of this is exemplified in *Lebanon Valley Cookery* (Figure 4-17), published in 1926 in New York: "Concerning our Advertisers: The Ladies of the Guild deal daily with the firms here advertised and heartily recommend them to others. Our gardens are planted, our homes and kitchens are furnished and our farms are equipped by these makers and dealers. You will find none better. . . ." One unusual group, the Steamer Hose Company of Cooperstown, New York, benefited from a compiled cookbook in 1908 (they needed clothing for their "official life as firemen" and for parades). In addition to linking their interest in cookery to their belief that roasting was discovered when a house burned down, the firemen also extended thanks to local advertisers and gave a boost to those who participated: "We believe it will be not without benefit to [the advertisers], inasmuch as the merchants

Fig. 4-17 Founded in eighteenth-century England, the Shakers were a religious sect known for dancing during worship, as well as for their beliefs in celibacy, hard work, fine craftsmanship, and good cooking. The latter has been celebrated in several books; *Lebanon Valley Cookery* (1926), with recipes from the 1880s through the 1920s, focuses on an early period of the group. The West Pittsfield, Church Family, Mount Lebanon, and Florida Shakers all provided recipes for the book, and several photos of Shaker ladies at work and rest appear throughout the pages, offering a personal look into Shaker kitchens.

who show themselves most ready to support enterprises that involve the general welfare of the community are those that deserve and receive the more generous public patronage."

Advertisements are important to collectors for several reasons. One, they identify the commercial community of a locality, allowing a reader to enjoy a visit to a vanished Main Street of long ago. While knowing that Mrs. Eggerton had a hat shop in Weeksville, New York, in 1920 might not make the recipes of a particular book any more interesting, it does help to identify the cookbook with a particular social niche. Two, ads can help to determine a publication date for a charity cookbook. Although many of the books can be dated by their copyright page or even by the title (for example, *Arkville's Centennial Cookbook: 1880–1980*), dates for some of the early books remain a mystery. But if the ads in a book indicate that a 1905 White Steam Touring Car is available at an automobile dealer in Fresno, California, then a collector can ascertain an approximate date of publication. Another example of a helpful ad is one that was used by Walter Baker & Co., Ltd., maker of Baker's chocolate. A little arithmetic based on the years and numbers embedded in the ad can provide the careful reader with an approximate publication date for the book in which the ad appeared (see Figure 4-18). Another clue for collectors: an ad for Swansdown Flour appeared in books that were heavily sponsored by this company, and

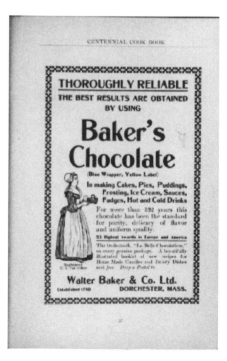

Fig. 4-18 Walter Baker & Company Ltd. not only produced chocolate, but it also inadvertently provided cookbook collectors with a way of estimating the age of a cookbook. As shown in this ad, the company was founded in 1780, and "for more than 132 years this chocolate has been the standard for purity. . . ." The resulting approximate date of 1912 is only one year off the known publishing date of 1913 for *The Centennial Cook Book,* in which this particular ad appeared; of course, Baker's changed the number of years in its ads as required for other cookbooks.

sometimes a date may be found at the bottom of the ad in very tiny type, along with a printer's code number or letter.

Although charity cookbook ads promoted many food-related items, such as baking powder, yeast, Cottolene (a shortening), flour, and other ingredients, some of the more interesting ads were for nonfood goods and services: ads for tin goods like the patent perforated pie plate from Troy (New York) Stamping Works, ladies shoes, undertakers, druggists, cigars, flowers, banks, tailors, lumber, vacation hotels, and hundreds of other products filled the cookbooks, lending a touch of local seasoning. And since charity cookbooks, which by their very nature were limited in their monetary resources and would often be pictureless, needed something to break up pages and pages of recipes, the ads also served to add visual interest to books by providing different typestyles and product pictures, or "cuts."

Fig. 4-19 By the 1880s, charity cookbooks had become, if not big business, at least going concerns for some organizations. *Chop Sticks,* from Troy, New York (1883), indicates the dining public's awareness of Chinese cooking, which was well-established in cities where an immigrant population opened restaurants to serve its own people. Despite the title, no Chinese recipes were included in the book; Americans would take a little longer to decide that such obviously "foreign" foods made for acceptable eating. This is an interesting charity cookbook, filled with detailed advertisements from local businesses such as the Troy Stamping Works and L. Burton & Company, sellers of Pratt's Astral Oil for lamps. Advertisements help the collector to place a cookbook in its social and mercantile niches.

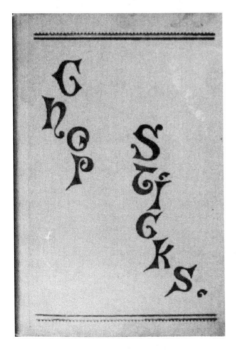

Food and Philosophy Dished Up Together

In addition to the copious amounts of information that can be gained from charity cookbooks in the way of recipes, local history, and social strata, offerings of humor and philosophy add to the interest and entertainment provided by the books. Besides all of its other functions, a charity cookbook often served as a vehicle for promoting the beliefs of a particular organization's membership, be it Lutheran clergymen's wives, hospital volunteers, or mothers of school-age children, and the editorial material usually set forth these beliefs in an amusing fashion. Cookbooks sponsored by religious groups might present essays on living the proper life. In *The Auxiliary Cook Book* (1909) of the Society of the Hebrew Sheltering Guardian Society of New York Orphan Asylum, an essay on "Laugh Lines" encourages the reader to clean out her heart and "fill it to the roof with simple, honest charity." In *Food for the Body, For the Soul* (1943), an essay entitled "Are You A Wilted Leaf Of Lettuce?" compares staying happy to learning to turn on the correct water faucet when washing lettuce: hot water, like envy, wilts; cold water, like happiness, restores the leaf (and, by analogy, the soul).

One popular charity cookbook style included quotes and poems about food presented throughout the book, but especially at the head of each chapter. Shakespeare was well-loved source ("My salad days, when I was green in judgement"), as were the works of poet James Whitcomb Riley ("When the Frost is on the Pumpkin"), Ogden Nash, and even Rudyard Kipling. Although some cookbook compilers did their own research when developing the quotes for their books, some of the commercial publishers who eventually dominated the charity cookbook world provided their clients with quotes and poems where necessary—not always accurate, well-rhymed, or well-reasoned, but still in the spirit of things. Women had little problem in laughing at themselves, recalling the mistakes made as new brides and the culinary messes that resulted:

> She measured out the butter with a very solemn air;
> The milk and sugar also; and she took the greatest care
> To count the eggs correctly, and to add a little bit
> Of baking powder, which, you know, beginners oft omit.
> Then she stirred it all together, and she baked it full an hour;
> But she never quite forgave herself for leaving out the flour.

Mock recipes are another characteristic of charity cookbooks, where philosophy was transformed into kitchen wisdom through language all could understand. "How To Preserve A Husband" was one of the most popular "recipes," appearing in various forms in both prose and verse:

> Be careful in your selection; do not choose too young, and take only such as have been reared in a good moral atmosphere. Some insist in keeping them in

a pickle, while other keep them in hot water. . . . Even poor varieties may be made sweet, tender and good by garnishing them with patience, well sweetened with smiles and flavored with kisses to taste. . . . Keep warm with a steady fire of domestic devotion and serve with peaches and cream. When thus prepared they will keep for years.

Other recipes included Home Happiness Cake, A Housekeeper's Epitaph, Recipe for an Ideal Woman's Club, and a Recipe for Quarreling: "Take a root of sassafras and steep in a pint of water and put in a bottle and when your husband comes in to quarrel fill your mouth with it and hold until he has gone away. A sure cure."

Tips for Collecting Charity Cookbooks

Depending upon the age of the books, charity cookbooks offer collectors one of the most available and least expensive ways to assemble or add to a cookbook library. No one is certain how many of the books were published or remain on the market, but if the twentieth century is any example then literally millions of charity cookbooks from the 1890s to the 1990s are still available to be collected. Thousands are still turned out by specialty fund-raising cookbook publishers each year, while others are now being offered by larger, commercial publishers, who issue the books in support of Olympic teams, women's groups, and other worthy organizations.

Comb-bound and wire-bound books are two of the most popular types found by collectors; these binding styles, which date from the late 1920s, made it easy to use the book while cooking, since it would lie open and flat on a table or counter. Sometimes the pages have become loosened or worn near the binding from rubbing up against the wire and plastic teeth, so look to make certain all pages are in place. Earlier books were bound in more traditional hardcover or softcover perfect styles, which may also show loose or missing pages. Charity cookbooks received a lot of wear, including staining, tears, tape repairs, and handwritten annotations, so prices may range from $2 to $3 at used book sales or garage sales for more recent publications to more than $100 for rare copies of early examples in good condition. Late nineteenth and early twentieth century hardcover examples in good condition can command prices in the $25 to $50 range. Collectors of charity cookbooks, more than other collectors, tend to let themselves become overwhelmed by their books, since there are so many on the market, and the temptation to add just one more is difficult to resist. Limiting collecting to "charities" from a certain region (like New York State) or a particular group (DAR cookbooks) can result in a fascinating, but controllable, collection.

Careful collectors will discover that the closer a book is found to its original location, the more expensive it usually is. A 1915 cookbook from Lancaster, Pennsylvania, sold in Lancaster may be priced at $60 by a dealer;

the same book offered in Anaheim, California, may be priced at $35 or less. Since cookbooks were often purchased as gifts or sent to distant relations and friends, it pays to explore used bookstores and book dealers everywhere, not just those near the original locality of the book.

Charity cookbooks are also excellent buys when purchased new; not only because of the enjoyment they provide to cooks, but because they are often printed in limited numbers and may go out of print quickly. Some of the most interesting in the way of regional or ethnic books are issued by historical societies or congregations of churches like Greek or Russian Orthodox. Buy them when you see them, since they offer excellent starting points for a new collection and provide a continually expanding dimension for more established cookbook libraries.

5 ❘ The Modern Kitchen

Twentieth-Century Cookbooks

Americans have been faced with so many advances and changes in food and diet in the last ninety years that it seems impossible to believe cookbooks could keep up with the demand for new recipes to support those changes. The twentieth century has seen kitchen technology "come a long way," starting in the early years when elaborate, chrome-bedecked woodstoves replaced the kitchen hearth, and ending with microwaves, convection ovens, genetically engineered foods, and sleek indoor grills guaranteed to make food taste like it was cooked (oddly enough) on a woodstove. At the beginning of the twentieth century, cookbooks were still using recipes from the early 1800s; now, as we near the end of the century, even the "average" cook is able to select a recipe from a book, push a few buttons, and serve up culinary treasures from Thailand, Australia, or the Caribbean islands.

Meeting the Challenge of Change

During this century, American food was removed from its insulated self-assurance and opened up to the newest taste, the newest texture, and the newest speeds: fast and faster. In addition to technological changes, there were vast rearrangements of society, as the shores of America welcomed immigrants from dozens of countries, provinces, and possessions. With the new settlers came culinary tastes for such "strange" dishes as sheep's head, highly pungent fish sauces, rich borschts, and exotic fruits and vegetables, like guava and plantains. The recipes were preserved by memory and passed along through families or were found in native cookbooks that were brought to America. Few immigrants in this century ever found complete acceptance

Fig. 5-1 The *Pan-Pacific Cook Book* was issued in conjunction with the 1915 World's Fair held in San Francisco and used an early version of the California bear mascot. Compiled by a single author, the book contains recipes from around the world, reflecting the nature of the exhibits. Dishes from places as far-flung as India, New Zealand, Guatemala, and the Isle de Miquelon show how expositions and fairs played a large part in bringing new foods and tastes to the attention of American cooks.

in their early years as citizens-in-waiting, but their food would eventually enter the mainstream of American cooking through the medium of cookbooks and change the way everyone ate.

Even the American homemaker would be forced to learn some hard lessons about fitting in, first finding herself honored as a good mother until the 1950s, then reviled as a drudge and drone in the 1970s, and finally receiving some respect for her skills again in the 1990s. Families would move during this century from being the perfect unit of mom, dad, grandparents, and kids to consisting of single or same-sex parents and children who often cook as well as any adult. And right along with the revolution in the American lifestyle came the cookbooks: tens of thousands upon tens of thousands, recording culinary changes, classics-in-the-making, fads, and mistakes.

Cookbook classics received an early start in the twentieth century, with the publication in 1901 of *The Settlement Cook Book—The Way to a Man's Heart*. Although charity books had been used to raise funds in the four decades before *The Settlement Cook Book* made its appearance, this cookbook was one of the great favorites, a best-seller that sold more than 2 million copies over the years. It was unusual in its origin and dedicated in its purpose. In the years before World War I, Americans found that it was not enough to just accept the millions of new immigrants who were flooding in cities like New York, Boston, and Chicago, but that it was also necessary to teach them how to cope with the new world they so avidly sought. For immigrants, the

Fig. 5-2 The idea of a cookbook for a small-size family does not seem out of the ordinary today, but in 1910, when *The Small-Family Cook Book* was published, nearly every recipe in a regular cookbook would have had to have been reduced to be prepared for only two or three people. The book emphasized economy and careful management of money by the housewife; the black-and-white photographs took the unusual step of offering the recipe printed beneath the picture of the food.

United States was an overwhelming brew of new language, clothing, currency, manners, mores, and traditions, and for those desperate to fit in, settlement houses must have been a welcome beacon. At these facilities, American women volunteered (and still do) their time by teaching classes in sewing, cooking, and housekeeping, and by helping the newcomers find a way to ease into a confusing life.

At The Settlement in Milwaukee, a home away from home for Jewish immigrants, one volunteer, Mrs. Lizzie Kander, taught cooking classes. While doing so, she also collected recipes from friends and students for use in a cookbook that she proposed to publish and sell in order to benefit the institution. But the male board of directors took the suggestion lightly and told Mrs. Kander and her committee to publish the book themselves. In the time-honored tradition of charity cookbooks, the women began by selling advertising space, and *The Settlement Cookbook* became reality in 1901. Later, it was the source of revenues for a new building and became a commercially published classic cookbook.

The book contained not only helpful rules for running a Jewish household (although the book was supported by and had appeal for non-Jewish cooks as well) but also dishes that were a mixture of American classics, European sophistication, and peasant robustness. Some recipes were borrowed from the Settlement classes, although it was unlikely that the poor immigrant families feasted on the likes of champagne sherbet or lobster à la Thackery. But they certainly could enjoy corn fritters, jumbles, and New Orleans pralines, just like "real" Americans, although they certainly must have felt a little homesick when they came across directions for dishes like matzoh pancakes, goulash, and potato flour cake. Mrs. Kander made certain that her readers could read explanations for making meat "kosher," preparing an orange for the table, and learning the history of the chafing dish ("The chafing dish is king, and everyone is looking for new recipes with which to regale and surprise his friends at the evening lunch. . . . It is said that the chafing dish originated with the Israelite women, and that it has been used through each succeeding generation by both men and women.")

The Settlement Cook Book was to remain under the editorship of Mrs. Kander for many editions, although later books changed with the times, offering hundreds more recipes and eliminating the suggested course of instruction "as given by The Settlement Cooking Classes." But it never lost its feeling that recipes should come from the people who cook them, and it predated by nearly a century one of the main trends of the late-twentieth-century cookbook—that is, offering various ethnic and sophisticated recipes from around the world, written in a form simple enough for even the most inexperienced cook to follow. The book was also unusual in that it offered recipes for "everyday" European dishes like strudel, complete with poetic descriptions of the correct way to spread out dough until it was "as large as the table and thin as paper." Cookbooks like *The Settlement Cook Book* helped to preserve food traditions that might have been lost during the process of immigrant assimilation and also made the dishes accessible to cooks who otherwise might not have been exposed to ethnic cuisine.

As the twentieth century introduced the American cook to the joys of technology, cookbooks were needed to cope with the new foods and new preparation methods. The change in population centers, the automobile, the large world expositions and state fairs, which trumpeted the advances in agriculture, medicine, and technology—all of these made life more hectic and confusing, if not always better, for the cook. Most cookbooks published before World War I reflected the fact that Americans were largely country people, with more individuals living on farms than in the cities, and most living without the wonder of electricity. At this time, cookbooks were written with the rural life in mind, with directions for making tansy yeast from potatoes and tansy leaves, for cooking an ox cheek, or for cutting up a hog for barreling, all jobs done by hand and without any special equipment or power source.

As the twentieth century reached its teens, emphasis was increasingly being placed on the new wonders of science, like electricity and the advancement of at-home food preparation. First, the kitchen itself began to change, from what *The Institute Cook Book* (1913) called "the meanest and darkest room in the house" to one, as the book suggested, of spotless wooden and porcelain preparation areas, a glass-topped work table, and washable wall coverings—a place where the cook might begin to understand the necessity of "clean hands, clean floors, clean refrigerators and clean pots and pans. . . ." One of the most famous proponents of kitchen change was the Hoosier Manufacturing Company of Indiana, makers of the Hoosier cabinets that

Fig. 5-3 Ingredients have changed a great deal through the centuries, as the methods of production have evolved and new products have been developed for the harried cook. This advertisement shows "automatic" maize and flour, which turns out to be an interesting way of explaining self-rising flour mixes to a public ready for convenience.

combined food storage and work areas with closet space, coffee grinders, silverware drawers, spice racks, and bread boards. "Of course you've heard of the woman who, upon looking around her cluttered, disorderly kitchen, decided to go take a nap! Tired before she began! Some kitchens are like that," began an advertising booklet for the company. The perky text then went on to declare that "domestic science authorities say no kitchen can be really modern unless it is a tastefully appointed room, inviting to the mind; restful to the eye. And of course, it must be completely equipped, with every detail planned to save your time and strength."

Stoves and Refrigerators

One of the pieces of equipment that saved time and strength was the stove, and with the changes it afforded in heat control and temperature timing, cooking (and cookbooks) would never be the same. Gas, kerosene, and oil stoves were in common use until the 1930s. The New Perfection Fireless Cooking Oil Stoves appeared in company advertising cookbooks with the claim that "you have abundant heat always ready, like gas." These books offered detailed directions for setting up, lighting, and cooking with the stoves, using such helpful accessories as the New Perfection broiler, the Aladdin bread pan, and the round roaster pan. The books were detailed in text and photos, with one showing a little girl in a lacy apron, large hairbow, and white dress setting up the oven for baking. But the firm admonition "Do not attempt to operate stove until you have read all the directions, then keep them always handy in the pocket at the left end of stove" did not always allay the fears of the cook about the modern kitchen. However, once a cook could manage to avoid blowing up the dinner, she would learn to prepare the recipes for such dishes as Perfection bread (made with Graham and white flours), turnip soufflé, and roast goose for Christmas dinner—dishes that called for a little flair in cooking. (Collectors who come across advertising cookbooks put out by stove companies might also look for the annual inserts showing the latest in stoves; the inserts add to the general value of the books.)

Stoves underwent major improvements from the mid-1800s onward, adding to the cook's control over her environment. Oven thermometers were added by 1915, making the cook's job much more accurate, although the cookbook issued with the gas-heated Lorain stove in the 1920s still declared that "the times and temperatures given in the recipes in this book are suggested merely to serve as guides." But by this time, recipes had undergone a subtle change and now contained the indication that a dish should be baked

Fig. 5-4 Appliance cookbooks provide the collector with detailed instructions in the use and care of antique stoves, refrigerators, and other equipment. The illustrations from this Westinghouse cookbook show an early stove design with the oven at the side of the burners. The booklet has detailed directions for running the range and a chart on which a cook could record successes and mistakes.

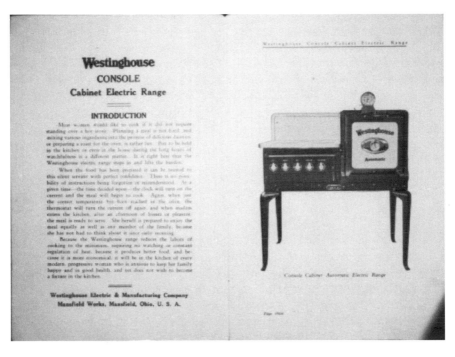

for a certain period of time at a certain temperature, a great advance over the tricky problems of managing a woodstove. Although earlier cookbooks did offer timing guidance, they relied upon the hope that a cook was experienced enough to estimate the heat of a moderate or fast oven, a confidence that was often shattered with burned cookies or a fallen cake. Now, with a flick of the wrist, even a new cook or baker could find the correct oven temperature and eventually discover the proper cooking time; soon, the days of "cook until done" would be a memory.

Cookbooks of the teens and twenties also contained a new way of preparing meals, brought about by the remarkable ability of the stove to maintain a constant temperature over a period of time. No longer would the cook have to start dinner hours ahead of time, making one dish, keeping it hot, making another dish and so on; now she could use recipes developed to be cooked together, in one oven. As indicated in the *Lorain Cooking Cookbook:* "It is a great saving of time to be able to place a whole meal in the oven, adjust the . . . wheel to the desired temperature and then go away and forget the meal until the end of the time for properly cooking it." Although it was never quite as simple as that, the cookbook suggested such combinations as canned fruit, eggs poached in milk, popovers, and coffee for breakfast, and baked veal cutlets, scalloped potatoes, yellow beans, individual chocolate puddings, and custard sauce for dinner.

Electric stoves, such as those produced by Westinghouse (see Figure 5-5) in the 1930s, caught on long after they were introduced in 1893 at the Chicago World's Fair. While the stoves were clean and safe to use, many households did not have access to standard electrical power sources, particularly homes in rural areas, and the true widespread introduction of the electric stove had to wait until after World War II, when wartime factories turned to peacetime production. Stove designers as late as the 1940s capitalized on the "new" method of electric cooking, adding such modern touches as bottle sterilizers, oven lights, warming drawers, and even cigarette lighters. One cookbook showed a photo of a happy housewife puffing away, noting that "midnight snacks in the kitchen are usually accompanied by a cigarette."

At the other end of the preparation spectrum, away from the heat of stoves, was the constant cool offered by the new refrigerators. Although keeping foods cool through the use of ice and insulation like earth or sawdust was known to housewives of the seventeenth century, self-contained refrigeration did not become common in the American kitchen until the 1940s. Before then, iceboxes were the primary refrigeration method. Chunks of ice were placed in an insulated box in the icebox, and as the ice melted, it cooled the food. As late as 1928, the cookbook that accompanied the General Electric Refrigerator, *Electric Refrigerator Recipes and Menus,* noted: "To many people, electric refrigeration is still such a novelty that they scarcely realize the range of its possibilities. It is almost like having an Aladdin's lamp and not knowing the right way to rub it."

Fig. 5-5 The electric range was not a new idea in the 1930s, but because many homes, especially those in rural areas, did not have dependable electric power, companies like Westinghouse had to work hard to get the public interested in their products. After telling the housewife that electric cookery was clean, flameless, safe, accurate, and fumeless, the advertising booklet went on to advise that the automatic (clock) feature would free the woman from the kitchen and she could "return to find dinner ready to serve, beautifully cooked at the appointed time. It means to her more leisure, more playtime. . . ." Sample menus were given to help organize the cook; note also that corrections were made to the page numbers. The cover bears a likeness of a fireplace, while the title emphasizes the old-fashioned flavors made with new technology.

Of course, while the refrigerator was wonderful for storing foods, it took some imagination to compile a cookbook based only on recipes for cold food. Refrigerator cookbooks offered detailed directions for using the new appliance, and the recipes were designed to appeal to the woman who enjoyed a radical social idea: more leisure time. Recipes and menus were included for luncheons, buffet suppers, and porch dinners, and cookbooks pointed out that "electric refrigeration means so much in health, in comfort and in common sense economy that the modern American homemaker no longer regards it as a summer luxury. . . . Sick people often need ice bags, ice cream and partly frozen nourishment of various kinds. . . . For these reasons and many more, an adequate refrigerator becomes a necessity in most homes." Cold and jellied soups, frozen salads, ices, sherbets, frozen fruits, mousses, and ice creams gained new status with the advent of refrigeration. Gone were the days when an arm-powered ice cream machine was cranked forever; now a housewife could take a cookbook's advice when it asked, "Why go out to the soda fountain when you can have a chocolate sundae at an instant's notice . . . ?" Cookbooks also began to offer recipes for dishes like molded shrimp with cucumber sauce, ice cubes with violet flowers frozen inside, chilled fruit cocktails, and the soon-to-be classic, refrigerator rolls.

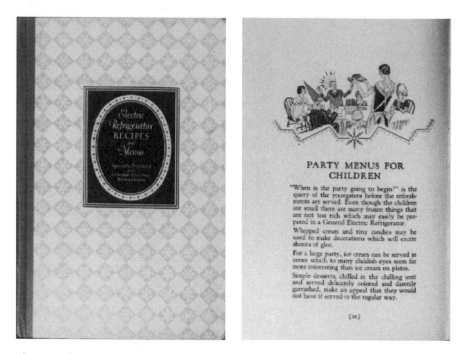

PARTY MENUS FOR CHILDREN

"When is the party going to begin?" is the query of the youngsters before the refreshments are served. Even though the children are small there are many frozen things that are not too rich which may easily be prepared in a General Electric Refrigerator.

Whipped cream and tiny candies may be used to make decorations which will excite shouts of glee.

For a large party, ice cream can be served in cones which to many childish eyes seem far more interesting than ice cream on plates.

Simple desserts, chilled in the chilling unit and served delicately colored and daintily garnished, make an appeal that they would not have if served in the regular way.

[24]

Fig. 5-6 When electric refrigerators began to replace the old, clumsy icebox, cookbooks were issued that extolled the virtues of the new appliance. This classic, from General Electric, first appeared in 1927 and presented recipes for informal luncheons, weekend guests, and children's parties. The color illustrations are charming and stylish. The recipes tended towards salads, ices, and other frozen dainties, as the cookbook concentrated on proving that new dishes would result from owning a refrigerator, rather than emphasizing the fact that food storage would be made simpler.

Along with the recipes, the refrigerator cookbooks offered colorful illustrations of frozen dishes, which probably helped as much to sell the refrigerators as any other advertising. Some of these books were expensive for the time ($2 a copy was a good bit of money in the 1920s), and while stove companies emphasized the safety and affordability of their products, refrigerator companies used cookbooks to emphasize the convenience of their product and usually showed women in comfortable circumstances entertaining equally comfortable guests. Refrigerator companies had learned early that publicizing an idea or a lifestyle was more important, in some cases, than focusing on the product.

Canning and Freezing

In addition to the storage and cooking advances that changed the reality of cooking and the look of cookbooks came two food preservation techniques: canning and freezing. Canning had been developed in the early nineteenth century with the encouragement of an unlikely booster. Napoleon Bonaparte needed food for his troops that would remain safe to eat over long periods of time, and his offer of a prize led to the development of a storage method in which foods were cooked, canned, and processed with heat. The idea worked, and commercial canning was introduced to this country by 1819. But Americans were wary of the commercial process, which did not always consider quality control as a primary goal; they preferred to do their own "canning" at home, using glass jars to store the processed foods. Cooks were slow to accept commercially canned "convenience" foods until the canning industry at the turn of the century finally emphasized clean, inspected food production and cans lined with nonreactive material. Canned food was promoted as a safe, convenient, healthy, and less wasteful alternative to fresh food, and for women who wanted to spend less time in the kitchen, opening up a can of baked beans certainly beat waiting hours for the beans to cook the old way.

The effect of canned goods on cookbooks was enormous, even as they played an important role in the downfall of cooking from scratch. Where recipes had once contained lists of fresh ingredients, by the 1920s cookbooks spoke in terms of cans, calling perhaps for one can of crushed pineapple and syrup or one cup canned potted shrimp. Cookbooks like those in the "Bettina" series (*A Thousand Ways to Please a Husband, A Thousand Ways to Please a Family, Bettina's Best Desserts,* and *Bettina's Best Salads;* see Figure 5-7), which appeared between 1917 and 1925, glorified the ease of food prepared from cans. In the books, wife Bettina and husband Bob appear in stories that revolved about her wonderful household skills and recipes. Although not especially well written, the books offered a look into the daily life of a housewife and her pantry just after the first World War. In the chapter "Home at Last," when Bettina returns from her honeymoon, she makes a dinner ("Bettina fastened a trim percale bungalow apron over her traveling suit, and swiftly and surely assembled the little meal,") and then organizes her emergency cupboard, complete with plenty of canned goods, which were gaining strong acceptance in the home kitchen. Foodstuffs like pimentos, tuna, salmon, dried beef, corn, peas, lima and string beans, devilled ham, tomatoes, pickles, olives, condensed milk, salted codfish, and other goods were stored on shelves, waiting for the time when the cupboard was bare and the shops were shut. Such convenience was a true luxury for cooks who had been used to working for hours just to devil the ham for luncheon.

Condensed soups, which first appeared on grocery shelves in the 1890s, became the basis for many dinners, casseroles in particular. The use of cans also demanded that cookbook users know which can contained the right amount of food: for reasons known only to the can companies, can sizes ran from the No. ½ flat (1 cup of salmon) to the No. 10 (institutional size). Many community cookbooks began recipes with the direction "1 #2 can of green beans" or "one 35¢ can of turkey," so the cookbooks also often printed listings of can sizes and amounts to help the confused cook complete preparations

Fig. 5-7 The Bettina cookbook series begain in 1915 with *A Thousand Ways to Please a Husband* and continued through three additional titles. The book boasted that it was not "the usual dull plodding kitchen cook book," but followed the "life and adventures of Bob and Bettina, who sail into the complexities of housekeeping the moment the wedding journey is at an end." The early books were enlivened with black and white drawings of Bettina at work and play, sometimes assisted by kitchen cherubs; later books contained stylized color illustrations of food.

for dinner. (Even the American Can Company booklet, *Choice Recipes and Menus Using Canned Foods,* used the can numbering system in its recipes.) By the 1950s, it was unthinkable that the cook should even try to manage without canned goods on her kitchen shelves; the Canco Company listed nearly two hundred foods available in cans, including unusual selections like beef and kidneys, youngberries, shad roe, and cream of shrimp soup, and *The Can-Opener Cookbook* by Poppy Cannon became a best-seller. Cannon's recipes were of course based on canned foods, from soups to fruits, and directions included how to sclect and buy a can opener and how to plan a "Can-Opener Party" in which most of the foods were made from ready-to-use canned ingredients.

Frozen foods, another preserved-food convenience, were developed for commercial use by Clarence Birdseye. As a geologist doing fieldwork in Labrador, Birdseye noticed that fish that were quickly frozen by the frigid temperatures could later be thawed and cooked with little or no loss of quality. Freezing foods for preservation was a method used by early cooks,

Fig. 5-8 Gail Borden perfected the system of preserving milk in cans through the use of sugar, and by the 1920s, women had developed recipes that took advantage of the product. Eagle Brand Sweetened Condensed Milk was used in this cookbook, which contained photographs and line drawings of happy housewives, husbands, and children mixing up cookies, cakes, and dressings ("Yes, even a man can make this mayonnaise"). Some of the recipes are still found in modern cookbooks, showing that the need for quick-to-fix recipes endures.

and cookbooks referred to the habit of storing frozen meat, fish, and pies in the ice house or in a snowbank. *The Pocumtuc Housewife,* a Massachusetts cookbook with recipes from the early 1800s, noted that freezing a fish would enable it keep for weeks. The same book also noted that at Thanksgiving time, it "saves labor to make seventy-five or a hundred pies and keep them on hand. Freeze them and slip the covered ones from the plates. Pack them in an earthen crock or large chest, one upon another and thaw as needed." Presumably, the pie containers were then kept in a cold room. Commercial freezing was used as early as the 1860s, but cookbooks took little notice of this innovation since the frozen foods were not for home use.

Birdseye actually developed a method for flash freezing and perfected it by 1928, but it took years before there were refrigerated trucks for shipping the products and home freezers for storing them. Few stores had ways to display or sell frozen foods properly, and the industry was near collapse in the late 1930s. But frozen foods took off in popularity during World War II, when it was discovered that the housewife could get more preserved foods than fresh food with her rationing points, and frozen foods did not require storage in metal cans, which could then be saved for use in defense work. Locker plants also popped up in the 1940s, and a housewife who didn't have the luxury of a home freezer could rent one and store her foods there. A manager would remain at the locker site to help the housewife freeze her poultry, meat, vegetables and fruit, and in *Facts About Freezing Foods* (1947), the text noted that "the locker makes it practical for you to purchase your Thanksgiving turkey and your Christmas goose well in advance of the high prices and sometimes limited supply during the holiday seasons."

Home freezers were in use by the late 1940s and contained such amenities as removable metal baskets, ice-cube trays, serving trays, "counter balanced finger-lift lids," automatic interior lights, temperature control, and even a warning alarm. (Home refrigerators gained their freezer compartments around the same time.) Cookbooks issued by freezer manufacturers contained many familiar recipes, the difference being that the cook was no longer forced to wait until June to use fresh strawberries; she reached into her freezer and pulled out the taste of summer. Iced beverages were now more than just chilled tea—there were ching-a-lings (orange juice and vanilla ice cream) and tropicocktail (a blend of orange, grapefruit and lime juices). New dishes included the proudly named Servel Electrolux Cheese Cake (from the Electrolux freezer), cardinal salad ("for left-over beets"), shamrock salad (cabbage, green peppers, olives, cottage cheese, pineapple, and nuts), and other delights. Of course, certain cookbooks got carried away with the convenience of frozen foods: *Miracle Meals* from Seabrook Farms had a recipe for lima bean and bourbon cake, and International Harvester thought pickle-burgers would make a good lunch in *How To Freeze Foods.*

Cookbooks issued by appliance companies contained extensive photographs and drawings of the equipment, along with the recipes, and the books played an important part in getting cooks to accept new technology and food products. Microwave ovens began to appear in kitchens in the 1940s, but

Fig. 5-9 Any cook who has struggled with cast-iron baking implements must have appreciated the changes that aluminum utensils brought into the kitchen. The pans and pots did not need to be seasoned for cooking, they cleaned easily, and they were relatively light in weight. Club Aluminum offered the cook a wide variety of kitchen equipment, including broilers, waffle irons, and donut bakers. This advertising cookbook contains recipes suggested for use with Club ware and has detailed illustrations of the products. Although all the letters of endorsement in the booklet came from women, a man appears on the cover in deference to the masculine ideal of a club.

unless the cook had attended a rare class, the only way to learn how the machine worked was to read about it in a cookbook.

Unfortunately, as all the standardization and time-saving methods assumed a place in the American kitchen, so too did cookbooks start to assume a bland standard of their own: fruit whip, baked meats, cornflake kisses, macaroni and meat. Few dishes were enlivened with unique flavors, and catchy names like "variety pie" (3 cups cooked leftover meat, 1 can vegetable soup, bread crumbs, butter, salt and pepper) tried to hide the fact that speed, and not taste, was a new kitchen credo. The Canco Kitchens even offered *Quick Trick Cookery* as the title of their cookbook, which promoted "table-ready" foods. Some of the more bizarre dishes that began to appear on family tables were conveyed there by cookbooks that highlighted the ingredients made by food producers and manufacturers. Two cookbooks, *Best Recipes from the Backs of Boxes, Bottles, Cans and Jars* and *Even More Recipes from the Backs of Boxes, Bottles, Cans and Jars* (1979 and 1982 by Ceil Dyer), contain hundreds of recipes calling for brand-name ingredients found on the supermarket shelves. While classic angel cake was included, cooks were also faced with some odd concoctions like Della Robbia holiday pie (made with cookie crumbs, candied fruits, and an almond liqueur) and tuna shortcake. Hundreds of product cookbooks still appear annually. Not unexpectedly, some of the strangest recipes came from the "table-ready" food makers, while growers and producers of crops like almonds, cauliflower, and sugar tended to offer classic recipes made from scratch.

Fig. 5-10 A flirtatious cook offers a steaming casserole to the reader in *Home Helps,* one of the advertising pieces published by Cottolene in 1910. The cover shows that even on simple "giveaways," artwork and salesmanship was used in conjunction with famous names of the cooking world.

Some Stars of the 1930s

The twentieth century was a sprawling time for cookbooks, as cooking became easier and faster, communication was no longer limited to weekly newspapers, and the ability to market a product made cookbooks interesting to hundreds of smaller companies eager to get the word out about their spices, flavorings, beans, dates, sweeteners, and a thousand other foodstuffs. The 1930s brought to cookbooks some unusual themes and consequences of the changes in cooking and shopping.

One of the most famous food publications to emerge made its debut as a formally printed book in 1931—*The Joy of Cooking,* by Irma Rombauer. Mrs. Rombauer's first collections of recipes consisted of mimeographed sheets used in a cooking course; her book was not published until her family suggested she print it privately. The first edition of 3,000 copies was sold by Irma and family; eventually, the book was printed by Bobbs-Merrill, and it still remains a best-seller, with new and old editions alike being snapped up by cooks and collectors at prices that would have amazed the author.

The Joy of Cooking was a special cookbook that touched not only the palates but the hearts of its readers. "I have attempted to make palatable dishes with simple means and to lift everyday cooking out of the commonplace. In spite of the fact that the book is compiled with one eye on the family purse and the other on the bathroom scale, there are, of course, occasional lapses into indulgence," stated Mrs. Rombauer. The book was a thorough compilation of recipes, explanations of cooking techniques, encouragement, and gentle humor of the type that would make all but most frightened cook comfortable in the kitchen. The early editions of *Joy* are eagerly sought after by collectors, who seek them out as much for their memories of a favorite dish as for the book itself.

Magazines began to promote their own cookbooks during this period as well, so that a cook who enjoyed *The Household Magazine* could turn to *The Household Searchlight Recipe Book* (Figure 5-11), in which the introduction noted, "In this seven-room house lives a family of specialists whose entire time is spent in working out the problems of homemaking common to every woman. . . ." In the book's pages were directions for such enticing dishes as codfish omelets, prune pickles, and popcorn fruit cookies, along with many standard recipes. *My Better Homes and Gardens Cook Book* (Figure 5-13) boasted that every recipe had been tested in the Better Homes and Gardens Tasting-Test Kitchen. And for every woman who bought the basic cookbook, there was a membership in the Cooks' Round Table, a recipe exchange that was enjoyed by tens of thousands of cooks across the country. The idea was to create a personal cookbook for all the participants; a book of recipes for "the beginner as well as the experienced cook," with the convenience of a filing cabinet and but not the inconvenience of recipe card files.

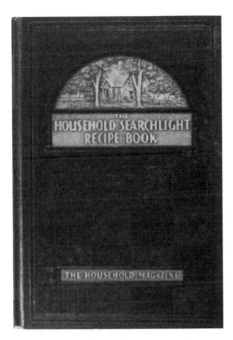

Fig. 5-11 The Household Searchlight was a testing and development kitchen for *The Household Magazine,* and its cookbook was a collection of recipes from readers, from the testing kitchen, and from "manufacturers whose food products have been entered for Searchlight approval." The types of recipes accepted were decided upon by a questionnaire sent to readers of the magazine; the resulting chapters included, besides breads, cakes, and other basics, sections on cereals, gelatin, pudding, and game. The embossed cover resembled a patchwork quilt, and chapters were divided by thumb tabs.

Fig. 5-12 Woman's World was a popular monthly magazine with a readership of more than 1 million in the 1930s, and this cookbook was one of the many published by magazines to take advantage of their built-in readership of cooks. The book was dedicated to providing readers with a modern manual of cookery and the latest advances of food scientists. To take advantage of the public's interest in dietetics and healthful eating, author Lily Haxworth Wallace presented sections on marketing, balanced menus, and the mechanics of cookery and entertaining, with such titles as "My 6 Best One-dollar Dinners for 4" and "My 12 Best Church Suppers." Photos, charts, and illustrations guided the cook, and even the cover was modern, being made of Leatherode, a varnished waterproof fabric that could be cleaned with a moist cloth.

Cookbooks were becoming standardized, and due to the popularity of certain cookbooks, so were the foods—everyone who owned a certain cookbook had access to the same "endorsed recipes," which had been tested for accuracy and which used the canned and convenience foods that were

Fig. 5-13 *My Better Homes and Gardens Cook Book* has continued in popularity for more than a half century. It was originally developed to be a "lifetime cookbook," one in which the cook could store recipes clipped from other sources, as well as using those that came with the book. The earlier editions (this one is from 1936) were silver with black type; later editions, like the 1953 version, were very colorful, with a "gingham" cover, bright illustrations of kitchens and food, and many more kitchen hints. Elaborate charts were also included to help the cook make nutritious meals and keep up with the latest in food science.

beginning to be found on grocery shelves. Now, Texas cooks made pineapple parfait pie and Utah cooks made frozen strawberry-pineapple salad, instead of plain, local recipes that once would have been the standard.

The golden age of radio in 1920s and 1930s also played its part in the development of the American cookbook and paved the way for a new method of advertising the printed recipe. Chatty radio programs were popular with housewives, who worked at home and could listen to soap operas, comedy shows, and housekeeping hints programs during the day. The shows often produced their own cookbooks based on recipes sent in by listeners or provided by the sponsors of a program. Proctor and Gamble issued *Good Things to Eat from Out of the Air* in 1932, with dishes enjoyed by radio stars. These celebrities, along with "their most requested recipes," included the likes of Guy Lombardo (meat pie), Helen Nugent (peach cobbler), Singin' Sam the Barbasol Man (fricassee of chicken), and Wamp Carlson "of the Tastyeast Jesters" (chocolate sundae pie). WFBL in Syracuse, New York, made the connection in 1945 between the listening and dining audiences, noting in its cookbook: "Since radio listeners become friends with their favorite radio entertainers, they most naturally are interested in how they look, the steps in their rise to entertainment fame, what they enjoy doing as

Kate Smith's Favorite Recipes

Fig. 5-14 Singer Kate Smith was not just famous for "God Bless America," she was also a well-known cook who acted as a spokesperson for various companies, which sponsored her popular radio show: "And was I tickled when the makers of my two best baking friends—Swansdown Cake Flour and Calumet Baking Powder—asked me to go on the air with a new Kate Smith show, and helped me prepare this book of my favorite recipes." Unlike other celebrity chefs in advertising cookbooks, Smith was actually an excellent baker. This full-size (8½" × 11") booklet is from 1939 and is filled with black-and-white photos of Kate at work in the kitchen and serving her cakes to appreciative guests.

well as what they like to eat (and who doesn't like to eat). . . ." Each recipe was accompanied by a photo of the "star" and a description of his or her career. Thus, the mysterious "Man in Black" host of the radio show "Suspense" was also known to enjoy a slice of Roma Cream Pie, which was prepared with the sponsoring company's product, Roma wine.

The tone of these cookbooks was usually gushing and sentimental; in *Mother Barbour's Favorite Recipes*, an offspring of the radio soap opera "One Man's Family," the characters are presented as a real family, complete with history, photos, and "family" recipes. The inimitable Gertrude Berg created the character Molly Goldberg for radio, and "Molly's" cookbook (Figure 5-15) had recipes and humor, just like that heard over the airwaves; in her introduction to stuffed cabbage, Molly noted that she always made the recipe with two pots, one for tasting and one for serving.

Even the government got into the cookbook act with a series called *Aunt Sammy's Radio Recipes* presented by the Bureau of Home Economics in the Department of Agriculture ("Aunt Sammy" was Uncle Sam's wife). These books were compiled from recipes offered during the "Housekeepers' Chat" broadcasts and were meant to provide well-balanced meals and simple recipes. The names of the dishes were plain (foamy sauce, onions fried in deep fat, brownies), lacking the inventiveness of later cookbook salesmanship, and in typical government fashion, many of the dishes were standardized through measurement and taste until little or no hint remained of their origin. Classics like bread pudding or creamed potatoes were still there, but the added touches of regional names or flavorings had been removed, so that a creamed potato in Boston would taste the same as a creamed potato

Fig. 5-15 "Molly Goldberg" was a radio character created by actress Gertrude Berg, and Molly's recipes reflected early twentieth century Jewish food traditions of New York City. The book was originally issued as *The Molly Goldberg Cookbook;* the change in title may have reflected additions to the text, or the fact that Jewish cooking was attracting an audience on its own without the help of a fictional character. Although difficult to see in the photo, the gold foil dust jacket on the example pictured is in good condition, even with the scuffing and fold seen at the top of the book.

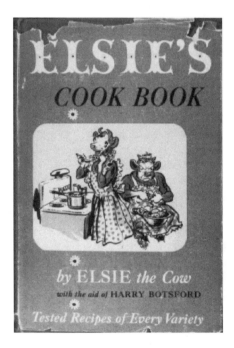

Fig. 5-16 Using celebrities to sell cookbooks is not new, but using animal cartoon characters was somewhat unusual in 1952, when *Elsie's Cook Book* was published. Elsie and husband, Elmer, were spokescows for the Bond Wheelwright Company, appearing at country fairs, at universities, and on radio. The book contains standard recipes (lamb chops, cheese potato casserole) and essays from Elsie about life with Elmer. The dust jacket is in poor condition on this example, although the book is in very good condition and contains a picture of Elsie embossed in gold on the front cover.

in San Francisco; at least, as far as these cookbooks were concerned. The American middle class was defining itself more thoroughly than it ever had done so before, and in the process, it was beginning remove the flavorings that had made regional cooking unique.

As if the onslaught of communications and food technology were not enough for cookbooks to absorb, along came another innovation that made food books even more popular and more easily available to the reader. In 1930, a store in Jamaica, New York, became the first American "supermarket," combining wholesale food purchases, self-service, and plain surroundings to reduce prices for the shopper. The markets brought a wider selection of foodstuffs to the housewife, with fruits and vegetables becoming available and affordable year-round (although not necessarily better in quality or taste). The author of *The Super Market Cook Book,* which celebrated the silver anniversary of the stores in 1955, noted that within that period of time more than 20,000 supermarkets had opened. Cookbooks reflected these changes, calling for canned and convenience goods, prepackaged meats, and, eventually, more product brands. By the 1960s, supermarkets were offering cookbooks as premiums, and collectors can still complete a set of *The Woman's Day Cookbook Library,* which was distributed by supermarkets, or discover copies of cookbooks sponsored by the Great Atlantic and Pacific Tea Company (A&P), Grand Union (Figure 5-17), and other market outlets.

Fig. 5-17 The Grand Union Tea Company was established in 1872 and became a major supplier of groceries a few years later. Their delivery carts were well known in neighborhoods, and their cookbook, offered in 1902, presented customers with hundreds of recipes backed by the guarantee of the compiler. Like many other inexpensive advertising books, this one contains a mixture of old and new dishes, and awkward photographs of food. One, a pile of brown bread rounds filled with cream, is captioned "Manhattan sandwiches," for what reason it may never be known.

The Role of Cookbooks in the War Years

Wars affect cookbooks in many ways—the returning soldiers bring recipes home to their kitchens, cookbooks are written as fund-raisers for the needs of soldiers and their families, and cookbooks help to raise morale by encouraging the homefront cook. During World War II, a massive change in cookbooks reflected the problems facing those who stayed at home. For the first time in American history, millions of troops were scattered around the

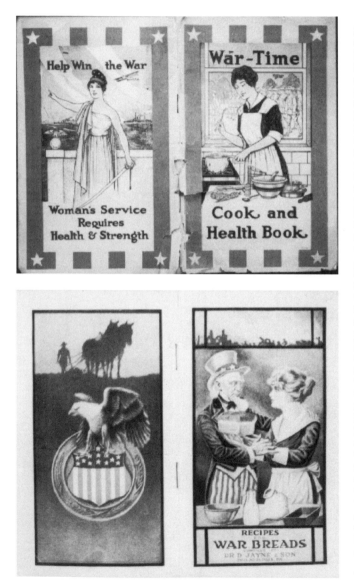

Fig. 5-18 The role of women in war may have been limited on the battlefields, but as shown in these two advertising booklets, women helped Uncle Sam in the kitchen. Both books were issued by companies that specialized in patent medicine preparations: *War-Time Cook and Health Book* was produced by the Lydia Pinkham Medicine Company (1917), and *Recipes for War Breads* was put out by Dr. D. Jayne & Son (1918). The booklets gave health advice and recipes that took into account the shortages of flour, sugar, and shortening plaguing the baker. Pinkham's booklet described in loving detail such problems as "falling of the womb," while chirpily providing recipes for apple brown betty; Dr. Jayne's was no better, touting the company's expectorant tablets opposite directions for rice and cornmeal waffles. Note the tears on this copy of the *War-Time Cook Book*, which is in poor condition; on the other hand, this example of *Recipes for War Breads* is in very good condition, with few signs of use.

world and had to receive food, supplies, and support, a massive problem which created shortages back in the United States. In order to try to ensure that everyone got his or her fair share of available foods, rationing was instituted. This system required a juggling of points for food purchases, and since cooks were never really sure what would be on hand when they went shopping, cookbooks appeared to explain the variety of ways in which a housewife could substitute ingredients or change a recipe in order to use whatever ingredients she could find. As Betty Crocker noted in a 1943 cookbook from General Mills:

> Hail to the women of America! You have taken up your heritage from the brave women of the past. Just as did the women of other wars, you have taken your positions as soldiers on the Home Front. You have been strengthening your country's defenses—as plane watchers—as flyers—as members of the armed forces—as producers, in war plants and homes—in Red Cross and Civilian Defense activities. The efforts and accomplishments of women today are boundless! But whatever else you do—you are, first and foremost, home-makers. . . .

The art of rationing involved booklets of tickets that allowed a purchaser a certain amount of a particular food, like sugar, each month. As *The Modern Hostess Cook Book, Patriotic Edition* (1942) clearly explained to house-wives, "Sugar is needed in the manufacture of explosives, and explosives are needed for Victory." The cookbook went on to encourage housewives with the thought that Americans ate too much sugar anyway and that rationing would also ensure the availability of sugar for "patriotic" canning and pre-serving. Sugar-saving recipes were highlighted throughout the book, and careful housewives could stretch their rations and still satisfy the family's sweet tooth with chocolate crumb cookies of breadcrumbs, chocolate, and sweetened condensed milk; brownies made with honey; and peach melba enlivened with corn syrup. Even local women's clubs got into the spirit, issuing books like *Ration By-Pass,* from the Garden Club of Daytona Beach, Florida. These recipes took advantage of local produce and resulted in the likes of shrimp Finchbull, pokeweed salad, loquat pie, and the suggestion that rosa rugosa petals and wisteria and red bud flowers made nice additions to a salad.

Cookbooks got behind the war effort 100 percent, with the scores of booklets, books, and brochures published by book companies, food conglom-erates, and product associations emphasizing ways to make food enjoyable and tasty, regardless of the limitations placed on the kitchen. *Meat in the Meal for Health Defense,* issued by the National Live Stock and Meat Board in 1942, encouraged the cook with notes like "Always wins acclaim" (Swiss steak with onions), "Thrift with a Smile" (roast stuffed veal breast), "Old American Favorite Up to Date" (Defense Scrapple), and even "One the Men Will Cheer" (beef brisket with onion sauce).

Other books were published in conjunction with cookbooks and were meant to help the woman plan meals and keep the spirit up at home (it was almost always a woman who entertained, even if she worked 10 hours a day in a defense plant). *Wartime Entertaining—Nothing Counts But Victory* offered the thought that "fun and relaxation help us all do a better job whether we are on leave from the service or doing our part at home." Fund-raising parties, benefit teas, bakery sales, and money-raising games were all suggestions, complete with recipes for the cook, who could read homilies on each page as she baked the bacon franks for a farewell party: "Brave hearts at home make brave soldiers on the field." Cookbooks assumed an unusual role during the war, acting as instruction books for rationing, morale boosters for the weary cook, chatty "kaffeklatches" in print for lonely women, and even propaganda devices, reassuring readers that, after all, if millions of others could ration food and cook successfully, so could they.

The military, in return, did its part, publishing cookbooks that were usually issued for use by the Quartermaster Corps and were filled with scientific, nutritional and technical data. The books were "survival manuals" for the so-called chefs in the armed forces, who had often spent little time in a kitchen before military duty called. Collectors will find in the classic text *Army Food and Messing* (Figure 5-19), written in 1942, detailed photographs of various edible livers, directions for inspecting onions and turnips, and hundreds of recipes that seemed to indicate that when possible, troops were treated to hearty meals. There are recipes for such dishes as smothered ham, "Southern creoles" (pickled pork hocks), Irish stew, stew el rancho, cheesed potatoes, and chocolate cake. The book gave directions for preparing and cooking food so that the troops would eat well, noting, for example, that "the salad should be attractively served [and] garnished with shredded carrots, whole radishes, cherries or grapes" and that "only appetizing and palatable desserts should be served in the Army mess. It is better to use plain canned fruit for dessert than a dessert like plain cornstarch pudding." There was even a section on tea and advice for the Army cook on how to select the proper leaves: "Congou liquor is a reddish brown in color and generally has a toasty flavor. . . ." Here, a cookbook offers collectors an unexpected glimpse of military life that was a little more sophisticated than foxholes and C-rations.

Regional Gems

Cookbooks were constantly being affected by changes in social thought, food technology, and government. For example, when the country was coming out of the Great Depression, food was not something to be elaborately celebrated, even in cookbooks, since few families escaped the sting of poverty or the feeling that the evening's dinner might be their last meal for a while. When Franklin Roosevelt instituted various programs as part of the federal government's attempt to employ scholars and artists, some of the work was directed

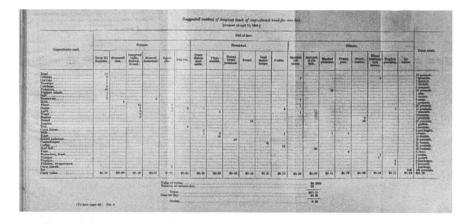

Fig. 5-19 The military has had a tremendous effect on food through the centuries, and the United States Army has taken its share of joking over its food and food service. But for all the grumbling from troops, the Quartermaster Corps struggled to produce well-balanced, hot meals in the field whenever possible. The manuals for cooks and food managers varied in their depth; the World War I manual was a small booklet with pull-out charts indicating how much food would serve a certain number of people. The World War II book, *Army Food and Messing*, contained directions for setting up a field kitchen, maintaining sanitation, and even selecting the best tea to serve the troops.

toward recording the folklore and traditions of regional America and its folkways. This interest was partly focused on food, and a trend in cookbooks from the 1930s and 1940s was to explore the varied tastes found from New York delis to Native American reservations. People were also starting to travel the country on the new national highways, or flying from one city to another, tasting and discovering the differences that made American food so special, and adding to the public's interest in regional cooking.

Some of these regional cookbooks, like *Two Hundred Years of Charleston Cooking*, by Blanche Rhett and Lettie Gay (1930), narrowed the study

Fig. 5-20 Duncan Hines was a traveling salesman who realized that Americans had no way of evaluating the dining spots and lodging along the byways of the 1930s. His first book was *Adventures in Good Eating,* a guidebook, and it became a best-seller, going through forty-six editions; he later licensed the use of his name on certain publications and products. *The Art of Grilling, Baking, Barbecuing* was published in 1952 for the RCA Estate Appliance Corporation, manufacturer of kitchen ranges, and contained a general selection of recipes including a dozen from Hines' personal scrapbook. Unlike many writers, Hines credited the sources of his recipes, from Lindy's in New York to Richards Treat Cafeteria in Minneapolis, and he was among the first Americans to use food as a guide for the traveler.

Fig. 5-21 In the early days of public rail travel, eating was done between stops or from a picnic basket; later trains had well-stocked dining cars and professional chefs along for the ride. The Southern Pacific was a transcontinental railroad and according to its cookbooklet operated 140 dining cars, 26 all-day lunch cars, 36 club cars, 7 hotels and restaurants, and 20 steamer restaurants; they also served more than 7 million meals each year. Diners who took advantage of the railroad food might enjoy Indian chutney, chicken gumbo Southern Pacific, pork pie, and something called an "omelet eclair," a dessert omelet served with chocolate syrup and whipped cream.

to a specific city, and often contained recipes that had never been written down (for example, Mr. Hughes' boned turkey with pecan dressing). Collectors who enjoy cookbooks of this type will find the all-but-forgotten feeling that a good family recipe was a gem to be protected and used to maintain

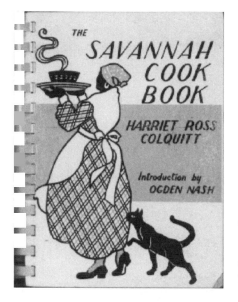

Fig. 5-22 For collectors of regional cookbooks, *The Savannah Cook Book,* which first appeared in 1933, is one of the best. The author collected recipes from old South Carolina family cookbooks and offers them up in a very direct style: "Before you go to bed that night, scald the possum with lye and scrape off the hair. (Or have it done, which would be altogether more pleasant all around.)" Poet Ogden Nash offered some poetry for the pages, and tiny, stick-figure drawings add a touch of eccentricity to the text. The cover depicts a stereotypical version of the African-American cook; some African-American recipes, like benne seed candy, were included.

stature in the kitchen; a last gasp of individual cooking before the homogenization of America's food was completed by magazines and newspapers. According to the writers, "The gathering of these recipes turned out to be a long job. . . . These recipes are treasured as closely as is the old sideboard from which dinners have been served for a hundred and fifty years. Not only have they never before been published, but they have never even been given to friends. . . ." Recipes like sweet potato pie, peanut dressing, and oyster stew with mace are accompanied by sensual descriptions so often lacking in modern cookbooks: "This sweet potato pie is a mouth-watering affair in a big, round dish oozing with brown richness."

Of course, the south was not the only region with great recipes, and cookbooks from defined areas appeared from California to Maine. *Good Maine Food,* by Marjorie Mosser, with notes by historic novelist Kenneth Roberts, appeared in 1939, praising the taste of everything from cod's tongues and cheeks to ham muffins and cranberry pie. *The Mary Cullen's Northwest Cook Book, North Carolina and Old Salem Cookery, The Connecticut Cookbook,* and hundreds of other commercially published regional books appeared until the 1960s, when the trend towards European cooking relegated American food to the back burner of many, although not all, cooks.

In *The United States Regional Cook Book,* by Ruth Berolzheimer (1939), the regions of the country were divided into cooking sections, including a few uncommon areas: Wisconsin and Michigan and Pennsylvania Dutch, Minnesota Scandinavian, Creole, southern and even the Mississippi Valley (midwestern dishes). Because many of the recipes were gathered directly from

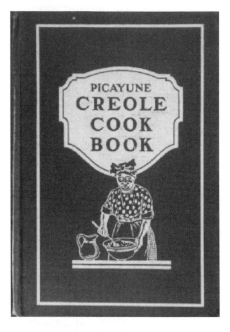

Fig. 5-23 The Times-Picayune Publishing Company began to issue *The Original Picayune Creole Cook Book* in 1901, and many editions later it is still popular with collectors. The recipes were accompanied by detailed notes on the history of Creole and French cooking, although many of the dishes can be considered Cajun, and the flavors of Africa (note the stereotypical "Mammy" on the cover) make their appearances as well. Interesting chapters on local beverages, candies, and menus make this an excellent regional sourcebook.

Fig. 5-24 The hearty Pennsylvania-Dutch food of the Anderson Hotel in Wabasha, Minnesota, was known throughout the midwest; the recipes in the book were collected by Mother Anderson's grandchildren. Cookbooks with a regional flavor sometimes offer recipes that were passed down by tradition, rather than by publication.

housewives and cooks by food editors working in the field, regional cookbooks allow the reader to visit little-known celebrations like the Escanaba Michigan Smelt Jamboree, or a real New England clambake. Recipes for delights like lemon catchup, possum and sweet taters, and Baltimore goldenrod eggs were collected and written by contributors who often had experienced pioneer life firsthand. It was to the credit of the regional cookbook writers that they did not remove recipes that were difficult or even impossible to make: "For mead, take 40 pounds of honey, 10 gallons water, 15 yeast cakes, and 1 quart of brandy or sack," begins one optimistic set of directions. The books usually consisted of recipes gathered from forty-eight states (Alaska and Hawaii didn't participate until statehood), along with comments upon the history or presentation of a recipe ("Pine bark stew is so named because it is prepared on the bank of the river where the fish are caught and pine bark is used to build a quick fire").

Writers like Sheila Hibben, who authored *The National Cookbook, A Kitchen Americana* in 1932 and *American Regional Cookery* in 1946, and the Brown family, which wrote *America Cooks* (Figure 5-25) in 1940, provided a last look at some cuisines that were fast losing their individuality. Hibben noted in *The National Cookbook:* "Writing this cookbook has been like writing a history of the country, for the recipes I have set down are not without historical interest. . . . But the feeling with which I end my work is that of a special sort of patriotism, a real enthusiasm for the riches and

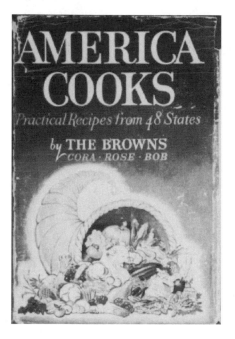

Fig. 5-25 One of the most interesting regional cookbooks published in this century, *America Cooks* (1940), contains more than 1,600 recipes from forty-eight states. The authors were well-known cookery writers, and they collected recipes that ranged from real Kentucky burgoo (given to the contributor by "Mr. Bob Roberts of Mayfield, who is a good cook as well as a good funeral director") to bean fudge from Wyoming. Collections like this often contain unusual recipes rarely recorded in commercial cookbooks. The book pictured is itself in good condition, but the dust jacket shows wear; the copyright page states that the book is a first edition.

Fig. 5-26 The Culinary Arts Press of Pennsylvania issued regional and specialty cookbooks in the 1930s. The recipes were collected from older books, and some carry unusual names: "hog's back son of a seacook" (salt codfish), paradise jelly (apples and cranberries), and Baptist cookies. But what sets this series of books apart is the cover—several books were available with painted, wooden covers held in place with plastic rings.

traditions of America, astonishment at the variety and flavor of the victuals native to all our old communities and delight at the . . . passion, with which armies of editorial writers can be raised to defend sectional recipes for potlicker or pan dowdy." Not many years later, she bemoaned the fact that ready-mixes and food editors had removed much of the sparkle from cooking. "There was a time," Hibben deplored, "when the phrase *this is the best thing I ever tasted* came to people as naturally as sneezing. . . . If only our tongues can again feel fresh and delighted over the taste of the best buttered muffins, or the best rabbit stew, there will come to us a salutory impatience with the graceless routine of eating out of packages and cans."

Collectors should watch for books that credit the origin of each recipe, rather than just printing all the pies or soups together, leaving the reader to guess where the dishes originally hailed from. In *America Cooks,* many recipes receive detailed descriptions regarding ingredients, preparation, and history of the food ("Snow picnics play such a frequent part in the social affairs of the . . . boys and girls of New Hampshire that it seems strange to hear other folk ask 'What is a snow picnic?'"). Photographs of the food or food producers are also something to watch for in regional cookbooks, since the way a dish was to be presented is often not revealed in the recipe.

Other books that offer a look at American foods include cookbooks from the series produced by the Ford Motor Company, *The Ford Treasury of Favorite Recipes from Famous Restaurants* (Figure 5-27), with their colorful illustrations, recipes, and descriptions of restaurants across the

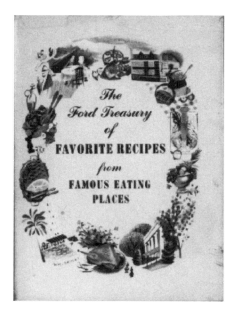

Fig. 5-27 Travel and food always went hand in hand, and as Americans took to the highways, they needed books that described just what it was they were eating out there. The Ford Motor Company issued a series of cookbooks, beginning in 1950, based on articles in its travel magazines. These treasuries were divided up into regional sections, in which restaurants were described and illustrated and a popular recipe offered to the cook. Reading the books today is a trip into inns and eateries long closed or remodeled, although some, like Antoine's and Trader Vic's, still flourish. The first edition was spiral bound; later editions were hardcovers, and an anniversary edition was issued in an oversized version, but it lacks the charm of the originals. The books are sometimes stamped with the name of the Ford dealer who presented it to his or her customer.

country, and *Adventures in Good Cooking,* by Duncan Hines (Figure 5-28), which began in the 1930s as a guide to eating and lodging across the country. Eventually, Hines leased his name to several other commercial ventures (including cake mixes), but his recipes are all credited as to their sources and his books are interesting collections of food by the side of the road in the early traveling days of this century.

More recent classics to watch for include Mary-Margaret McBride's *Harvest of American Cooking; Fading Feast,* by Ramond Sokolov (not a cookbook, but a look at traditional foods and celebrations); *The Grassroots Cookbook,* by Jeanne Anderson (first published in 1974); and *I Hear America Cooking,* by Betty Fussell, an excellent look at where regional food is heading in the latter part of the twentieth century. Time-Life Books also presented a Foods of America series in the 1970s, which consisted of twelve volumes and twelve recipe books, each set dedicated to a specific region of America's food.

Food Establishment Cookbooks

Although cookbooks from the nineteenth century sometimes provided recipes from famous hotels and dining establishments, it was not until this century that the idea of establishment cookbooks arrived. These were books penned by people who either owned or managed famous dining spots, and collectors will discover a rich selection of cookbooks in this category. Readers can "listen in" as George Rector tells behind-the-scenes stories of such

Fig. 5-28 Duncan Hines was the first writer to provide traveling Americans with a guide to lodging and food across country; his cookbooks used recipes borrowed from famous restaurants and out-of-the way stops. These two books were published fifteen years apart, in 1943 and 1957; the earlier example, on the left, is in fair condition, while the one on the right is in very good condition. For collectors interested in the foods served in dining establishments during the mid-twentieth century, *Adventures in Good Cooking* is a fascinating sourcebook.

luminaries as Diamond Jim Brady, in *The Rector Cook Book* (1928), or read in *Old Waldorf Bar Days* the hundreds of drink recipes that are accompanied by stories about Bat Masterson and Gentleman Jimmie Walker. Also telling tales and sharing recipes were inn owners, including Ruth Wakefield, whose Toll House gave the world a famous chocolate chip cookie; Elsie Masterson, with her Blueberry Hill inn series; and owners of the Brown Derby, the White Turkey Inn, Old Hundred, Mother Anderson's Dutch Kitchens, Patricia Murphy's, the Old Coventry Inn, and many other establishments, most no longer in existence.

Establishment cookbooks were sometimes sold as souveniers of the establishment. *How It Is Done,* from the McDonald Tea Room in Gallatin, Missouri, not only provided a selection of recipes (tuna salad shaped to represent a pond lily, strawberry jam cup cakes) but was also filled with testimonial letters, as well as an essay encouraging women to open their own tearooms, penned by the very successful owner, Virginia McDonald: "Make

Fig. 5-29 The White Turkey Inn was located in Connecticut and styled after an old world teahouse. *Let's Talk Turkey* tells the history of the establishment, along with recipes from the tearoom and restaurant. Cookbook and food historians might find it interesting to know that the book also offers a recipe for Lady Baltimore cake, a rich, frosted confection. The owners of the inn received it from their cousins, who were considered the original inventors of the cake; this is an example of a cookbook preserving popular food history.

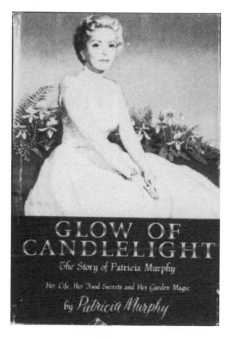

Fig. 5-30 Patricia Murphy was a well-known restauranteur, who started in New York with a broken-down tearoom. Her later establishments were famous for their lush flowers, elegant service, and hot popovers served with the meals. Books like this memoir add background and history to a cookbook collection, bringing chefs and their dishes to life and recording the history of dining establishments long closed.

up your minds to work on Sundays and holidays—that is when the money is made, as people like to go out to Sunday dinners and roam around on holidays." The cookbooks were often illustrated with photographs of an establishment in its heyday, providing collectors with a look inside the tearooms and lunchrooms that are no longer part of America's culinary landscape. Modern establishments still issue cookbooks, and the collector can watch for offerings from the Marriott Hot Shoppes, Moosewood Restaurant, Moody's Diner, and other classic eating spots.

Cookbooks in Modern Times

As the middle class began to experience postwar growth and prosperity in the 1950s, cookbooks were there to advise the housewife on the changes in food and fashions. After the relative freedom and equality of the war years, when women had worked in factories or flew planes, most women had gone back to the kitchen or to other more "suitable" jobs. New, affordable housing developments began to spring up, as did appropriate cookbooks such as *What Cooks in Suburbia* (1961; see Figure 5-31), by Lila Perl, which offered a look at life in the kitchens of middle-class women. "Here is that rarity of rarities," proclaimed the book's jacket, "a cookbook with a new and unusual twist, designed and arranged specifically for the special meal occasions that the average suburban housewife must face every day." Recipes and menus offered guidance to the wife who had to prepare teas, luncheons, and dinners

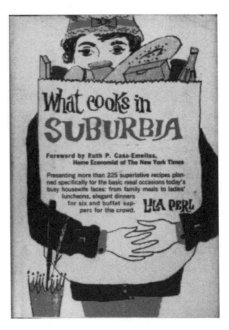

Fig. 5-31 Suburbia grew quickly after World War II, when tens of thousands of returning veterans and their families moved from the cities to new development towns and villages where housing was affordable and the surroundings were somewhere between rural and urban. Cookbooks soon entered the suburban kitchen to help the harried housewife juggle family, card parties, and other aspects of suburban life. The copy of *What Cooks in Suburbia* (1961) pictured is in very good condition, including the dust jacket.

for six. Must-have directions for popular cocktail dishes like sour cream and caviar dip were presented along with standbys such as chicken almond, jambalaya and sausage patties, and lemon pudding tarts. The recipes in *What Cooks in Suburbia* call for few convenience foods, perhaps indicating that cooks were still poised between the worlds of home-baked and get-me-out-of-the-kitchen.

Cooks and cookbooks were greatly affected by the advent of television, which now brought commercials for new products, new ingredients, and new cooking methods into the home every night. TV dinners were served by housewives anxious to watch Uncle Miltie and Ed Sullivan, and the television also provided viewers with a new look at food. Commercials made their pitches several times an hour, convincing the cook that she needed a new refrigerator, a better stove, or a food slicer that would whisk her into the living room faster. Soon, cookbooks influenced by television were turning up on the shelves of neighborhood shops. The books were sponsored by programs, like "Queen for a Day" or Josie McCarthy's cooking show, or authored by well-known television figures, like Betty Furness, spokeswoman for Westinghouse, who honestly noted in her introduction to *The Betty Furness Westinghouse Cookbook* in 1963 that, although she owned a Westinghouse kitchen, she wasn't the most experienced cook and needed help in writing the book.

The recipes found in television cookbooks were almost always touted as being easy, simple, and quick to make, and the cook was usually thanked

Fig. 5-32 ZaSu Pitts was a popular actress who starred opposite Mary Pickford in early film comedies; ZaSu was also famous on movie back lots for her candy-making skills. Besides being an excellent cookbook, *Candy Hits* offers a special inside look at Hollywood, with illustrations from the silent films to the advent of television.

by the author in the introduction for her part in preparing three meals a day for the family and delighting in the work. This TV cookbook trend has continued for more than forty years, and collectors can find moderately priced examples based on shows like "All In The Family" (written by "Edith Bunker"), "The Mike Douglas Show," and "Dallas," along with English cookbooks from public television shows like "The Irish R.M." and "Upstairs, Downstairs."

During the 1950s and 1960s, African-American cookbooks began to attract attention from white cooks, although it took until the 1970s, when the interest in "soul food" blossomed, for traditional black cooking to receive its due historically and culturally. One of the earliest books to address the art of black cooking was *A Date with a Dish,* written in 1949 by Freda De Knight, food editor at *Ebony* magazine. Even at this late date, she felt it necessary to note in her introduction that "it is a fallacy long disproved, that Negro cooks, chefs, caterers and housewives can adapt themselves only to the standard Southern dishes, such as fried chicken, greens, corn pone, hot breads and so forth." De Knight provided recipes that were collected from African-American cooks all across America, and her introductions brought many unknown and unsung chefs to light.

Other books often either were coauthored by white writers or the recipes were gathered by a white writer from an African-American cook, making the collections less personal and authentic and separating the reader from the source. *Plantation Recipes,* by Lessie Bowers (1959), the owner of The Virginian restaurant in New York, and *Jesse's Book of Creole and Deep South Recipes* were two in this category. The latter appeared in 1954 (it has been reprinted) and gave the favorite recipes of Jesse Willis Lewis, a well-respected chef. Both books contained recipes with African-American roots as well as sophisticated southern and European cuisine. Later books by various writers, including Pearl Bailey, Norma Jean and Carole Darden *(Spoonbread and Strawberry Wine),* and Vertamae Smart-Grosvenor *(Vibration Cooking or the Travel Notes of a Geechee Girl),* presented African-American food in a more personal way. Many traditional recipes were passed down in church cookbooks or kept alive through an oral tradition in places like the Sea Islands off the coast of South Carolina. Eventually, African-American cookbooks came to reflect the pride and shared traditions of many people; cookbooks are now appearing that help to celebrate the holiday, Kwanzaa.

By the 1960s, cookbooks were facing the problem of representing the varied thoughts on the changing places of women, in home and office, kitchen and boardroom. *The Working Wives' Cook Book* (Figure 5-33), by Theodora Zavin and Freda Stuart (1963), offered cook-ahead recipes designed so women could make dinner the night before, get to work, get home, reheat dinner, and then serve it again the next night. The working wife would use the cookbook so that meals would be ready to go, since "[dinner

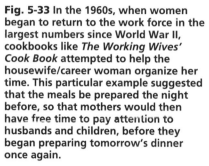

Fig. 5-33 In the 1960s, when women began to return to the work force in the largest numbers since World War II, cookbooks like *The Working Wives' Cook Book* attempted to help the housewife/career woman organize her time. This particular example suggested that the meals be prepared the night before, so that mothers would then have free time to pay attention to husbands and children, before they began preparing tomorrow's dinner once again.

hour] is just . . . the time that children (and husbands, too!) want and deserve attention." *The How To Keep Him After You've Caught Him Cookbook* (1968) was a tongue-in-cheek look at married life and how to smooth its edges with food ("armistice artichokes" for serving after a spat, and fresh strawberries for keeping the magic in the marriage), while Helen Gurley Brown offered cooking (and other) advice in the *Single Girl's Cookbook* (1969), a compendium of recipes geared to make the unmarried "girl" a cook good enough to snare a man (and please visiting relatives). Even as early as the 1930s, cookbooks for were available for women "live-aloners." One handy guide, *Corned Beef and Caviar,* included recipes for dinners from a can, as well as advice like "Never ask a man to balance his plate on his knee."

Cookbooks aimed at single diners had first appeared early in the century, when *A Bachelor's Cupboard* guided the stag male through the terrors of the kitchen. (It is interesting to note that as times changed, male chefs began to feel the need to justify just why it was they had entered the kitchen in the first place. One radio personality of the 1930s and 1940s called himself "The Mystery Chef" and hosted a popular cooking program. In *The Mystery Chef's Own Cook Book* [Figure 5-34], published in 1945, he writes, "Why do I call myself The Mystery Chef? . . . My dear mother, who was alive at that time, was horrified when she first heard that I had taken to cooking as a hobby. . . ." He then explains how his mother taught his sisters to manage a household, but it was a different matter for a *son* to know how to cook.) Later books for

Fig. 5-34 The Mystery Chef cookbook series began when a Scottish advertising executive filled in for his friend on a radio program; the resulting blend of food and chat was so popular that the "chef" received his own show. Calling himself The Mystery Chef in order to prevent his mother from being embarrassed (in the 1930s, men usually didn't admit to cooking), John MacPherson wrote several books, starting in 1934. The book pictured has a worn dust jacket and has a wipe-clean cover; this particular copy has added value because it was signed by the chef.

singles include *The Bachelor's Cookbook* (Figure 5-35), published in 1962, which taught how to prepare "food most men enjoy" like fried eggs, spaghetti and clam sauce, and even Welsh rabbit for a poker night. But lest the bachelor become confused in the cupboard, sections were provided with advice on opening tin cans, dealing with mice, and preparing game ("We know a man who pins his grouse to the back-porch washline; he pulls at a bird's leg every day until the bone comes away in his hand, then he unpins his birds and expects his wife to cook them. You may have other ideas").

The 1960s helped women admit that not everyone was suited for domestic life or had a love affair with the kitchen. The perky author Peg Bracken struck this nerve with her series of books filled with easy recipes and advice on running a household on little time and even less interest. The bestselling *I Hate To Cook Book, Appendix to The I Hate To Cook Book,* and *The I Hate To Cook Book Almanac* all reassured a housewife that if she didn't like cooking and cleaning, she was not alone in her thoughts, and that life could be lived reasonably well with only a minimum of kitchen effort.

By the 1970s and 1980s, cookbooks were pouring out of publishing houses at an astounding rate—hundreds of new titles jostling for space on bookstore and grocery shelves, along with books with classic names (Fannie Farmer was still selling strong) and unusual topics. The Age of Aquarius and the hippie era were entwined with the new interest in "natural" and healthful cooking. Vegetarian cookbooks emerged from behind the casserole dishes and took their rightful place on the shelf along with brown rice, bean sprouts, and tofu.

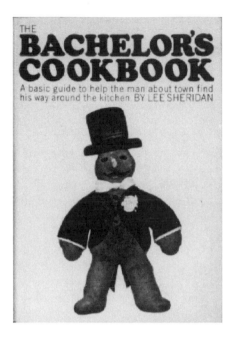

THE
BACHELOR'S COOKBOOK
A basic guide to help the man about town find
his way around the kitchen BY LEE SHERIDAN

Fig. 5-35 Books like *The Bachelor's Cookbook* took advantage of the fact that until the 1970s, many men did not know how to cook, beyond boiling water or defrosting a TV dinner. The recipes in the various cookbooks aimed at male novices usually began with a description of kitchen equipment and ended with a party menu that even the clumsiest male cook could handle; in between were many pages of encouragement and the repeated belief that cooking was manageable by everyone.

The Moosewood Cookbook, from the Moosewood Restaurant in Ithaca, New York, helped popularize what many had viewed as food for radicals and stargazers. Books like *Meatless Cooking Celebrity Style* (1975) contained vegetarian recipes and quotes from "names" as diverse as Shelley Winters and Yehudi Menuhin, and books like this helped to take the exoticness out of meatless meals and make the mysteries of vegetarian dishes more accessible.

Along with vegetarian cookbooks came books that considered food from many different angles. Books appeared touting organic foods (those without additives or artificial coloring and flavorings), health foods (a fuzzily defined area), herbs (self-proclaimed witch Sybil Leek wrote her own cookbook on this topic), and aphrodisiac cookery (try "stud spuds" or connubial onions). Even hippie communes had their food views enshrined in cookbooks; The True Light Beavers from Woodstock, New York, penned *Feast,* a book filled with suggestions for self-sufficient living, including cooking with a few untraditional kitchen ingredients, like morning glory seeds and an illegal plant or two. The Greenwich Village Peace Center in New York City financed its 1970s antiwar work with *Peacemeal,* a collection of recipes from people who believed in peace, love, and good dining. Zodiac cookbooks connected good eating to the stars, and books like *The Solar Cookbook* (1981) began to introduce the idea of environmentally responsible kitchens (all the recipes were based on cooking with free energy from the sun). Other cookbooks had suggestions for recycling, composting, and reducing kitchen waste, tucked in along with the recipes.

Cookbooks were important repositories of trends, from *The Junk Food Cookbook* (which promised "healthy" junk food from the home kitchen) to make-your-own-mix cookbooks to books about bagels, chocolate, chicken, homemade baby foods, and on and on. If there was a trend, there was a cookbook. The "no" cookbooks became popular, providing recipes for dishes with no salt, sugar, cholesterol, fats, or additives, while diet books surged to the front of cookbook sales, carried there by "classics" like *The Beverly Hills Diet, The I Love America Diet, The Pritikin Diet Cookbook,* and *The Weight Watcher's Cookbook.* (There were also gems like *Martinis and Whipped Cream* and *The Rice Diet.*)

By the end of the 1980s and the start of the 1990s, commercially published cookbooks were being produced at the rate of nearly 800 new books a year, and that did not include charity cookbooks or the 10,000 cookbooks that remained in print and were available to cooks and collectors alike. Cookbooks were no longer purchased solely in bookstores but were also available through catalogs, in museum gift shops, from book clubs, at checkout counters, through television offers, and even in shops dedicated only to cookbooks. That so many cookbooks were being produced, unfortunately, did not mean that either writers or editors knew what they were doing, even after nearly two centuries of practice. Collectors will still discover books with inaccurate ingredients listings, poorly written directions, and recipes that just don't work, although as publishers like Better Home & Gardens, Good Housekeeping, and Pillsbury have always insisted upon using only rigorously tested recipes. Some publishers tried to avoid the threatened move to the metric system that haunted the 1970s by creating books to satisfy everyone, resulting in recipes were that were cursed with two or three different types of measurements for each ingredient.

Classic Cooks

Like avid readers of mystery novels, many cookbook collectors find a favorite author, then wait eagerly for the writer's next book to come along to provide a good read on a cosy evening. (Interestingly, it wasn't unusual for a woman editor in a publishing house to be assigned all the cookbooks and mysteries that came through the door, since they were lumped together under "women's interests" in the minds of company executives.) Like the nineteenth century, the twentieth century has been rich in writers who elevated food to the level of high art and helped others discover that there was life beyond meatloaf and TV dinners.

James Beard was one of the first chef/authors to consider American food as a cuisine, and not just a means of nutrition. His classic *James Beard's American Cookery* (1972) is a grand view of this country's foods, from the traditional, like basic boiled beef dinner, to the more continental, like chicken Kiev. His writing style harks back to the early period of cookery, when cooks like Amelia Simmons offered comments on the food and its preparation entwined with the actual recipes. Indeed, his title was a reworking of the title of Simmons's book, *American Cookery.* James Beard authored many cookbooks, including works on grilling; outdoor cookery; and fish, fowl, and game cookery. His *Fireside Cookbook* offered readers a unique cover which unfolded into a display poster (finding this cover in good condition—which is difficult to do—adds to the value of the book).

Another of the great cookbook writers who provides collectors with fascinating provender is Julia Child, author of classics like *Mastering the Art of French Cooking,* written with Simone Beck and Louisette Bertholle in 1961. For Americans thoroughly frightened by seemingly impossible French culinary techniques, Child's writing and presentation style was a commonsensical rock, upon which could be built the fussiest of French dishes. Child was also a pioneer in televised cooking shows, all the time maintaining a sense of humor and proportion when it came to food. Her later shows included "Julia Child and Company" and "Julia Child and More Company," which produced cookbooks of the same names.

Those book collectors who like to read even a little more than they like to cook should consider the works of Mary Francis Kennedy Fisher (M.F.K. Fisher), one of the finest of all food writers. Her essays and recipes appeared in many books, beginning with *Serve It Forth,* her earliest work, but collectors who did not have the foresight to capture her first editions upon publication will now have to pay heavily for the privilege of owning them. Other outstanding modern food writers whose books should tempt the collector while enriching his or her understanding of American cooking include Jeff Smith, the Frugal Gourmet; Graham Kerr, the Australian chef better known as the Galloping Gourmet; Alice Waters, who established the light, sophisticated fare known as the "new American cuisine"; Lee Bailey, whose lusciously photographed books about food are personal and fascinating; William Woys Weaver, an outstanding writer who examines American culinary history; and Jane and Michael Stern, who take cooks on a visit down the highways and interstates of yesteryear in books like *American Gourmet* and *Roadfood and Goodfood.* This list only hints at the number of fine cookbooks recently published and ready for collecting, good news to collectors who may have limited monetary means but a wide interest in food.

Tips for Collecting Twentieth-Century Cookbooks

The collectors of twentieth-century cookbooks will have to limit their libraries or lose their minds, since there is such a variety of books of all prices on the market. Advertising cookbooks are usually inexpensive (unless illustrated by a well-known artist) and offer excellent views of the changes that overtook the American kitchen, family, and women in the last century. Appliance cookbooks are an underrated collectible and generally can be found in the $8 to $10 range, especially the books that accompanied some of the more faddish electric items found in the kitchen, like hotdog steamers, Crockpots, and crepe pans. Watch for the notebook-style cookbooks from blender and microwave manufacturers, which are usually very well made, with wipe-clean plastic binders, but are too often tossed out when an appliance breaks.

Television and radio cookbooks were sometimes inexpensive giveaways or, as in the case of books from the Mystery Chef radio series and the Galloping Gourmet television series, could be purchased. Cookbooks from local radio stations, containing recipes sent by listeners from the broadcast area, make excellent regional collectibles; the prices of these books are often affected by the fame of the "stars" who contributed recipes, but $15 and under is a common value.

First editions by any of the legends in the culinary field, especially James Beard, Julia Child, M.F.K. Fisher, and others of that caliber, are always a solid addition to any collection, but don't ignore the essay-style books by lesser-known writers, like Della Lutes and Haydn Pearson, who captured the charm of country cooking long before it was fashionable to do so ("For dessert with fish chowder, nothing yet invented equals a thick slice of cold, rich, moist, smooth, cinnamon-flavored squash pie").

American cookbooks no longer consider American food only, and there is a large selection on the market for collectors who are interested in foods from other countries (note that books representing countries that no longer exist have an almost built-in collectibility). For those who enjoy watching the quirky changes in American tastes over the years, diet cookbooks are another overlooked collectible source and are generally priced at $8 and under, even for the more bizarre examples.

There seems to be little concern that cookbooks will cease to appear during the next century or so. The so-called video cookbooks—actually, tapes of cooking demonstrations with recipes—failed to take off in the way that many producers had hoped. While the tapes are interesting to watch, bringing, in a sense, a chef into the home kitchen, the techniques are not always easily transferred to the kitchen; also, the user has to depend upon the recipe cards that accompany the tapes for actual cooking directions. However, for cooks who can't attend classes at a cooking school, the tapes are good learning tools and make an interesting addition to a collection that focuses on modern cooking.

Cookbooks have continued in some cases to plead for a social conscience along with their food values, although in the last few years the tendency has been for books to be oversized, lavishly illustrated, and at times overpriced, with newly published books sometimes retailing for $50 and more. Trends of the last part of the twentieth century include a wide interest in cookbooks from exotic countries, like Vietnam, and little-known regional areas, like southern Italy. Also in vogue are fresh looks at food from the midwest, northwest, Amish and Mennonite kitchens, Broadway, prisons, diners, in short, just about anywhere food is served. University and college presses have published many excellent studies of food lore and history in recent years; *The Sensible Cook,* by Peter Rose (Syracuse University Press), is one example of this highly collectible format. Although the books are not strictly cookbooks, their insights into the tradition, preparation, and history of regional foods make the books invaluable research guides. Celebrity chefs continue to hold their own in the pantry, while books dedicated to chocolate never seem to lose their hold on popular tastes.

Cookbook writers have also turned their interest to creating recipe collections meant to soothe the nerves of a modern-day, overscheduled, frazzled cook with books on suppers, nursery food, waffles, and at-home dining (part of "cocooning" trend) being offered. The advent of desktop publishing has also brought a number of cookbooks to the marketplace which would not ordinarily arrive there. Many times, the subjects are unusual, like Welsh or Cornish cooking, recipes from a sea captain's wife's diary, religious holiday meals, or foods for the person who cannot chew. These kinds of cookbooks are ordinarily ignored by large publishers who have neither the means nor the interest in handling narrow cookbook topics. As far as collectibility is involved, independent presses can often produce something as well-done as any commercial press can offer, and the books tend to be issued in limited numbers. Of course, quality varies widely, and the collector is advised to watch for books that will add depth to a collection.

What's in store for collectors? Everytime it seems the cookbook industry has saturated the market and that no one could possibly have a fresh idea left about food, along comes a writer to prove everyone wrong. (Who ever thought that cookbooks about popcorn, grits, fudge, or crackers would sell? But they did.) Trends are always difficult to predict, and this is part of the fun of collecting. Nostalgic cookbooks, like the lighthearted looks at food provided by Jane and Michael Stern in their books *Square Meals* and *American Gourmet,* will continue to tug at the memories of food lovers and cooks who can never forget Grandma's meatloaf or Uncle Joe's chili. Older cooking techniques will continue to be the focus of new cookbooks, with grilling, convection cooking, steaming, pressure cooking, and other time-honored methods receiving updates. Books by new immigrants will begin to display the blending of cooking cultures from around the world with American cuisine. Of course, charity cookbooks will go on raising funds for deserving organizations, and Junior League books will no doubt maintain the sophistication and innovation they have displayed in the last dozen or so years. And while cookbooks have long been directed towards women and traditional families, new cookbooks are beginning to take into account that while families differ in their makeup, beliefs, and economic backgrounds, food is a universal joy that may be shared in many ways. There is something very satisfying about sitting down in a cozy kitchen with a cup of tea and a cookbook from a prior age; perhaps it is the feeling that cooks can still talk to each other, and their feelings and tastes can cross the centuries.

6 ❘ Ephemera

And Cookbook-Related Collectibles

When it comes to making additions to a collection, truly dedicated "cookbookers" rarely stop with the original item; such collectors cannot resist adding things that are not, strictly speaking, cookbooks. Culinary ephemera and food-related books can deepen the scope of a library, providing a more comprehensive look at cookbook history through the study of related fields and interests. There are literally millions of pieces of ephemera available to the collector, from advertising booklets and product-related leaflets to recipe card sets and even paperback books. Much of it is exceedingly affordable, and the supply is continually renewed, since food companies continue to publish leaflets and brochures that highlight a special ingredient or product and which, in turn, enter the world of collectible cookbooks. For those who care to collect only books, etiquette manuals may provide a better understanding of manners of times past, while medical guides dispense information about nineteenth-century cookery and household management, along with directions for curing rabies. Fascinating reading, indeed, and the following are only a few of the cookbook-related items, some unusual, some very common, that are available to the collector in a wide range of prices.

Advertising Booklets

Advertising booklets and brochures have been popular giveaways since the nineteenth century, and these colorful sales tools ranged from miniature booklets that were tucked into the product or attached to the outside of the box to full-sized magazines complete with color illustrations. (The term "booklets" is relatively vague when it comes to determining the number of

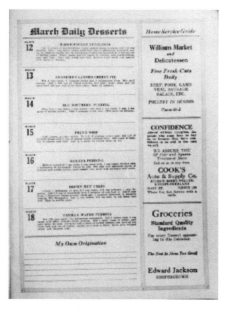

Fig. 6-1 Advertising cookbooks used many ways to reach readers and gain customers. In *The Daily Dessert Calendar* issued in 1924, cooks could find a dessert a day for one year, along with ads from local businesses in Cooperstown, New York. Recipes provided by Margaret Wayne, of the American Culinary Guild, presented the cook with dishes as comfortable as steamed apple pudding and as odd as Indian dainties (an Indian pudding dressed up with custard and cherries). The booklet pictured had no writing or other marks on the blank recipe pages, and no folds on the covers; if an advertising book like this is in good or better condition, It usually means the book had been tucked away and rarely used by the original owner.

Fig. 6-2 The Pebeco Tooth Paste Company issued this advertising booklet just after the motion picture version of "Gone With The Wind" captured the public's imagination. According to the booklet, readers would be able to "enjoy the Lacy Corn Cakes, Scarlett's thick Crab and Okra Gumbo, Aunt Pittypats's delicate Cocoanut Pudding or Melanie's Sweet Potato Pie." The fact that these dishes existed, as the booklet admitted, only "in the mind's eye" of the viewer was not important; recipes were created in the spirit of the movie or borrowed from famous cooks, like Mary Randolph. This booklet is in very good condition; a hardcover reprint was issued in 1992.

pages that make the difference between a book and a booklet; in most cases, a booklet is made up of fewer than fifty pages. A brochure is usually only a few pages and is folded, not bound.) The advertiser offered recipes using its products, and the housewife got a chance to try out the latest tastes and received a bonus cookbook in the bargain. The booklets were usually colorful and well-illustrated, providing collectors with detailed views of how the food was styled and served. The story of social diversions and entertainments is also depicted in these collections, which show how hostesses moved from chafing dish suppers and waffle dinners to outdoor barbecues and microwave snacks. The artwork reflected the styles and fads of the moment, and in fact, because they advertised a product that had to appeal directly and quickly to the customer and cook, these booklets were often better illustrated than many full-length cookbooks. Recipes ranged from the lyrically named ("Aladdin melting potatoes") to the unusual (potato spice cookies) to the downright bizarre (toast water for invalids: soak well-browned toast in water for an hour, then serve the liquid to the convalescing person).

Self-promotion was the bottom line with these advertising pieces, and the publishers had no problem fulfilling this requirement. According to the booklet *Say good-bye to hand beating!* not only did the Star-Rite Electric Magic Maid Beater mix, beat, and stir, but it roasted coffee, popped corn, polished silver, and sharpened knives as well. Promotion material for Brer Rabbit Molasses turned to an argument for bribing children with food, noting that "the rich store of iron and lime makes [the molasses] an especially wholesome sweet for children [and] your child is actually encouraged to eat more if there is gingerbread waiting for her at the end of the meal." And in the days before fat-conscious Americans would turn to lighter cooking oils, the Lever Brothers Company advertised in one of their dozens of Spry shortening booklets that "Spry is one of the richest sources of energy for your family. It makes all foods more nutritious. Spry supplies valuable Vitamin E, important in a well-balanced diet. The smart lithographed can is easy to keep clean."

Advertisers knew how to reach the housewife, whether it was 1890 or 1990—the product had to be different from the rest of the field, it needed to offer speed and convenience, and it had to be viewed by the housewife as improving home life. The families depicted within the pages of recipes were invariably white, happy, and of a comfortable economic background. In the history of advertising, African Americans were often represented as "characters," such as this mammy/cook from a 1935 baking leaflet: "Laws, Honey, it don't take no time at all. I use . . . batter to fry my chicken in, and folks tell me my chicken has the real old Southern flavor." Booklets emphasized the thriftiness of a product ("It was found . . . that making pancakes with our mix saves almost half the time . . . and costs less than one-seventh of a cent more than old methods") while showing the "good life" that Americans hoped to achieve.

Early advertisers turned first to well-known teachers and cooks for suggested recipes, and then to the new American royalty—movie stars like Dick Powell and Bing Crosby and society ladies like "Mrs. Marten Gregory." This charmed group provided menus for golf club buffet suppers, hunt club breakfasts, and yachting and hunting lodge luncheons (the latter came from Mr. Clark Gable) and endorsed products that they probably had never tasted. Overall, the advertising did what it set out to do: sell a product. The booklets

SLADE'S
COOKING SCHOOL
RECIPES

BY TWENTY-FIVE COOKING SCHOOL TEACHERS

PRICE 10 CENTS

Fig. 6-3 Anyone reading the title of *Slade's Cooking School Recipes* in 1909 might think that Slade's was a school; in reality, it was a food company that distributed and produced extracts, baking powders, and other kitchen goods. Of course, these ingredients were well mentioned in the recipes from twenty-five cooking school teachers, many of whom worked for the Boston Cooking School in Slade's hometown. The recipes are interspersed with comments like "Congress Baking Powder has been on the market for over 60 years. If it had not possessed superior merits, it would have been driven from the market a generation ago." In the spirit of advertising booklets, it is sometimes difficult to tell where the recipes start and the promotional material stops.

themselves were colorful, cheerful, encouraging, and filled with advice, and they offered all this to the consumer free of charge or for only a few cents in postage. If the books also mixed a little glamour and stardust in with the pancake batter, then all the better for the advertiser and even, perhaps, the reader.

Advertising cookbooklets also provide important resources for kitchen equipment collectors. Because they were distributed as promotional items and/or given to buyers, the cookbooklets could serve as user's manuals and order guides for kitchenware. Stove companies, like Home Comfort, sent out books, and along with the recipes for delectables like "Home Comfort cream candy" went pictures of the company factory, illustrations of prizes won at national expositions, and scores of letters from satisfied customers in every state in the union, including the Indiana governor's daughter. Also included were detailed pictures of range parts and suggestions for making the most of the Home Comfort stove. On a smaller scale, the Keystone Manufacturing Company produced the Keystone beater, and the advertising cookbook contains pictures of the various beaters and attachments, useful to collectors who wonder if what they own is a complete model or is perhaps missing that all-important rotary wheel. The booklet also had testimonials from the famous, including Sara Rorer, who composed a letter on the hows and whys of beating eggs, and bombastic store owner John Wanamaker, who stated, "Here's a machine that's bound to make a stir in the world. . . . Given a few

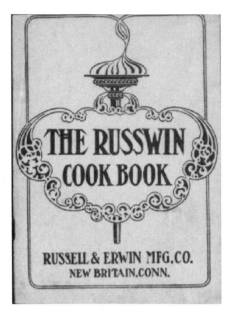

Fig. 6-4 The Russwin Food Cutter, manufactured by Russell & Erwin Mfg. Co., was actually a tabletop grinder, used to mince and cut meats, nuts, bread, suet, and vegetables. The cover of this cookbook has a graceful design, which belies the practicality of the equipment described inside. Photographs of a cook, along with her ungrammatical descriptions of how the cutter worked, were meant to demonstrate to the lady of the house that her lower-class servants could produce more work with the proper kitchenware.

more such inventions and the cook that prepares the feast of Lucullus may have ample leisure for Latin classics." (It would be interesting to know how many of the beaters were sold in his stores!)

Despite the fact that some products have disappeared from the market, a remarkable number have survived along with their advertising. Sweetened condensed milk booklets from the 1930s offer many of the same recipes as the ones available today (except for the boiled custard in the can, which could explode). Baking powder, cornstarch, dates, coconut, gelatin, and chocolate are all still around, along with some of the original companies and many of the original booklets. Look for examples from Walter Baker Chocolate Company, Swans Down Cake Flour, Bisquick, Spry Shortening, and Brer Rabbit Molasses; these companies published many versions of their booklets. Although some convenience foods (for example, instant rennet custards) have lost popularity through the years, others, including Jell-O gelatin, have continued to produce interesting collectibles. Jell-O debuted its "Jell-O Girl" in 1904 and through the years has issued untold numbers of booklets based on her travels and cooking adventures. The company has continued to issue collectible material in recent times, from movable booklets with wheels that turn to change recipes, to children's cookbooks, like *Amazing Magical Jell-O Desserts* (1977), which has recipes for cakes baked right in ice cream cones, instructions for creating frozen "pudding-wiches," and directions for simple magic tricks. Everything is fair game for cookbooklets; just when it seemed that potato chips must be left out of the recipe booklet competition, some bright copywriter managed to come up with recipes including gems like cinnamon rolls, brownies, and even chip brittle candy, all made with potato chips and proudly recorded in booklet form.

Without doubt, the majority of advertising cookbooklets were printed for food companies, but there were some exceptions, the most common ones concerning patent medicines. Americans through the centuries often depended more upon self-administered cures than on visits to the doctor, and there were scores of patent medicines on the market to fill a family's needs. As early as the seventeenth century, ointments, drops, pills, and laxatives were concocted and sold as cure-alls by doctors, farmers, cads, and con artists. Some of the medicines contained nothing more than pure liquor or morphine, certain to numb any pain if taken in sufficient quantity; other products were based on traditional herbal mixtures that provided some natural comfort.

Patent medicine manufacturers published many giveaways, complete with testimonial letters, ads for the medicine, and recipes. These booklets were odd combinations of old-time medicine shows and inadvertant humor. In *Henry's Cook Book,* the standard preparations for sale included Denton's Magnetic Balm, Boardman's French Worm Confections, and Sure Death to Rats; on the opposite page, the cake recipes begin. One of the most famous "vegetable compound" medicines was sold by Lydia E. Pinkham, who developed her pills and liquids for women going through "the three trying periods of maturity, maternity and middle life." In one of the Pinkham cookbooks, the recipe for upside-down cake appropriately if perhaps inadvertently appears just before a letter entitled "Was A Nervous Wreck." The F.W. McNess Company cookbook had ads for everything from fly chaser to vanishing cream, along with recipes calling for McNess spices, but collectors may never discover if the cold cream ad was actually supposed to be put underneath the recipes for frozen desserts. Another well-known patent name was Ayer's Standard Family Medicines, producer of the famous Ayer's sassparilla. The company's advertising booklet, *Ayer's Book of Pies and Puddings,* contained facing pages of creamy, rich recipes and descriptions of physical ailments—an unusual and somewhat unsettling combination.

Collectors should look for buys in cookbook advertising leaflets and brochures at flea markets, although bookstores specializing in used books often price the pieces moderately. Many dealers carry these items at book shows or antique shows, but the prices are generally higher because of the items' recognized value as advertising collectibles. If the illustrations in a booklet were done by a well-known artist, collectors can expect the price to be accordingly higher. Some of the more colorful publications had center spreads showing the subject food in all its glory—don't pay top dollar for a booklet if it has lost its center spread.

Advertising items also came in die-cut designs, that is, the booklet itself was shaped to resemble something else. Watch for these in the form of milk bottles, cans, bread loaves, shoes, and other unusual designs; few modern advertisers use die-cut designs because of the printing costs. Another style

Fig. 6-5 Some advertising booklets were designed to resemble the product they endorsed—in this case, a piecrust. These die-cut books sometimes show wear or have tears along the cut edges, or are missing pieces where the design was delicate. This example from 1977 is only in fair condition because of the folds in the cover.

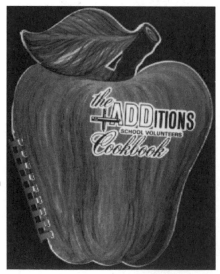

Fig. 6-6 Die-cut advertising booklets are popular collectibles and are sometimes hard to find; die-cut cookbooks are even more difficult to collect, although in recent years, several have been issued. This example was published by a group of school volunteers in Florida; other cookbooks have been found in the shape of a cowboy boot and a moose, among others.

to watch for is the mechanical, a book that has moving parts. Usually, these consist of wheels which can be turned to give different types of information about a food or allow the user to change recipes quickly.

Patent medicine cookbooks and almanacs are most easily found from the years between 1890 and 1930; the earlier and more colorful the piece, the more expensive it is likely to be. Advertising items that used the Shakers, a nineteenth-century religious group, as a selling point are rare and are sought after by both cookbook collectors and many non-cookbook collectors. (When you have to compete with collectors other than those in your field, you face the problem of "crossover" buying or collecting.) One other unusual collectible is the recipe card, usually a series of printed cards with recipes that are stored in a box provided by the publisher (in many cases, a food product manufacturer). The cards seem to have first appeared in the early 1920s and were offered by flour companies, so the recipes on these early cards have an emphasis on baked goods. Although they did not become nearly as popular as cookbooks, recipe cards are still being printed in sets and collected by cooks. Look for complete early sets (sometimes the cards were numbered and listed in a separate index) and the original box.

Even advertising pieces that are recent can be considered future collectibles, especially if they feature a personality or a food fad or they highlight an historic celebration, such as the centennial of Ellis Island or the Statue of Liberty. Booklets take up much less storage room than do cookbooks, and they have a quirky charm hidden in the self-promotion, making them a first-rate and fun collectible.

Medical Guides and Household Books

Related to cookbooks in their use of recipes and household ingredients, the medical guides and household receipt books of the nineteenth century still make interesting reading. Because so many parts of America lacked doctors, craftsmen, and skilled laborers, the pioneer and settler had to depend upon books that provided information on making things that could not be readily bought and on curing ills that would never see a doctor's visit.

One of the most famous books to appear on the shelves was *Dr. Chase's Recipes or Information for Everybody,* first published in Michigan in 1865. Chase was at various times a grocer, a druggist, a physician, and a writer, and his books sold in the hundreds of thousands, an enormous number for the time. Readers discovered directions for making everything from artificial skin for burns, to the proper way of saving bacon for winter. The recipes came from many sources and often contained a testimonial from the contributor. Remedies for both animal and human afflictions were included, along with many folk cures, like toad ointment, which was considered "hard on the toads" but a sure cure for sprains and bad backs. Other books trumpeted their

Fig. 6-7 Household manuals sought to provide a woman with all the necessary information for running a home, raising a family, and fulfilling her obligations as a mother and wife. The books often had chapters on cooking, medicine, and baby care, the latter a sad reminder of the days of when heavy infant mortality was a fact of life. *The Hearthstone* (1888) is a typical example of this kind of book, combining practical advice and maudlin sentimentality and containing engravings like "Baby's Welcome," "A Floral Window," and "The Dearest Pet." While these books showed daily life in its most ideal (and unattainable) form, modern readers can still see the problems and fears that faced the nineteenth-century housewife.

contents as being "worth their weight in gold" or a "complete library," and chapters offered instruction on everything from building a barn to making paint varnish. The household sections usually contain medical and cooking recipes and are interesting windows into the responsibilities of a housewife as nurse and doctor combined. Depending upon condition, the books usually range in price from $15 to $45; first editions, especially those of the Chase book, are higher. The books are sometimes shelved with cookbooks and other times are in with the medical works at bookstores, so ask the bookseller if you are unable to find any examples in his or her shop.

Etiquette Guides

A logical extension of a cookbook collection is etiquette guides, books written with a view toward changing eating into dining and everyday behavior into more refined etiquette. Rules for proper behavior have existed almost as long as people have gotten together to share a meal, although books about manners did not receive much attention until 1530. In that year, a short work appeared by the philosopher and teacher, Erasmus, entitled *On the Civility of the Behavior of Boys*. Until the Renaissance, manners were something for the nobility to be concerned about, and even they spent much more time planning amorous meetings or political behaviour in the court, rather than concentrating on achieving civilized behavior at the table. But by the seventeenth century, people had become aware that certain actions—among them belching, removing fleas from the body, and trimming the fingernails—were just not acceptable at the table. Eventually, the Victorians took up the

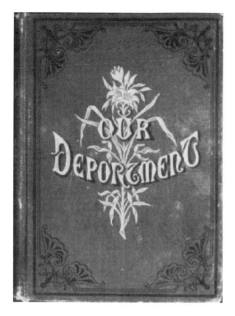

Fig. 6-8 Etiquette books were guides to the increasingly complex world of American manners and morals. *Our Deportment* presented rules for manners, conduct, and dress of the "most refined society" and helped to answer questions about such thorny issues as greediness, conduct in church, and authority over daughters. The book was published in 1882, and the copy pictured here shows wear to the corners; however, the gilt lettering, although difficult to see in a photograph, is clear and clean, making the overall condition good.

etiquette question with a vengeance, because the newly rich wanted to fit in with the wealthy, who supposedly already knew how to behave. So it was necessary for ladies and gentlemen to turn to manuals and etiquette books for guidance through the difficult terrain of acting and eating correctly. Hundreds of the manuals were published between 1830 and 1922, when Emily Post began the modern fascination with manners.

People did not study etiquette manuals in order to stand out from the crowd, but rather to blend into that hazy background dubbed "refinement." Petrified that they would use the wrong fork, say the wrong thing, dress the wrong way, call at the wrong hour, and look like ill-trained bumpkins, the new American middle class was faced with learning too many rules in too little time. But where there was a book, there was a way to avoid a social solecism, and etiquette manuals filled the void. Armed with Mrs. Ward's *Sensible Etiquette of the Best Society* (1878), a woman would be able to fulfill "the duty of the American woman to do all in their power toward the formation of so high a standard of morals and manners that the tendency of society will be upward instead of downward, seeking to make it in every respect equal to the best society of any nation. Manners and morals are indissolubly allied, and no society can be good where they are bad." The book contains seventeen chapters on topics as wide-ranging as "Proofs of Good Breeding," "The Lobred Type of Woman," and "The Immortal Life" (good manners did not stop in this world). The book was not just for the benefit of women who wished to act properly at a five o'clock tea or at the newer "kettledrum" (a late afternoon reception); here are some of its suggestions for a young man:

> The properly trained youth does not annoy those next to whom he sits by fidgeting in his chair, moving his feet, playing with his bread or with any of the table equipage. Neither does he chew his food with his mouth open, talk with it in his mouth, or make any of those noises in eating which are the characteristics of vulgarity. . . . He handles his knife and fork properly, and not "overhand" as a clown would. . . . He does not leave his coffee-spoon or tea-spoon in his cup. He avoids using his handkerchief unnecessarily, or disgusting those who are eating by trumpet-like performances with it.

As shown by this example, part of the need for etiquette manuals arose from the new and bewildering cutlery and service pieces which came into style and onto the American table in the nineteenth century. Even the common fork could prove to be a vehicle for poor etiquette, as discussed in *Manners and Social Usages* (1887) by Mrs. John Sherwood: "To take meat and vegetables and pack them on the poor fork, as if it were a beast of burden, is a common American vulgarity, born of our hurried way of eating at railway-stations and hotels. But it is an unhealthy and an ill-mannered habit. To take but little on the fork at a time, a moderate mouthful, shows good manners and refinement. The knife must never be put into the mouth at any time—that is a remnant of barbarism." Sometimes, the manuals reveal a unique problem of the period, one that is unnecessary to mention in modern manners books:

> The lighting of rooms by means of lamps and candles is giving hostesses great annoyance. There is scarcely a dinner-party but the candles set fire to their fringed shades, and a conflagration ensues. . . . But if a candle screen takes fire, have the coolness to let it burn itself up without touching it, as thus it will be entirely innocuous, although rather appalling to look at. Move a plate under it to catch the flying fragments, and no harm will be done; but a well-intentioned effort to blow it out or to remove it generally results in a very much more wide-spread conflagration.

Emily Post's book, *Etiquette,* first published in 1922, was a modern standard that still sells, along with "new" classics by writers like "Miss Manners" and even the notorious blue-blooded Mayflower Madam (the head of a house of ill repute). As times changed, so did manners and mores, so twentieth-century manuals had to consider such problems as whether a stenographer should rise when a business associate enters the room or how to issue proper war-time wedding announcements. Etiquette manuals fell into disrepute by the 1970s, but a recent interest in polite behavior has resulted in new publications, which, dealing as they do with topics such as sexual courtesy and same-sex relationships, should become as collectible in the future as the older examples are now.

Etiquette books can be found at antiquarian book fairs and shops, although at least one dealer specializes in the field (see Sources at the end of this book). Many older etiquette book do not contain illustrations; those that have pictures—for example, of the proper way to greet a lady or the proper way to set a table—usually command higher prices. Collectors should not overlook the etiquette sections contained in the household encyclopedias, which often have extensive chapters on behavior and manners, complete with how-to pictures for such skills as napkin folding and orange carving.

Trade and Seed Catalogs

Reading about food in cookbooks is only part of the culinary story, and collectors can explore another part of the story through trade and seed catalogs. Issued by companies to describe their wares, these catalogs are well-illustrated and highly collectible, so cookbook buyers will have to compete with other collectors in this crossover category.

Trade catalogs run the gamut from the annual Sears, Roebuck & Company extravaganzas to Hotpoint manuals, with their drawings and photographs of stoves and electrical appliances. Other catalogs help identify kitchenware and equipment mentioned in recipes (gem pans, cat tongue pans, and so on), while some booklets blur into cookbooks, as in the case of Pyrex, whose catalogs contained photos of the Pyrex dishes available (Figure 6-9), along with recipes to be used with the product.

Fig. 6-9 The Corning Glass Company still produces Pyrex, and this cookbook (1925) placed emphasis on the elegance of cooking and serving with the glass cookware. The text suggested that "the work, of preparing the daily meals will be more interesting, the dishwashing will be easier, and the dining table more attractive" if the hostess used Pyrex. Illustrations like this one display not only the company's products but also a view of how foods were served over the years.

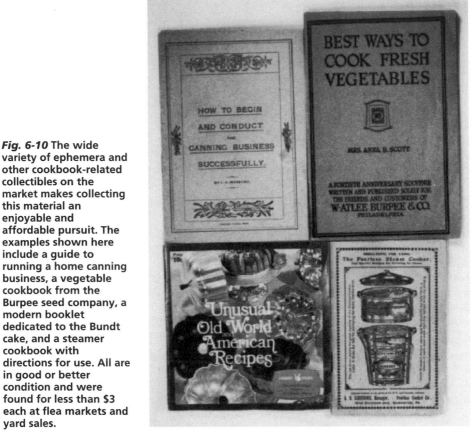

Fig. 6-10 The wide variety of ephemera and other cookbook-related collectibles on the market makes collecting this material an enjoyable and affordable pursuit. The examples shown here include a guide to running a home canning business, a vegetable cookbook from the Burpee seed company, a modern booklet dedicated to the Bundt cake, and a steamer cookbook with directions for use. All are in good or better condition and were found for less than $3 each at flea markets and yard sales.

American seed catalogs have been published since the eighteenth century, but the most interesting examples span the 1870s to the 1930s. Some of the catalogs boasted colorful covers and several pages of floral, fruit, and vegetable illustrations, while others relied on detailed line drawings to describe their products. The catalogs are an interesting accompaniment to old cookbooks, since the pictures and descriptions often are for fruits and vegetables called for in recipes from long ago but often no longer available to the modern cook. The rattlesnake watermelon, lightning early valentine beans, dandelions, apple pie squash, and strawberry tomato are only few of the hundreds of heritage plants used by cooks of the past but rarely, if ever, grown today for cookery.

When buying trade and seed catalogs, check to make sure no full-page illustrations have been removed by previous owners (the pictures were favorites for decorating). The covers should be intact, and although some of the catalogs were printed on rather thin paper, the pages should be in good condition and, of course, readable; in the case of seed catalogs, a separate order sheet with prices may have been enclosed. Trade and seed catalogs may range in price from a few dollars to $50 or more, depending upon condition, rarity, and subject matter. Seed catalogs, in particular, can be priced high if the dealer is selling them as examples of the printer's art; if the seller does not happen to specialize in the topic, prices will often be more moderate. Prices for catalogs can vary widely even at a single antiquarian book show or antiques and flea market, so get to such events early in order to do some comparison shopping.

Menus

Since cookbooks result in menus, many collectors are attracted to menu listings of food and beverages from the past. Menus were printed for private parties, political dinners, tearooms, ice cream parlors—anywhere people gathered to enjoy a meal—and these listings are still available from ephemera dealers, at flea markets and book shows. Some booklet-style menus had photographs of the diners, along with their signatures; others, like those published by the Dutch Treat Club, were elaborate programs for their scandalous dinners in New York in the 1930s. Mystery or puzzle menus were sometimes presented at fund-raisers and consisted of riddles based on the foods to be served or quotations from the classics that were food-related. Besides being easy to store, menus can also be framed and displayed with a cookbook collection. (Note that framing materials should fulfill archival requirements.) Prices begin at around $2 for a single-page ice cream parlor menu from the 1940s and can top $100 and more for menus from nineteenth-century grand hotels and private dinners. Collectors should note that there has been a resurgence in interest in menu design over the past several years, and modern examples should prove to be excellent future collectibles; a few restaurants have made their menus available for purchase to patrons.

Pillsbury Bake-Off Booklets

Probably the most well-known collectible in the cookbook world, outside of books themselves, are the Pillsbury Bake-Off booklets (Figure 6-11). The contest began life in 1949 as The Grand National Recipe and Baking Contest (a member of the press dubbed it "the bake-off"), and it was immediately popular. Thousands of cooks participated, with the hope of being one of the 100 people selected to march into the Waldorf-Astoria Hotel in New York and prepare their best recipes at the finals. Both adult and junior cooks participated; there were celebrity hosts, like Art Linkletter and Arthur Godfrey; and the top prize of $25,000 represented the price of a house at the time (in fact, some winners bought houses).

Fig. 6-11 The Pillsbury Bake-Offs were famous for their booklets, which featured winning recipes from the contests; however, collectors should also look for this Bake-Off collection cookbook issued in 1959. The selection is filled with 1,000 recipes from the first ten Bake-Offs, along with a history of the contest, a list of the judges (many of them well-known cookbook writers), and dozens of photographs, including one of an awards dinner. The book pictured is in fine condition.

The recipes were gathered into annual collections, and the detailed instructions and photographs made the booklets instant hits. In fact, many of the recipes went on to become kitchen standards. Watch for Bake-Off booklets at yard sales and flea markets in particular; the scarce Bake-Off #1

Fig. 6-12 Although the Pillsbury Bake-Offs are probably the most well-known recipe contest in America, they were not the first. Food companies often sponsored awards for recipes that used a specific product, like chocolate or flour. In the case of *101 Prize Recipes,* Postum Cereal Company in Battle Creek, Michigan, offered $7,550 in prizes. The judging was done in 1924 by the Good Housekeeping Institute of *Good Housekeeping Magazine,* and the winners were selected from more than 8,000 entries; the winning recipe was Grape-Nuts Omelet California. At a time when an apartment could be rented for $30 a month, the grand prize of $1,000 must have meant a great deal to the winner. The effect that contest booklets had on other cookbooks was large; by 1925, the winning recipes were already appearing in community cookbooks.

booklet has been known to command $80 to $100 from collectors intent on completing their sets, although it can be found for less; the other booklets sell for $10 or less.

Paperback Cookbooks

During approximately the last thirty years or so, publishing houses have followed the practice of first offering a cookbook in a hardcover version and then releasing a much cheaper paperback version a year or two later. (Paperback editions of a cookbook should not be confused with the better-made softcover editions.) These paperback books were rarely the first edition of a cookbook and in many cases lacked the illustrations found in the original edition. The paper was brittle and the books were inconvenient to use in the kitchen, since they didn't lie flat for easy reading and, if the spine was spread at all, the cook faced the prospect of losing pages completely. As collectibles, paperbacks have little value ($1 to $2 is a fair market price for most of them), but if a hardcover book is difficult to find, the paperback can temporarily fill a gap in a collection. Some of these books were used as tie-ins with television shows, movies, or other promotions and may be found with an autograph of the author or other celebrity; such books command a few dollars more than unsigned examples.

Children's Cookbooks

Learning to cook is a hands-on skill, and most children begin to enjoy kitchen work while helping or watching a relative prepare meals. Children's activity books of the nineteenth century, like *The Girl's Own Indoor Book* (1888), sometimes contained chapters on cookery (the unfortunate illustration shows a young girl holding her cookbook open with her mixing spoon), but children's cookbooks did not become popular until the early twentieth century. Early examples include *The Mary Frances Cook Book* (1912), wherein kitchen implements help the heroine learn to cook, and *The Child Life Cook Book* (Figure 6-13), published in 1926, which contains lovely silhouette illustrations of young people at work in the kitchen. Later books were offered by "Fannie Farmer" (the *Fannie Farmer Junior Cook Book* book was written in her name in 1942; see Figure 6-14), *Better Homes and Gardens* and *Farm Journal,* and Helen Evans Brown, who authored *The Boys' Own Cook Book* in 1959, which had recipes designed to meet the needs of male teenagers and others of the sex who needed to survive when mom was away.

The books present a special view of how children and their skills have been viewed through the last few generations, and modern collectors might be surprised at the types of recipes or cooking methods the young chefs were entrusted with (for example, fried doughnuts, broiled bacon, and escalloped

Fig. 6-13 In the early days of cookbooks, children learned kitchen skills by watching their mothers; the idea of a children's cookbook was unknown. By the end of the nineteenth century, however, juvenile cookbooks had begun to appear, and they gained popularity in the 1920s. The books often contained essays on food and cooking along with the recipes, many of which were unsuitable for children unless under adult supervision. The *Child Life Cook Book* appeared in 1926 contains lovely silhouette artwork, as shown by the cover. The recipes were offered in both paragraph and two-part form, and they ranged in difficulty from beef with carrots and Christmas pudding to grilled peanut butter sandwiches and broiled bacon. Surprisingly for the time, there are even illustrations of little boys baking and cooking. Children's cookbooks are usually expensive when found in fine condition, as was this example; unfortunately, many young cooks often used the books for coloring and drawing as well.

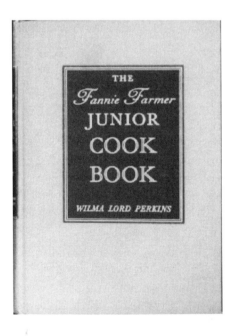

Fig. 6-14 Because she was a cooking instructor, Fannie Farmer might not have been surprised to see a cookbook for young people with her name on it. But *The Fannie Farmer Junior Cook Book* was actually written by Wilma Perkins in 1942, to fill a need for cookbooks directed toward beginning cooks. The book is not typical of later children's cookbooks; the recipes have few illustrations and offer some complicated cooking challenges, like shrimp jambalaya, ice cream flowerpots, and baking powder biscuits.

cabbage that was hand-chopped). In the last several years, children's cookbooks have begun to appear in number, some accompanied by small cooking implements, others written for use with microwaves or special cooking classes, and it looks as if the early editions of these may become collectible.

Older cookbooks for children are usually found at book shows and antiquarian book stores, while the newer versions can be discovered at flea markets and house sales. Check children's cookbooks carefully before you buy them; a book might have received a lot of use or been employed as a coloring or drawing pad in addition to a recipe source. Prices for examples from the nineteenth and early twentieth centuries in good or better condition can top $80 or more.

7 ❦ The Complete Collector

Hands-on Collecting

To be a complete collector, you will have to be able to find, evaluate, buy, research, care for, insure, and just generally know about your cookbook collection. There are nearly unlimited numbers of cookbooks available on the market, and even books that have been out of print only a few years can increase in value, particularly those with an unusual slant, like the cookbooks offered during the Ellis Island restoration or America's Bicentennial.

Finding Cookbooks

A collector can add to his or her library in a number of ways: finding cookbooks is not a problem, but finding certain cookbooks in a particular price range may be. Begin your search close to home, even for scarce and hard-to-find items. Cookbooks are often undervalued and ignored at flea markets, yard sales, and garage sales, so the savvy buyer should ask if any have been tucked out of sight in the kitchen or beneath a table. Talk to tag sale organizers and auctioneers, and make sure they know you are interested in cookbooks. Oftentimes, they do not want to haul a large collection down out of an attic or transport it back to the auction house where general buyers may be uninterested in the books, so they may be willing to work out a sale between you and the book's owners.

Stores that sell used books often have a constantly changing stock of cookbooks, as do thrift shops and fund-raising organizations like hospital auxiliaries; not surprisingly, collectors can locate some excellent ephemera at these places as well. You might have to pull out boxes or sift through stacks of leaflets jumbled together on shelves, but since most people ignore advertising booklets and recipe leaflets, the time (and dust) can be worth

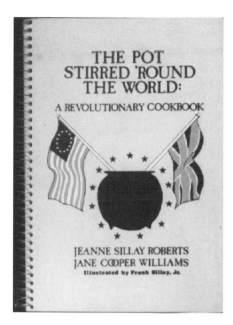

Fig. 7-1 Historic events can trigger the writing of cookbooks, and America's Bicentennial resulted in many looks back at eighteenth-century food. This example was printed by the authors, who offered anecdotes about the Revolution along with the recipes, which ranged from the colonial beverage called flip, to old-fashioned steamed ginger pudding. Collectors should watch for cookbooks issued to commemorate such events as town or county centennials, restorations of famous buildings like those at Ellis Island, or even a local event, like the Woodstock Festival.

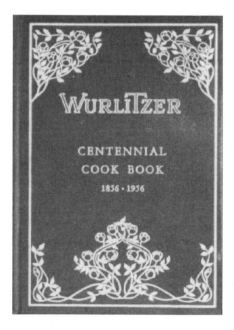

Fig. 7-2 The Wurlitzer family is best known for its musical instruments, but it also issued a heritage cookbook in 1956 to commemorate the centennial of the family business. The book contains color illustrations and black-and-white family photographs, and the recipes were collected from family, friends, business associates, and employees. There is even a signature page where a Wurlitzer member would sign the book when presenting it to a customer. Heritage cookbooks are an offshoot of the early family "receipt" books and are still published by family organizations or businesses.

the search. Large book sales, like the Vassar College fund-raisers with their tens of thousands of books, may offer substantial cookbook sections that attract little attention from dealers and collectors; patrons of such sales perhaps intent on discovering a first edition *Ulysses* may ignore an early

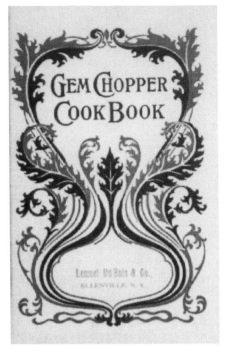

Fig. 7-3 This *Gem Chopper Cook Book* (1902) was an unusual find, since it came in its original mailing envelope. The book contains recipes calling for foods prepared with the Gem Chopper, as well as detailed illustrations of the chopper and its attachments. The text is full of examples from the golden age of self-promotion, including a drawing of Japanese women seated around a Gem Chopper with this caption: "It is the same everywhere. Things have to be chopped during the preparation of the meals and all housekeepers find that Sargent's Gem Food Chopper enables them to lessen the labor." Note that the cover has been stamped with the place of sale: Lemuel Du Bois & Co., Ellenville, N.Y.

Fig. 7-4 One collectible that fits in well with cookbooks is the kitchen advice book, which gained popularity in the 1950s. *Kitchen Kinks* was issued as a giveaway by a life insurance company and is typical of the subject. The book was written and produced by a publishing firm, then "personalized" for a specific company and given away to customers. Suggestions like "Watch him grin from ear to ear the first time you poach his egg in tomato juice" were aimed at the housewife, as was the typically silly 1950s advertising art that accompanied the chapters.

edition of *Joy of Cooking*. Library sales, however, can be disappointing if the books have been deaccessioned from the collections, since the wear on the books is usually very obvious and library bindings replace the original covers. Don't ignore remainder tables in bookstores, either, where first editions often turn up and where the prices can be a fraction of the original cost. Sometimes oversize picture cookbooks or cookbooks produced by overseas presses are well-represented at the remainder sign, and although the books may be new, the fact that they are no longer in print makes them collectible. Historical associations and sites are also good locations for finding cookbooks—their bookstores sometimes carry locally published cookbooks or fund-raising cookbooks that are difficult to locate anywhere outside a specific region.

Placing an ad in a specialty antiques newspaper or even in a local newspaper can lead to the purchase of full cookbook collections, but you will have to be willing to spend the time checking out each and every offering. One way around this is by noting in the ad that you would like a list of available books, along with the asking price of the seller. If the seller doesn't provide the asking price or says that he or she simply has no idea of the books' values, then you will have to do some research to come up with an offering price. Of course, you can locate books by attending as many antiquarian book fairs as possible every year, where you can make contact with dealers who know, understand, and like cookbooks. If you have a "want list" (a listing of books you are searching for), make copies and keep them with you to hand out. Dealers who take tables at shows only bring a tiny portion of their stock along, but they will be able to tell you what they have at home, and you may locate hard-to-find items in this manner.

There are many rare book dealers who specialize in cookbooks and domestic science books (see Sources at the end of this book), and nearly all of these dealers offer catalog, booklist, and mail-order sales. The books are carefully described, and the buyer pays for shipping and insurance. Book dealers will usually allow you to return a book if you feel that it was not fairly represented by the catalog description, but since each dealer sets her or his own business rules, you need to ask what the time limits and return policies are *before* you buy. Prices asked by specialty dealers will generally be higher than those placed on books found in a secondhand store, but the cookbooks they list are often hard-to-find or rare, are in good or better condition, and are carefully described. Be aware that catalog sales are done on a first come, first served basis, so once the catalogs are mailed, the dealer will fill orders based upon who responds most quickly. Some catalog dealers will allow you to phone in an order and reserve a book until your check is received; others require a check with an order, so call ahead to check on the availability of a title. Dealers sometimes offer search and appraisal services in addition to their book catalogs, or they may offer to put a buyer in touch with someone who might have a book the buyer seeks.

A good relationship with a cookbook dealer can provide a collector with an outstanding source for acquisitions, as well as a friendly guide who will assist the collector in developing a fine collection over the years. Even if you think you are the most inexperienced collector on the block, never hesitate to call a dealer and inquire about a book. Dealers tend to stock a wide range of titles, which may range in value from $10 to several thousand dollars, and the experienced dealer knows that a beginning collector will not remain a beginning collector forever, and may eventually purchase a large number of cookbooks.

Cookbooks and ephemera can also be found by advertising in special interest publications, including *AB Bookman's Weekly; Buy Books Where, Sell Books Where; The Cookbook Collector's Exchange;* and the Ephemera Society of America's newsletter, or by contacting book searchers. The latter specialists will attempt to locate a book for you and then report back with a price. Searchers spend money on advertising, phone calls, and other location methods, and a searcher will often charge a small fee in addition to the book's price to cover the search costs; some searchers also require an exclusive on a search for a specific time. Make certain that you understand a book searcher's requirements, and discuss the amount you are willing to spend on a title; book searchers are not magicians, and they won't find you a rare book for a few dollars.

Fig. 7-5 Book designs reflected the styles and trends of the time, whether they included the Gibson Girl look or the lithe curves of Art Nouveau. *The Silver Sheaf Cook Book* an undated book published to benefit a nursing society, shows the influence of Art Deco, with its angular edges. The cover was printed with black ink on a silver sheet, but for all its modern styling, the recipes in the book are old-fashioned and plain.

Fig. 7-6 The strong design of this cookbook is a little unusual since it appears on the cover as well as on the dust jacket. First printed in 1901, the *Inglenook Cook Book* was compiled by the Brethren Publishing House of Elgin, Illinois, and was given as a premium to subscribers of *The Inglenook Magazine.* Both magazine and book were written for the Church of Brethren women, who had strong ties to the Pennsylvania-Dutch tradition; the signed recipes identified the contributors as "Sister," and the foods included such unusual items as "smearcase" pie, cucumber catsup, and breads made with "spook" yeast.

Making a Purchase—Dealers and Auctions

Although collectors usually have some idea of what they want to pay for a cookbook, they can also be unrealistic about price when it comes to actually buying the book, and this dichotomy occurs for a number of reasons. If you began collecting twenty years ago, then stopped for whatever reason and now are looking to expand your collection, you may think that the prices being asked by modern dealers are insane, unfair, and generally detestable. Why, you complain, should a book you once bought for $5 now cost you $25 to replace? How in the world did the dealer come up with that price? Cookbook dealers, like other antiques and collectibles dealers, are also businesspeople. They search out and purchase their stock, research its history, maintain its physical well-being, insure and advertise the stock, do mailings of booklists and catalogs, set up at shows, and sometimes maintain bookstores. Along with the general overhead of running a book business, these dealers understand the value of their books and ephemera, from M. F. K. Fisher first editions to advertising cookbooklets with the likes of Kate Smith on the cover. Why is this any different than a print dealer understanding the value of a Currier and Ives collection, and asking a fair price based on personal knowledge and the knowledge of the market?

Cookbooks need to be evaluated in the same manner as any other collectible. Value is based on rarity, condition, subject (for example, diet cookbooks are unpopular, while some regional cookbooks fly off the shelves), edition, age, illustrations, popular taste, and a sixth sense of what customers want and are willing to pay. A dealer might refer to a guide such as the one provided at the end of this book to see what others are asking and paying for a book, but he or she will usually price a book based on a personal knowledge of the market, developed over the years. As cookbooks continue to gain in popularity, and as collectors begin to place their books in historic and social perspectives, it is inevitable that certain prices will rise. But while these increases may put some books out of the reach of the "average" buyer, if there truly is such a person, collectors must also acknowledge the fact that their own books are growing in value as well, both from a dollar perspective and from an information perspective. Remember that collecting can take place on many levels of interest and cost, and because one cookbook collector is willing to spend $100 on a Pillsbury Bake-Off #1 while another wouldn't dream of giving more than $5 does not mean that either is incorrect: it just emphasizes the fact that a buyer has to decide which type of cookbook source is comfortable, monetarily or otherwise, for the buyer to work with in building a collection. You may think that setting limits on the price you are willing to pay for a book is wise, and sometimes it is. But if you continually walk away from books that you want or need for your collection, then the prices you seek may be unrealistically low and you may need to adjust your thinking somewhat.

Whether you purchase cookbooks from a dealer, an auction, or a flea market, there are some rules of buying etiquette that are too often ignored by collectors, both old and new. Flea markets and yard sales usually have proprietors who are willing to make a deal on a purchase, just so that they don't have to drag the box of books out again the next weekend. On the other hand, bookstore owners who carry used or secondhand books may be less flexible on the price of their stock, since they know that while you might not want to pay a certain price, someone else will. Regardless of what you think a book is worth, the seller has established the price and this needs to be respected. If a book is marked $50, you may ask politely if the dealer can do any better on the sale, especially if you are purchasing several books. On the other hand, comments like "I'll give you $10" and "I just saw that book for a dollar at a yard sale" are unrealistic and they treat the dealer as less than a professional.

If you are shopping in a store with a general used or antique book selection, you might consider asking the proprietor if he or she would be willing to accept other books you may own in trade against the cookbooks; this is one way to buy "up" even if you didn't think you could afford to. In the case of professional cookbook dealers, they are usually pleased to talk with a collector, and most will spend time answering questions and making suggestions for your library. If you are unsure of how or why the dealer has priced a cookbook a certain way, just ask—you will probably learn more than you expected about bibliography, book collecting, and cookbook history.

Fig. 7-7 Agricultural fairs began in the early nineteenth century, and they still hold an important place in the world of home cooking. For country cooks, winning a blue ribbon for a pie or jam was the end result of a year of developing and testing a recipe over and over. *The State Fair Blue Ribbon Cook Book* first appeared in 1950 and was one of the earliest cookbooks to present readers with the recipes, foods, and techniques for winning at a fair. The colorful dust jacket emphasized the variety of fair foods found in the competitions.

Fig. 7-8 The Walter M. Lowney Company produced cocoa and chocolate goods, including Lowney's vanilla sweet chocolate; according to the company, "Price is a secondary consideration in buying the materials for this eating chocolate. The main thing is to make it perfect." Although the publishers hoped that the average household would purchase *Lowney's Cook Book* in 1907, the preface apologized for recipes like salmi of game and chocolate Swedish meringues by stating that "thousands of our most valued customers cannot afford to prepare many of these dishes very often for their tables. But there are special occasions when we all feel that we can have the best for ourselves and our guests." On the cover, the trademark Lowney girl salutes the reader with a cup of cocoa. Inside, the book contains several lovely color plates showing chocolate desserts; the frozen chocolate soufflé is served nestled in a water lily.

No matter where or when you purchase a book, ask for a detailed receipt (one listing the title, author, date of sale, and cost of purchase), since you will need to keep this for insurance purposes. If a dealer represents a book in a particular way, such as a first edition or as being signed by the author, but refuses to offer you written confirmation of the description, then buy from someone else. A good dealer will stand by his or her stock.

Auctions, both in person and by mail, are also a source of cookbooks, although prices can go higher than usual because of the competition. With mail auctions, like those held by rare book businesses, you purchase a descriptive catalog that contains directions on how to bid on a book. There is a deadline for mail-in bidding, although phone bids may be accepted on the day of the sale as well. The catalog contains photos of some books, descriptions of all the books, and often estimated bids arrived at by the auction house's experts, so you can tell generally what price a book is expected to bring. Before you bid, however, find out if the auction imposes a buyer's premium, that is, a percentage above the final purchase price, in addition to tax, shipping, and insurance; adding all these onto the actual buying price may result in your paying far more for a book than you expected to when you sent in your bid. One drawback with mail auctions is that unless you are very familiar with a particular cookbook beforehand, your bid is based on a written description alone, but book auction houses, like Swann's in New York, are very careful in their description. However, if the book is expected to bring a high price, and you want to know about the item, you can request more information from the auction house; some houses will also send photos of the book for a fee.

At standard "in person" book auctions or general estate auctions you are able to examine a book before. A good book auction will guarantee that the cookbook is sold in the condition it was displayed in—that is, that nothing has happened to it between the preauction viewing and the sale. Less formal auctions will tell you that you are buying the book "as is, where is," meaning, for example, if the cover was wrenched off by a careless looker before the sale, then you, as the buyer, must beware; thus, if you are not happy with your purchase, there is not much you will be able to do about it. But don't let that one caution discourage you from attending auctions. One of the best sources for cookbooks can be at country sales, where "box lots" may have an unusual book or two tossed in with the contents of the kitchen drawers (note that even lowly box lots can be the subject of switching by unethical bidders, so keep a careful eye on your hoped-for treasure). At an auction, you register for a number (some auctions require a refundable deposit), which allows you to bid on a certain item or group of items known as a "lot." As you bid, feel free to ask the auctioneer to clarify your bid if you don't understand what he is saying. "One" can refer to one dollar, one hundred dollars, or, rarely, one thousand dollars, and in a fast-paced, high-priced auction you can get confused and spend far more on a single cookbook or lot than you intended.

Fig. 7-9 Sponsored by the retail giant, the *Macy's Salad Dessert Book* is an interesting collectible. The title is misleading, since the author provided recipes for many main dish meals along with the salads and desserts. The photo section offers settings and suggestions for men's and ladies' luncheons, teas, buffets, and holiday meals, and there are directions for getting the most out of a refrigerator. Unusual for a cookbook in 1933, each recipe was accompanied with tested preparation times, and most could be prepared in under 15 minutes.

Buying Smart

When you locate the cookbook you want, then the next consideration in the process is price. Sometimes you are just not sure if you should spend $45 on a book, no matter how much you want it. Othertimes, you may think the cookbook is a good buy, but you may be attending a one-day show and you know that you may never see the dealer, or the book, again, or you may be at an auction and you have to make decisions very quickly. Of course, there are no absolute recipes for solving these problems, but there are the "Four Cs of Cookbooks" to help you decide if a book is worth the price asked.

1 *Condition:* Is the condition of the book good or better? Remember, only buy a cookbook in less than good condition if the book is rare or unusual.

2 *Collection:* Do you need the cookbook to enhance your collection, and does it fit in with your overall plan for your library? Does the book duplicate material in your collection—for example, in the case of charity cookbooks, how many Hummingbird Cake recipes from rural fire department auxiliaries do you really need?—or, if the book does duplicate material you have, does it also contain some different recipes you have been looking for?

3 *Cost:* Have you seen the book recently, at another price? Does the price seem to fit in with books of the same date, subject, and condition? If you are at a book show, does one dealer have it for $25, another for $20, and still another for $26?

4   *Craving:* Have you been looking for this book for more than a year without finding it? Do you expect to use this book or just stick it on a shelf because you think it belongs with your collection? Finally, how much is the enjoyment of the book worth to you? If you've lusted after a first edition cookbook by the author Zane Grey, and you have only seen it once before, ten years ago, then perhaps it is time for you to spend $45 on the book when you discover it at a show.

Once you've answered the preceding questions to your own satisfaction (not that of the dealer or the price guide), you can decide if the cookbook will be a solid addition to your collection and worth the price marked. There is also a "law" in cookbook collecting called the "But It Was There 10 Minutes Ago Law": once you walk away, there is no guarantee the book will be there later on, so buy it when you see it.

With all these warnings, caveats, and suggestions, by this time a beginner may feel shaky about buying even a 50¢ leaflet for fear of appearing stupid or uninformed. Don't ever be afraid to buy on instinct or take a chance on a book. Once you understand the basics of collecting and you have explored cookbook history, you will be surprised how many times you will buy the right books based on your instinct. And don't be upset when you make a mistake— it happens to every collector, and your mistakes help you learn what to avoid or pursue the next time that you are out on the hunt.

Evaluating and Caring for Your Cookbooks and Ephemera

If you buy books regularly at book fairs, book shops, and other retail outlets, you need to consider the physical cookbook, along with the textual contents. It can't be emphasized enough that cookbooks receive more use and, therefore, more damage than any other publications found in a house. In most cases, cookbooks in either good or better condition indicate that the owner was a reader, while those in fair or worse condition indicate that the owner was a cook and used the books on a regular basis. So evaluating and caring for cookbooks may take a little more effort than is required for other types of books and ephemera.

Before you start pulling your cookbooks off their shelves, first think about the shelves themselves. If you have a small collection of books that you use for preparing meals or planning party menus, you may decide to keep them within arm's reach in the cooking area. Although cookbooks were meant for the kitchen, older books do not stand up well to steam, grease, and other cooking by-products (just look at some of the older cookbook covers, with their coatings of tacky batter and cooking oil). Overall, the books are better off somewhere else in the house, away from stoves and sinks. But whether you have a separate library or a just a special book nook, you still need to store your books properly. Closed cabinets prevent dust from settling on books and may keep fireplace smoke, heating oil, and other airborne pollutants away from the pages, but these same cabinets also retain humidity in wetter climates, so don't lock your cookbooks up in an airtight case. Old cookbooks need to be dusted if they are kept in an open bookcase, but never vacuumed. Use a soft, large paintbrush for a light dusting, especially on older specimens. Cookbooks should be treated like other books and kept in a room where the temperature is below 70°F and the humidity is approximately 50 percent.

While open shelving, like that used in libraries, allows dust to settle on books, it also allows air to circulate, and, depending upon their size, these shelves lend themselves to flat storage of oversized books and document boxes. Metal shelves will not react with your books, while the finishes on some wooden shelves, particularly finishes containing formaldehyde, can cause destructive chemical reactions over a period of time. Library and archival storage supply companies sell nonreactive paper that can be placed under the books to protect them. The lowest shelf should be several inches above the floor to keep the books out of harm's way in the event of minor flooding or water problems, and there should be enough space to allow air to circulate underneath the books as well.

Handling your cookbooks carefully is essential to their preservation. Do not pull a book off a shelf by the head or foot of the spine, a practice that can

Fig. 7-10 The *New England Cook Book* was an uncommon blend of advertising and recipes. The book received its name from its publisher's location in Boston, and it contained directions for just about every dish imaginable, some of which had more than likely never seen the inside of a New England kitchen. But the publishers had something more in mind for their book: "The publishers . . . have introduced a department of Supplies, Furnishings, etc, which is a feature never before attempted. We have investigated the claims of manufacturers of and dealers in goods . . . and having satisfied ourselves as to the excellence of the goods. . . . We have allowed them to state in their own way their claims for recognition." Of course there is no mention that the manufacturers paid well for their advertising space, while the housewife paid $2 for the book. But there were enough recipes to make it worthwhile, and it must have been comforting to know that locally made Swampscott Sparkling Gelatine would produce a superb pressed chicken dish.

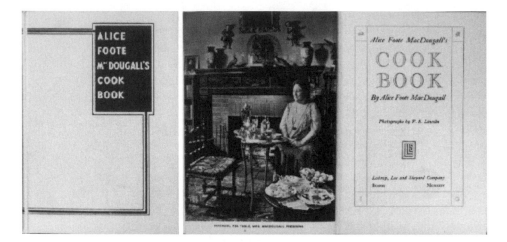

Fig. 7-11 If a woman author did not write mysteries or novels in the 1930s, she more than likely wrote a cookbook. Alice Foote MacDougall owned several restaurants and was known for the chatty, "you can do it too" encouragement that she offered throughout her books. She stressed economy, having suffered "through all the years of varying poverty, comfort, and return to poverty. . . . In clear dry weather, you can make fairly good soles for your little child's worn-out shoes by using carefully cut and shaped cardboard made from cereal cartons. I know. I did." As shown in the frontispiece photo of her book, she also belonged to the "overstuffed" school of decorating, although her tea table is a model of warmth and elegance.

cause the back strip to tear away or the cover to separate from the book. Instead, hold a cookbook by its sides and ease it off the shelf. Your cookbooks should not be crammed together or forced into place so that one book holds up another, since this not only causes rubbing of covers and catching and tearing of dust jackets but even, in extreme cases, distortion of the binding itself. Use bookends to hold the books upright. Don't forget to wash your hands before touching your books, because natural oils and perspiration, dust, dirt, cooking ingredients, and even makeup can be transferred to a book's pages all too easily. With older books, the covers sometimes shed fibers and dye, which are then wiped onto another book when you pick it up, resulting in an unsightly reddish mark that may not come off. So wash your hands frequently as you handle your books. And, since just about every collector has done something very dumb, one additional piece of advice: Remember to keep cigarettes, pens, markers, ink pads, and drinks out of your library or away from your bookshelves. These cookbook enemies are all too easy to drop, spill, and splash, and the damage they can inflict may cost you a lot of money to repair.

Cooks wanted their recipes where they could find them easily, and they often stuck clippings containing favorite recipes between the pages of a cookbook (this can lead to the discovery of some nice examples of culinary ephemera). A collector needs to examine the interior of a cookbook to see if any of the pages have loosened or become separated from the spine due to the expansion caused by the clippings. Also look to see if the pages have become discolored over the years from chemical reactions with the clippings (newspapers seem to have been the worst offenders). Although this staining cannot be corrected, it might have an effect on the readability of recipes or illustrations and thus reduce the book's condition from good to fair.

In certain books from the nineteenth century, particularly domestic books that showed ladies' fashions or household goods, sheets of tissue paper were sometimes placed before colored prints in order to prevent the inks from bleeding across the pages. The ink may have stained the tissue sheet along with the opposite illustration or text, and this cannot be corrected; since prints are an important part of a book, check each print carefully. Some conservators will remove the tissue sheets, but this is a decision best left to an expert, especially in the case of a valuable book.

Wormholes, silverfish and rodent damage, kitchen stains, glued-in recipe clippings, and other problems can make it impossible to read some of the recipes in a book, so examine a book carefully for such things if you are looking for a cookbook containing usable directions. It's certainly no fun to read the beginning of a recipe for Watermelon Cake and then find you do not have the complete, readable directions for assembling it. Another potential problem has to do with comments written in by a long-ago cook. Check the pages of a prospective purchase carefully. Pencilled or penned annotations may make the book charming and attractive to some buyers who appreciate a personal connection with the century-past owner; however, these same marks may be uninteresting and disappointing to those in search of very good to mint condition books. A once-popular method of protecting old cookbooks was to cover them with a plastic, paper, or oilcloth book cover. If these were glued in place or became attached to the covers through a combination of grease, heat, or other undefinables, don't let anyone convince you that you can just soak, scrape, peel, or pull the problem cover off the book. You shouldn't have to do that, and the book should be priced accordingly by the seller. If you want to protect your cookbooks, special nonreactive book covers, sleeves, and dust jackets are available from archival supply houses.

Also check the illustrations in a book carefully. In some older cookbooks, the illustrations provide fascinating examples of how food was served and dishes were prepared. The pictures also described serving pieces, suggested methods of setting tables, and even offered comic views of a woman's life (such as the day the maid quit on a newlywed bride, or the sketch of a waltzing oyster from a hand-drawn charity cookbook). Unfortunately, sometimes the illustrations were trimmed out of the book, so the careful buyer needs to check a list of illustrations against the actual illustrations (the listing may appear after the table of contents). Ephemera faced the same fate, with seed catalogs losing their lush pictures of apples and cabbages to someone in need of a print for the parlor wall, or pretty advertising cards being glued to a dressing screen for decoration. A book without its illustrations is practically valueless, and it sometimes takes a careful examination to discover whether pictures have been removed.

A problem found in some cookbook leaflets and advertising booklets is staining caused by the rusting of staples used during the binding process. This rusting can weaken pages or make them difficult to turn, resulting in tearing and discoloration of recipes. The only way to stop the problem is to remove the offending antique staples and replace them with nonrusting modern staples, but remember that you may cause as much damage with a poor repair as did the original problem. Another option is to take out the staples and store the loose pages in an archival folder or box.

Cookbooks and other paper culinary collectibles that were stored in musty basements, damp garages, and leaky attics offer a challenge to even the most dedicated collector. While glass can be wiped off and furniture reupholstered, books draw in and hold odors, mold, and other undesirables, and paper, by its very nature, swells with dampness and can be difficult, if not impossible, to clean. No matter what their age, books should not smell like a lakeside cabin that has been closed for the winter, so don't pay top price for a book that has a heavy musty odor. If you do happen to own a book that has a mold problem, try the following: gently wipe away the obvious mold infestation with a soft cloth, and stand the book on its edge with the pages carefully spread open for a few hours in a ventilated area. Placing a book in the sun for 45 minutes will also kill mold, although this can fade older covers and rot paper; use this method only as a last resort and only for more recent books (those from the 1950s on). It is unfortunate, but mold is as catching as the flu, so keep infected books away from "healthy" ones until the problem has been solved. Heavy mold problems require professional assistance for control.

As far as repairs go, there are only a few types that a nonprofessional is capable of doing, and even those are generally suspect. Remember that every repair done by an amateur needs to be completely reversible, so that the book or collectible won't be ruined by good intentions. "Conservation" means maintaining a cookbook or piece of ephemera in its original form; "preservation" seeks to stop the deterioration of a cookbook.

If you are in doubt about performing a cookbook repair, don't do it. Don't use tape, glue, or other adhesives in or on a book. Don't try to bleach a stain out of a page or unstick fragile pages that have clumped together. Don't use plastic or electrical tape to repair a weak binding. Don't do anything that can't be reversed easily. You may want to try to remove pencil marks with a very soft, low-abrasive eraser or an artist's kneading erasure, but keep in mind that every time you erase, you remove paper fibers and cause a slight thinning of the page, so avoid even this, if practical. Crayon, pen, and marker lines are essentially impossible for a nonprofessional to remove without adding more damage to the book (possibly because a mother would let her little ones keep busy at the kitchen table, cookbooks seem to have suffered the indignities of coloring and drawing at childish hands).

Regardless of where you keep your books, they must not be stored in direct sunlight, which can rot paper to pieces, particularly if the paper is cheap newsprint. Sunlight falling on books through a nearby window may also bleach the books' covers and weaken the binding fabric. If the books spend a lot of time under fluorescent lights, there are light filter sleeves available that slip over the bulbs to help reduce the destruction that ultraviolet light can cause.

Little piles of dust on your cookbook shelves may not mean that you are a terrible housekeeper, but they may indicate that some undesirables have settled in the pages. Insect infestation from silverfish, ants, and other creatures may be handled by placing the affected books in a plastic bag with a container of paradichlorobenzene (moth flakes) and tying the bag shut *(do not allow the books to touch the moth flakes);* leave the books for two weeks in order to be certain all eggs and adult insects have been destroyed. If you think there is any chance that new purchases have been infested with insects, then treat the suspect books immediately, before they join the rest of the collection—better to take this simple precaution rather than risk having your entire library crawling with uninvited species. Mice can also damage cookbooks, as indicated by the nibbled edges found on older examples, so keep an eye out for this problem as well.

Charity and fund-raising cookbooks were often bound with wire spirals or plastic comb binding—the latter become brittle with age and can crack if handled carelessly. If the plastic is dirty, you can wipe it carefully with warm, soapy water, then pat it dry. The plastic "teeth" may have bent out of the binding, and you can carefully attempt to move them back into place, but you may end up breaking off the teeth. In most instances it is better to leave them alone unless the broken teeth interfere with page turning. If a wire spiral has become bent, carefully reshape it, and wipe it clean with a soft cloth; rust was not usually a problem with this type of binding.

Older leather-bound books, especially those from the nineteenth century, may need treatment to keep the leather supple and in good condition. Various commercial preparations are available for preservation, cleaning, and restoration (see Sources in the back of this book), but if the book is rare or requires extensive work, it should be placed in the hands of a qualified conservator. To locate a paper conservator, contact a library or a historical association or museum; colleges and university libraries are also good sources, as are collectors' societies and professional organizations.

Dust jackets can add to the value and interest of certain books; for example, if a dust jacket from a 1920s book is intact and in good condition, it will add to the value of a book. If it has been torn, repaired, taped back into shape, or otherwise defaced, it may not add value but it can offer some insights to the book. Dust jackets can be sources of information on advertising, author biographies, even material about what other cookbooks were published by the same company or written by the same author. Since a dust jacket primarily served as a protective coating, it took the brunt of a book's wear and tear and was often discarded when no longer useful. Treasure all your dust jackets, not just the early examples, and protect them and the covers of your books with archival quality coverings.

If either the dust jacket or the cover of a book has an old price sticker in place, don't rush to pull it off, since you may remove more of the cover than you bargained for. You may want to carefully and slowly attempt to ease the sticker off in one piece, an action that might work if the surface of the book was originally coated or shiny, or if the glue on the sticker is of the rubber type that was meant to peel off. But an unsightly faded section might result, or you can end up removing part of the cover or jacket along with the sticker, so it is often better to leave it alone.

Culinary ephemera, which includes menus, advertising booklets, recipe card sets, instruction manuals for kitchenware, and other paper items, requires special treatment and storage. Many times fragile items survive because someone tucked the pieces into a cookbook or stored a menu away for personal memories. To keep these items in good condition for another century or so, use basically the same care rules for these paper goods as for cookbooks: do not use tape to repair tears, be careful about erasing any marks, be careful about removing a price tag (the glues from long ago really stuck), and don't store materials in plastic bags (which can't breathe and thus retain moisture, leading to mildew or insect problems). Instead, use Mylar sleeves or polyethylene bags and protectors, which can be ordered through archive catalogs. Magazines, like *The Boston Cooking School Magazine*, pose

Fig. 7-12 Slipcases were used to keep a series of books together, and some cookbooks were issued with the protective boxes. *A National Treasury of Cookery*, published in 1967, consisted of five small books covering the eras from Colonial to Victorian America. The set was a unique blend of talent: Mary and Vincent Price wrote the introduction, Helen Duprey Bullock (author of *The Williamsburg Art of Cookery*) was the editor, and artist Charles Wysocki provided many of the charming illustrations. A set of books like this can increase in value if the slipcase is present and in good condition.

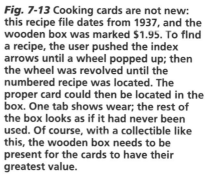

Fig. 7-13 Cooking cards are not new: this recipe file dates from 1937, and the wooden box was marked $1.95. To find a recipe, the user pushed the index arrows until a wheel popped up; then the wheel was revolved until the numbered recipe was located. The proper card could then be located in the box. One tab shows wear; the rest of the box looks as if it had never been used. Of course, with a collectible like this, the wooden box needs to be present for the cards to have their greatest value.

special problems, since they cannot stand up on shelves by themselves and their covers are usually fragile and susceptible to tears and chips. At the very least, use bookends to support these collectibles, although storing them flat in archive boxes is a better method. If you insist on storing the magazines in a pile, then at the very least don't overstack, and never put glossy covers on top of each other—if there is dampness or humidity, the covers may stick together.

One term you will come across when reading about conservation materials is "acid-free." This indicates that the paper used in framing, storage, or repair of items is itself free from the acids that occur naturally in many papers or that have been introduced by chemicals in the environment. These acids can destroy paper over a period of time; thus, the use of acid-free papers for storage purposes can greatly reduce the normal rate of decay. Any collection of loose or small paper items, odd-sized or tiny cookbooks that cannot be stored on shelves, or fragile handwritten recipe books should be kept in acid-free boxes or pamphlet binders for their own protection and for your future enjoyment.

Unlike many other books, cookbooks seemed to lend themselves to exotic methods of binding and covering, and caring for these oddities takes some care. Collectors will find examples bound with wooden covers (wipe with a damp cloth), "wipe clean" plastic or pseudo-leather (use mild soap and water only, no harsh abrasives or alcohol-based cleaners), "aluminum foil" or silver foil (just wipe lightly with a clean, dry cloth), fabric (dust lightly; don't try to wash or the colors may run), and printed boards (wipe lightly with a clean cloth).

Finding Out More About Your Cookbooks

Collectors who want to find out the histories of their cookbooks are in for a big disappointment: there is no one research source that will tell you about the books in your collection or the people who wrote them. Discovering the history of a book takes time, but what you turn up can make the recipes and the era come alive in your kitchen. Many excellent historic sourcebooks are listed in the Bibliography at the end of this book, and your local library should be able to locate most of them. If you have a book that was produced by a large company like General Foods, you may be able to write to the public information office and ask if they have information available on certain books (the Betty Crocker cookbooks have been carefully documented, along with Betty's looks down through the years). Of course, cookbook bibliographies are indispensable when it comes to providing researchers with information about the history of a book; the basic bibliographies are also listed in the Bibliography at the end of this book.

The men and women who wrote cookbooks were often listed in biographical dictionaries and encyclopedias, and some, like Isabella Beeton, have had entire books written about them. In the case of charity cookbooks the search for information can be more challenging, particularly if the organization that sponsored a cookbook did the work a half century ago. However, Granges, church groups, women's service circles, and other community organizations are often long-lived, so a call or letter to the state organization or even the local church that sponsored the book may help you get some background information on what appears to be a defunct group. If you are researching a charity cookbook from your region, you may want to take a chance at contacting people in the locality with the same last name as the donors of a signed recipe. Small towns have long memories, and much information about a group or even a recipe can be obtained with a little detective work. Old local newspapers are also good sources for material, as they often printed announcements of local cookbooks, authors, and such. Armed with a publication date, you may be able to track down an article in a paper published around that time period.

Don't forget to read about the historic period a particular book or piece of ephemera represents. Although this probably will not provide you with specific information about the book or menu you are researching, it will place the collectible in its historical perspective. It is nearly impossible to be interested in nineteenth-century cookbooks, for example, without discovering more about fireplace and woodstove cookery or middle-class dining customs, and understanding the economics of the antebellum South may explain the use of certain ingredients in those cookbooks.

One of the best ways to gain insight into a cookbook is by carefully reading its recipes. They indicate what foods and cooking methods were popular, what a housewife was expected to do in addition to baking and cooking, and what ingredients and equipment—for example Baker's chocolate or Home Comfort Ranges—were all the rage. Advertisements can provide the researcher with a jumping off point for further reading, so that even if you can't discover information specific to one particular cookbook, at the very least you will be able to fit that cookbook into its proper historical niche.

Insuring Cookbooks

Unfortunately, few people tend to think of their culinary collections as something that has a monetary value in addition to an historic and social value—that is, they don't think about the value until the collection is destroyed or damaged in a fire, flood, robbery, or other disaster. Let's face it, insurance companies will rarely replace a hundred or a thousand books on your word alone, even if you swear you can remember every title in your damaged collection. If you don't think your collection is valuable, try this test: Select from your bookshelf any twenty cookbooks in good or better condition. Look up their value (or comparable value) in a price guide, or, if the books are new, add their retail prices together. Chances are you will be surprised at the total, which can easily top $200 or more. Now, check your insurance policy to see what type of deductible you have and what your policy covers in general. If you have a high deductible, you would have to write off the cost of replacing the cookbooks; with some policies, you may not have cookbooks considered under the heading of "household goods." And if you are like many collectors who have spent years adding to their library, you will be faced with the loss of hundreds or thousands of books instead of twenty—and a monetary loss that could range into tens of thousands of dollars. Thus, if your collection is one that you cherish and would consider replacing in the event of a loss, you will need to insure it properly, and that is neither easy nor inexpensive to do.

Since each insurance company has different terms, it is necessary to check with your carrier and determine what part, if any, of your cookbook collection is covered in the event of a problem. Cookbooks may be insured under your homeowner's policy, since the books can be considered personal property, but it is wise to ask your agent to stop by and look at the collection; since he or she might be unaware of the size or complexity of it, you might discover that only a small portion would be recoverable. You need to know your personal property limit to insure that in the event of a fire, you have enough coverage to replace both your furniture and your cookbooks.

Homeowner's insurance may suffice for cookbooks that are fairly easy to replace (books from the 1970s and 1980s, for example), but if you have many books from the nineteenth and early twentieth centuries, you could be looking at items that fall under the category of "fine art" or "antiques" for insurance purposes. Adequate coverage can be expensive, and the insurer may require certain actions on your part (proper storage, fire or intrusion alarms, and so on) in order to provide the insurance. If you decide to forego any but the general household coverage for your collection, don't be surprised to discover that when you make a claim, you are reimbursed for what you *paid* for a book, not necessarily what it is *worth*. This is a wicked surprise if you found a bargain at a flea market that you know you could sell on the specialty market for $50 or more. There are no simple answers to the insurance problem. You have to decide if you could sustain a loss of your collection and replace it without insurance money (something which could take many years) or if you should pay higher premiums now, in case a problem occurs, and receive money later that would allow you to replace the books all at once at market price.

Whatever you decide, you need to keep careful records of your purchases for insurance and resale reasons. Value is, in most cases, subjective. Collectors with more than a few dozen books are usually surprised to learn that

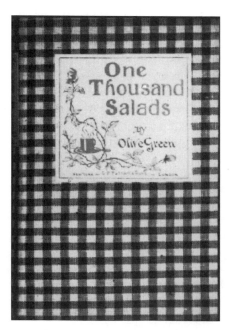

Fig. 7-14 "Salad making requires the best of materials, a deft touch, a sense of harmony and proportion and more than all, the artist's love of his art." This single-subject cookbook offers recipes for 6 different kinds of walnut salads, 21 orange salads, and 356 salad fillings (chopped chicken and ham seasoned with minced truffles, salt, pepper, mustard, and mushroom or tomato catsup was #321). The gingham fabric cover was a kitchen-y touch, as was Olive Green's humorous, possibly fictitious, name.

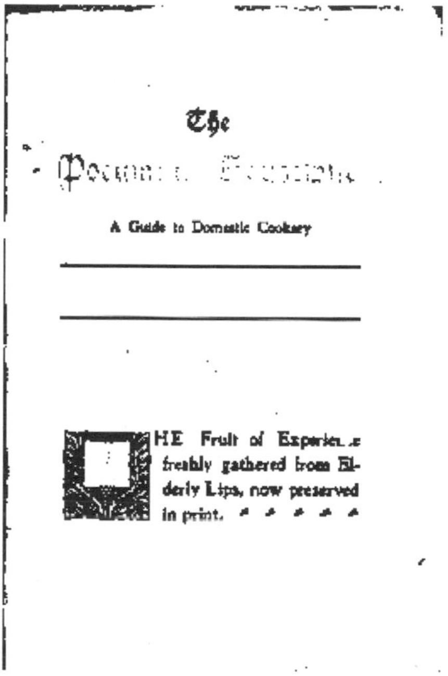

The

Pocumtuc Housewife

A Guide to Domestic Cookery

HE Fruit of Experience freshly gathered from Elderly Lips, now preserved in print. ♪ ♪ ♪ ♪ ♪

Fig. 7-15 The Pocumtuc Housewife was published as a revised fund-raising edition in 1906, but it selected some of its text from *The American Frugal Housewife* (1829). The ladies of the First Church of Deerfield, Connecticut, with tongue in cheek, said that their booklet was meant to help the young and ignorant wife "forget her stove-cooked food and Emulate the Past." The booklet was designed to look old, with heavy paper, old-style type, and a handmade cover. Old-fashioned recipes predominated, along with directions for making soap and dyeing fabrics. The advertisements in the book show the influence of the Colonial Revival movement on both cookbooks and crafts, with listings for artisans who reproduced colonial linen embroideries, woven rugs, and bayberry candles.

even their modest accumulations have "book value," or the value assigned by a price guide such as this one. If your books are worth $500 and it will cost you an additional $75 a year to insure them under a fine arts schedule to your present policy, you may want to think twice. If your books are worth $5,000 and include a few irreplaceable examples, and it will cost an extra $75 a year to insure them, you may decide to go with the extra coverage. Not insuring your books does not reduce their value as collectibles, or as resources; it does mean that you have little, if any, protection should the books be destroyed or damaged.

Keeping Records, Getting an Appraisal

Most likely you will assemble your cookbook collection over a period of time, and you will probably not be able to recall what each one cost at purchase time. Maintaining a record of purchase is simple, and either a simple notebook or a detailed fill-in-the-blanks register will do (see Sources at the end of this book). You will need to record, at the very least, the title, author, publishing date, condition, price paid, date, and place of purchase for each cookbook. Sounds like a lot of work? It is, and this is probably the most overlooked area of cookbook collecting, even though proper record keeping may save you a lot of money over the years. If you can record every purchase you make, that's wonderful and incredibly organized. But, like the majority of collectors, you may find that you will record only the "important" books—the ones you spent the most money on and the ones you value the most, whether for sentimental, historic, or other reasons.

One way to keep your records is to make certain you get a receipt for each cookbook you purchase, and then record the missing information on the back of the receipt. Store the receipts in an envelope and, while you may have to wade through a lot of pieces of paper to recover a specific piece of information, at least you will have it on hand. You should also consider taking photographs or a video of your books in order to strengthen your claim to ownership in the event of an insurance problem. Instant-camera-type photos are fine, as long as the books can be easily identified (several books to a photo will save time and money). Clip the photos to the appropriate sales slips and store in a safe place outside of your home, since fire and water don't discriminate between important papers and junk mail.

If you are a cookbook collector from way back, you may at this point be worrying that you have been collecting for lo these many years and have never, ever saved a single receipt. Perhaps now you want to insure the collection, bequeath it to heirs, donate it to a library, or just sell it. There is a way to overcome this problem: consider having your cookbooks appraised by a professional. The keyword here is "professional"—a person whom it may take some time to locate but whose skills are worth the search. Few areas require that an appraiser of any kind be licensed, and even that bastion of rules and regulations, the Internal Revenue Service (IRS), is vague on the subject: "A qualified appraiser is an individual who declares on the appraisal summary that he or she: holds himself or herself out to the public as an appraiser or performs appraisals on a regular basis; is qualified to make appraisals of the type of property being valued, because of his or her qualifications described in the appraisal. . . ." In other words, the appraiser must prove that he or she can do the job, accurately and fairly, even though there are few guidelines. Of course, there are professional appraisal associations that set forth strict rules for their members, who are often top experts in their fields. In addition to calling these organizations for membership listings, you can ask at your library, bank, or insurance office for recommendations. *AB Bookman's Yearbook* has a section on "cookbooks and cookery" with listings of cookbook specialists, some of whom may do appraisals; the listing of auction specialists is also a good source for names. The owner of a local bookstore specializing in used books may also be able to suggest someone appropriate for the job; however, do not have your books appraised by someone who also wants to purchase them from you. As honest as the dealer may be, this is a conflict of interest and will appear so to agencies like the IRS, which could someday examine your appraisal for tax purposes.

Once you've located an appraiser whom you think is appropriate, you need to discuss what the cost of the appraisal will be. The services of an appraiser do not come cheap—first, because appraisers represent a unique knowledge of a field, and second, because an appraiser will be willing to defend his or her decisions to you or other agencies. Appraisers may charge a straight fee for a small job or an hourly fee for a longer one; an extensive appraisal may cost $1,000 or more. Do not hire an appraiser who charges a percentage of the total appraised value, for regardless of how honest the appraiser is, this type of arrangement is prohibited by the IRS in conjunction with materials or collections that are being donated.

Once you have agreed on a fee, the appraiser will examine your books, list titles, condition, authors, and other information, and then write a report. What can you expect for your money? For one thing, an appraiser will provide you with a valuable record of your cookbook collection. For another, the appraiser will provide information for an insurance appraisal; that is, a valuation of your property based on the market replacement value of an item lost through fire, theft, or other catastrophes. There are also donation and estate valuations, necessary when you give your books to a library or you leave them as part of your estate, and your appraiser needs to know the difference (and your intentions) in order to provide you with the most accurate and IRS-acceptable prices. The appraisal itself must have several sections:

1 A statement of the owner's name, the date of appraisal, and a signature of the appraiser, along with the reason the appraisal is being made (this could indicate insurance purposes, donations, and so on). The IRS also requires an explanation of the fee agreement between the appraiser and customer.

2 A statement of the appraiser's qualifications (for example, cookbook dealer or specialty librarian).

3 The source of the valuations that appear in the appraisal (auction, catalog or sales prices, price guides).

4 A detailed listing and description of each of the cookbooks being appraised.

This last requirement refers to a "scheduled" appraisal, or one in which each book is listed and valued. You do not want to have an appraisal that states, "Collection of 350 cookbooks, 19th–20th centuries, good to better condition, $1900." What you *do* want are accurate, detailed entries, like "Hirtzler, Victor, *The Hotel St. Francis Cook Book,* 1919, Hotel Monthly Press, first edition. Cloth binding, gold stamped title on spine, 412 pages. Illustration of author on frontispiece. Very good. Bitting, page 231. $130" (Figure 7-16).

Although not all the entries may be this detailed, anyone—and for the IRS this means anyone not necessarily familiar with cookbooks—reading this description would be able to identify the book, which is the point for appraisals. It should be noted that appraisers, in general, do not take photos of your books; if you want photos, you will need to discuss this with the

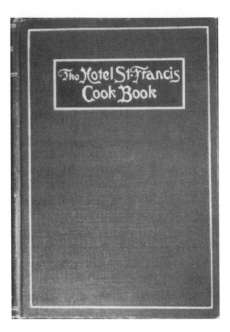

Fig. 7-16 The Hotel St. Francis was a well-known dining establishment in San Francisco, and the author, Chef Victor Hirtzler, adapted the hotel's dishes in 1919 for "every place where high class, wholesome cuisine is desired." This book is set up like a calendar, with daily menus for breakfasts, luncheon, and dinner on everyday and holiday occasions; listings of menus for special dinners, like the one given for the National Association of Professional Baseball in 1915; and the daily menu of the hotel, complete with prices (sirloin for four was $3.25). Books like *The Hotel St. Francis Cook Book* provided readers of the time with a chance to cook à la high society and appealed to the American fascination with wealthy lifestyles.

appraiser beforehand to determine whether or not the appraiser can provide this service.

Once your appraisal is completed, put the original copy in a safe place, away from your premises (a safety deposit box is recommended). To include recent acquisitions and because all collectibles and antiques, including cookbooks, have prices that fluctuate, it will be necessary to update your appraisal at least every other year, in order to be certain that you have adequate insurance for your treasures.

Selling Your Cookbooks

The time may come when you decide to sell all or part of your collection. For example, some collectors retire and move to smaller quarters and can keep only a few treasures, meaning the rest have to go. Other people sell collections on behalf of an elderly owner or as part of an estate. Still others have decided to specialize in one area and are ready to sell the books that no longer fit in with their current interests. Whatever the reason, selling cookbooks takes some work.

First, select the books you want to sell. Next, establish what you think your collection—or the group of books you wish to sell—is worth. This means making an inventory of the books to be sold, including title, author, publication year, illustrations, number of pages, and condition, including damages. Using price guides, including *American Books Prices Current* and specialty listings like this one, note the suggested value of the books. Once you have your inventory (which can also serve as your sale list), you can begin to locate buyers for the books. In many cases, cookbooks find a ready market, and an inexpensive ad in a shopping guide or newspaper may bring you some offers. Buyers can also be found through antiques specialty newspapers and cookbook newsletters. Try to locate one that contains offerings in the same price range as you expect to get for your books; collectors who limit themselves to books that cost under $20 are probably not the audience you want if your books start at $50 or more in value. If you send out your booklist with the prices, be certain to indicate that the buyer will have to pay for shipping and insurance as well. Selling directly to a collector can result in getting the best possible price, although it may take some time to sell a complete collection.

You can also contact used book or specialty book dealers. They will offer you a percentage of the books' value, anywhere from 10 percent to 50 percent, but rarely more. The prices you see in guides like this one are the prices being *asked* by sellers, so they will not offer you the same price because they of course work to make a profit. The plus side of selling to a dealer: they may arrange for shipping or pickup; they may purchase the entire collection, rather than one or two books; and they will pay you immediately for the entire collection, instead of your having to wait weeks or months to sell off the books one by one. The minus side, as alluded to above: you receive only a fraction of the collection's value.

If you have a collection of valuable cookbooks (usually from the nineteenth century or earlier) in very good or better condition, you may decide to sell them through an auction house (see Sources at the end of this book). Prices realized at auctions, including those for cookbooks, can be much higher than prices found in bookstores, since the bidders know they have competition and are usually specialist collectors. Here is where your booklist will be important: any auction house will require a detailed list of books (along with photos, if available) before they can decide on whether or not they are interested in your holdings. Call or write the auction house to find the name of the cookbook specialist, and send your list with a cover letter. Swann Galleries in New York suggests that the potential seller send along a copy of the title page of each book.

Do not send the auction house a list of prices you expect to get for the books; if the house decides to handle your cookbooks, the firm's experts will determine estimated values. Similarly, do not send the books or ephemera to the galleries unless asked to do so. Smaller, local auctions may contact you immediately, while the larger firms can take up to a month to respond to a letter. Most firms that handle fine book auctions set minimums for accepting consignments, so they expect a collection to bring at least $1,000 or, more unusually, an individual item to realize at least $500 at auction. Some auctions accept ephemera and hold sales especially for paper collectibles, including recipe leaflets. Other auction houses have what they call "shelf sales" where buyers can browse through shelves of books that didn't make it to the auction, and sometimes collectible cookbooks turn up here at bargain prices (at least "bargain" in comparison to the auction prices). Auction galleries usually charge the consigner (the seller) on a sliding fee scale—that is, if your books sell for under $500, you may pay 25 percent of the purchase price to the gallery; at $1,000, you may pay 15 percent of the purchase price; and so on. The auction gallery will provide you with a description of sales terms upon request. A local auction house may put your books up for sale right away, perhaps even a week or so after receiving them, while a larger firm may take six or eight months to get your books on the block.

Since many collectors have bought but not sold books, they need to be aware of some selling suggestions. First, you must describe a book's condition accurately, no matter where you are selling it. There is nothing worse than a buyer making a trip (or buying by mail) and discovering that "a very old cookbook in good condition for its age," as you have described it, turns out to be a water-stained, fifteenth edition copy of *The Boston Cooking-School Cookbook* with some pages missing. Second, you have to work in order to sell your cookbooks. For example, you cannot merely write or call a dealer in Ohio if you live in New York and tell the dealer you have 300 cookbooks for sale. You have to offer a booklist, and you have to be willing to ship the books. If you cannot or will not do this, then you need to consider taking less money for your collection and doing less work.

Cookbooks should never be considered as simple commodities to be bought and sold for profit only; nor should they be thought of as treasures that should always remain undervalued so that you never have to pay more than $5 for a book. In an ideal collecting world, all books would be affordable to all collectors and available in all editions, in fine condition and at low prices. Lacking this cookbook Eden, collectors have to settle for just enjoying the search and the creation of a cherished cookbook library, an avocation that provides more than enough fascination and instruction during a collecting lifetime.

Part Two

Bibliographical
Listings With Prices

A&P Cookbook and Shopping Guide
Sullivan, Barbara
Simon and Schuster, NY, 1975: 288 pp
Wraps; illustrated $8.00

Abalone to Zabaglione
Beilenson, Edna
Peter Pauper Press, Mt. Vernon, NY, 1957: 60
pp, hc
Dust jacket $10.00

About Lobsters
Prudden, Tim
Bond Wheelwright Co., Freeport, ME, 1962:
170 pp, hc
Illustrated $14.00

ADDitions School Volunteers Cookbook
ADDitions, Orlando, FL, 1977: 74 pp
Die-cut in shape of apple $10.00

**Adventures in Good Cooking and the Art of
Carving**
Hines, Duncan
Adventures in Good Eating, Inc., Bowling
Green, KY, 1943: 492 pp
Illustrated; local ads; carving directions $15.00

Adventures of the Galloping Gas Stove
Garis, Howard
Grosset and Dunlap, NY, 1926: 154 pp, hc
Illustrated $12.50

Airtight Woodstove Cookbook
Darling, Dale, Dyck, Julia
Brick House Publishing Co., Andover, MA,
1981: 124 pp
Wraps; illustrated $7.00

Akron Cook Book, The
First Methodist Church, Akron, NY, 1921: 96
pp
Wraps; signed recipes; local ads $12.50

Alexandre Dumas' Dictionary of Cuisine
Colman, Louis, editor
Simon and Schuster, NY, 1958: 242 pp,
hc $17.50

Alice B. Toklas Cook Book
Toklas, Alice
Harper and Brothers, NY, 1954: 288 pp, hc
Dust jacket $55.00

Alice Bradley Menu Cook-Book
Bradley, Alice
Macmillan Company, NY, 1937: 243 pp
Spiral; first edition $10.00

Alice Foote McDougall's Cook Book
McDougall, Alice
Lothrop, Lee and Shepard, 1935: 292 pp, hc
Illustrated; first edition $17.50

Alice's Restaurant Cookbook
Brock, Alice
Random House, NY, 1969: 148 pp, hc
With record $30.00

All About Apples
Martin, Alice
Houghton Mifflin Co., Boston, MA, 1976, 174
pp, hc
Illustrated; first edition $14.00

All Maine Cooking
Wiggin, Ruth, and Shibles, Loana
Courier of Maine Books, Rockland, ME, 1967:
186 pp
Spiral; signed recipes $9.00

All Star Cook Book
Palestine Chapter, Order of the Eastern Star,
1940: 67 pp
Spiral; local ads; signed recipes $12.50

Allied Cookery
Harrison, Grace, and Clerque, Gertrude
G.P. Putnam's, NY, 1916: 108 pp $25.00

Amana Recipes
Homestead Welfare Club, Homestead, IA,
1948: 120 pp
First edition; history; signed recipes $22.50

America Cooks
Browns, Cora, Rose, and Bob
W.W. Norton, 1940: 986 pp, hc
First edition; regional recipes $30.00

**America Cooks Favorite Recipes from North,
South, East, West**
Hardwick Stove Company, Cleveland TN,
1946: 64 pp
Wraps; illustrated $5.00

America Eats
Weaver, William Woys
Harper and Row, NY, 1989: 198 pp
Wraps; illustrated $17.00

**American Cookbooks & Wine Books,
1797–1950**
Longone, Janice and Daniel
University of Michigan, MI, 1984: 68 pp
Wraps; illustrated $20.00

American Cookery
Simmons, Amelia
Albany, NY, 1804: 72 pp
Wraps; third edition $4000.00

American Cookery Magazine
Boston Cooking School Magazine Co.,
Boston, MA, 1936: 320 pp
Wraps; illustrated; formerly The Boston
Cooking-School Magazine $6.00 an issue

American Cooking: Creole and Acadian
Time-Life Books, NY, 1970: 108 pp, hc
Illustrated; with recipe book $12.00

American Cooking: New England
Time-Life Books, NY, 1970: 108 pp, hc
Illustrated; with recipe book $12.00

American Cooking: The Melting Pot
Time-Life Books, NY, 1970: 108 pp, hc
Illustrated; with recipe book $12.00

American Cooking: the Northwest
Time-Life Books, NY, 1970: 108 pp, hc
Illustrated; with recipe book $12.00

American Drink Book, The
Field, S.S.
Farrar, Straus and Young, NY, 1957: 282 pp,
   hc
Illustrated $15.00

American Feasts
Williams, Sallie
William Morrow Company, NY, 1985, 288 pp,
   hc
Illustrated; dust jacket $12.50

American Folk Life Cookbook, An
Nathan, Joan
Schocken Books, NY, 1984: 336 pp, hc
Illustrated $20.00

American Food: The Gastronomic Story
Jones, Evan
E.P. Dutton, NY, 1975: 387 pp, hc $25.00

**American Heritage Cookbook and
Illustrated History**
Bullock, Helen D.
American Heritage Magazine; PA, 1964: 2
   vols., hc
Slipcase; illustrated; first edition $55.00

American Home Cook Book, The
Denison, Grace
Grosset and Dunlap; NY, 1932: 537 pp, hc
Illustrated $17.50

American Home Cooking
Hazelton, Nika
Viking, NY, 1980: 308 pp, hc $14.00

American Peoples Cookbook, The
DeProft, Melanie
Spencer Press, Inc. Chicago, IL, 1956: 600 pp,
   hc
Illustrated $25.00

**American Practical Cookery Book, A
Practical Housekeeper**
John E. Potter and Co., Philadelphia, PA,
   1859: 319 pp, hc
Illustrated $65.00

American Regional Cookbook, The
Hawkins, Nancy and Arthur
Greenwich House, NY, 1976: 301 pp,
   hc $12.50

American Regional Cookery
Hibben, Sheila
Little, Brown Company, Boston, MA, 1946:
   354 pp, hc $25.00

American Soda Book, The
American Soda Fountain Company, 1912:
   260 pp
Illustrated; guide to running a soda
   fountain $45.00

American Woman's Victory Cookbook
Berolzheimer, Ruth
Culinary Arts Institute, Chicago, IL, 1942: 800
   pp, hc
Illustrated; dedicated to General D.
   MacArthur $22.50

America's Charitable Cooks
Cook, Margaret
Kent: OH, 1971: 315 pp, hc
Illustrated $50.00

Amish Dutch Cookbook
Redcay, Ruth
Ben Herman Dutch Books, Kutztown, PA,
   1964: 64 pp
Wraps; illustrated $5.00

Amy Vanderbilt's Complete Cookbook
Vanderbilt, Amy
Doubleday, Garden City, NY, 1961: 811
   pp, hc $14.00

Annemarie's Personal Cook Book
Huste, Annemarie
Bartholemew House, 1968: 336 pp, hc
Illustrated $15.00

Any One Can Bake
Royal Baking Powder Co., NY, 1929: 100 pp,
   hc
Illustrated $14.00

Aphrodisiacs and Love Stimulants
Davenport, John
Lyle Stuart, NY, 1966: 254 pp, hc
Illustrated $12.00

**Apicius: Cooking and Dining in Imperial
Rome**
Vehling, Joseph
Chicago, 1936: 301 pp, hc
Numbered; limited edition $500.00

Appendix To The I Hate to Cook Book
Bracken, Peg
Harcourt, Brace, World, NY, 1966: 178 pp, hc
First edition $12.50

Apples of New York
Beach, S.A.
Dept. of Agriculture, State of New York,
   1905: 2 vols., hc
Illustrated $125.00

Approved Recipes For the Hotpoint Refrigerator
Edison General Electric Appliance Co., Chicago, IL, 1937: 64 pp
Wraps; illustrated $8.00

Army Food and Messing
Military Service Publishing Company, Harrisburg, PA, 1942: 418 pp, hc
Illustrated $22.50
Second edition; illustrated $25.00

Army Wife's Cookbook, An
Grierson, Alice Kirk
Ft. Davis National Historic Site, Globe, AZ, 1972: 71 pp
Spiral; illustrated $12.50

Art of American Indian Cooking, The
Kimball, Yeffe, and Anderson, Jean
Doubleday, NY, 1965: 215 pp, hc
First edition $15.00

Art of Confectionery
J. E. Tilton and Comp., Boston, 1866: 346 pp, hc $200.00

Art of Cooking with Love and Wheat Germ, The
Kinderlehrer, Jane
Rodale Press, Inc., Emmaus, PA, 1977: 355 pp, hc $10.50

Art of Creole Cookery, The
Kaufman, William, and Cooper, Mary
Doubleday Company, Garden City, NY, 1962: 227 pp, hc $15.00

Art of Entertaining, The
Sherwood, M.E.W.
Dodd, Mead & Co., NY, 1892: 404 pp, hc
Fine condition $35.00

Art of Fine Baking, The
Peck, Paula
Simon and Schuster; NY, 1961: 320 pp, hc
Illustrated; dust jacket $12.50

Art of Fish Cookery, The
Miloradovich, Milo
Doubleday Company, Garden City, NY, 1949: 456 pp, hc
Dust jacket $10.00

Art of Food Decorating, The
Townsend, Doris M.
Gallery Books, NY, 1973: 192 pp, hc
Dust jacket; illustrated $12.00

Art of Grilling, Baking and Barbecuing, The
Hines, Duncan
RCA Estate Appliance Corp., Hamilton, OH, 1952: 95 pp
Advertising $4.00

Art of Jewish Cooking, The
Grossinger, Jennie
Random House, NY, 1958: 238 pp, hc
Dust jacket $12.50

Art of Making Good Cookies Plain and Fancy, The
Ross, Annette, and Disney, Jean
Doubleday, Garden City, NY, 1963: 252 pp, hc $10.00
253 pp, hc
Illustrated $6.00

Art of Polish Cooking
Zeranska, Alina
Doubleday Company, NY, 1968: 366 pp, hc
First edition $15.00

Art of Serving Food Attractively, The
Wenker, Mary Albert
Doubleday and Company; Garden City, NY, 1951: 190 pp, hc
Dust jacket $12.50

Art of Southern Cooking, The
Warren, Mildred
Doubleday; Garden City, NY, 1969: 264 pp, hc
Dust jacket $10.00

Art of Syrian Cookery
Corey, Helen
Doubleday, Garden City, NY, 1962: 186 pp, hc
Illustrated $15.00

At Home on the Range
Westchester Ladies' Aux. of United Home for Aged Hebrews, 1937: 105 pp, hc
Local ads $15.00

Attic Cookbook, The
Wilkinson, Gertrude
Penguin Books, Baltimore, MD, 1972: 265 pp, hc
Dust jacket $11.00

Aunt Sammy's Radio Recipes Revised
Van Deman, Ruth, and Yeatman, Fanny
United States Department of Agriculture; Washington, DC, 1931: 142 pp
Wraps $11.00

Auxiliary Cook Book, The
Hebrew Sheltering Society; NY, 1909: 141 pp, hc
Local ads; essays on living well $25.00

Avon International Cookbook, The
Meredith Publishing Services, Des Moines, IA, 1983: 96 pp, hc
Illustrated; signed recipes $12.50

Ayer's Book of Pies and Puddings
Ayer, J.C.
Ayer & Company, Lowell: MA, 1892: 24 pp
Wraps $5.00

Bachelor's Cookbook, The
Sheridan, Lee
Crowell-Collier Press, 1962, 190 pp, hc
Dust jacket; first edition $12.50

Bachelor's Cupboard, A
Phillips, A.
Luce Co., 1906: 210 pp, hc $35.00

Bake Shop in a Book
Proctor and Gamble, 1979: 184 pp, hc
Three-ring binder $12.50

Baker's Best Chocolate Recipes
Walter Baker & Company, 1930: 60 pp
Wraps; illustrated; recipes for Baker
  chocolate; center spread of Baker
  products $6.00

Baker's Best Chocolate Recipes
Walter Baker & Company; Dorchester, MA,
  1932: 60 pp
Wraps; illustrated $6.00

Ballet Cook Book, The
LeClerq, Tanaquil
Stein and Day, NY, 1966: 424 pp, hc
Illustrated $50.00

Baptist Cook-A-Long
Flemington Baptist Church: Flemington, NJ,
  1972: 104 pp
Spiral; signed recipes $8.00

Barry's Fruit Garden
Barry, P.
Orange Judd Company, NY, 1890; 516 pp, hc
Illustrated $35.00

Beautiful Wive's Cookbook
Wilson, Rosemary, and Pool, Ruth
Prentice-Hall, Englewood Cliffs, NJ, 1970: 202
  pp, hc
Illustrated $14.00

Bel Canto Cookbook, The
Gravina, Peter
Doubleday and Co., New York, NY, 1964:
  219 pp, hc
Illustrated; first edition $12.00

Belgian Relief Cook Book
Belgian Relief Committee, Reading, PA, 1915:
  300 pp
Signed recipes; ring bound; celebrity
  recipes $45.00

Belle Terre Favorites
Belle Terre Garden Club, 1936: 160 pp
Spiral; signed recipes $15.00

Best Cookery in the Middle West
Clark, Grace G.
Doubleday, NY, 1955: 355 pp, hc
First edition $22.50

Best in American Cooking, The
Paddleford, Clementine
Charles Scribner's Sons, NY, 1970: 312 pp, hc
Dust jacket $25.00

Best in Pennsylvania Dutch Cooking, The
Ladies Aid, Elizabethtown, PA, 1954: 62 pp
Spiral; signed recipes; local ads $12.50

Best of Amish Cooking, The
Good, Phyllis
Good Books, Intercourse, PA, 1988: 224 pp,
  hc
Illustrated $15.00

Best of Shaker Cooking, The
Miller, Amy, and Fuller, Persis
Macmillan Publishing Co., NY, 1985: 496 pp,
  hc
Signed by authors $25.00

Best of Taste, The
SACLANT-NATO Cookbook Committee,
  Annapolis, MD, 1957: 191 pp, hc $20.00

**Best of the Bake-Off Collection: Pillsbury's
Best 100 Recipes**
Pillsbury, Ann
Consolidated Book Publishers, 1959: 608 pp,
  hc
Illustrated; signed recipes $45.00

Best Recipes from the Cookbook Guild
Fink, P.
Doubleday, Garden City, NY, 1972: 332 pp, hc
First edition; illustrated $12.50

Best Ways to Cook Fresh Vegetables
Scott, Anna B.
W. Atlee Burpee Co., 1916: 40 pp
Wraps; illustrated $8.00

**Better Homes and Gardens Golden Treasury
of Cooking**
Meredith Corporation, Des Moines, IA, 1973:
  302 pp, hc
Illustrated $20.00

**Better Homes and Gardens Good Food on a
Budget**
Meredith Corporation, Des Moines, IA, 1971:
  96 pp, hc
Illustrated $8.00

**Better Homes and Gardens Heritage Cook
Book**
Meredith Corporation, Des Moines, IA, 1975:
  398 pp, hc
Illustrated; first edition $40.00

**Better Homes and Gardens Homemade
Bread**
Meredith Corporation, Des Moines, IA, 1973:
  96 pp, hc
Illustrated $8.00

Better Homes and Gardens Hot and Spicy Cooking
Meredith Corporation, Des Moines, IA, 1984:
96 pp, hc
Illustrated $8.00

Better Homes and Gardens Junior Cook Book
Meredith Corporation, Des Moines, IA, 1955:
77 pp, hc
Illustrated $15.00

Better Homes and Gardens Meals with a Foreign Flair
Meredith Corporation, Des Moines, IA, 1963:
61 pp, hc
Illustrated $8.00

Better Homes and Gardens New Cookbook
Meredith Publishing, Des Moines, IA, 1953:
416 pp
Three ring binder; very good; first
edition $25.00

Better Homes and Gardens 1989 Best-Recipes Yearbook
Meredith Corporation, Des Moines, IA, 1989:
192 pp, hc
Illustrated; first edition $11.00

Bettina's Best Salads and What To Serve With Them
Weaver & LeCron
A.L. Burt Company, 1923: 215 pp, hc
Illustrated $20.00

Betty Crocker's Cake and Frosting Mix Cookbook
Golden Press; New York; 1966: 144 pp, hc
Spiral; illustrated; first edition $10.00

Betty Crocker's Dinner for Two Cookbook
Golden Press, NY, 1973: 160 pp
Spiral; illustrated; first edition $10.00

Betty Crocker's Kitchen Garden
Campbell, M.
Scribner's Sons, NY, 1971: 170 pp, hc
Illustrated $12.50

Betty Crocker's New Boys and Girls Cookbook
Golden Press, NY, 1965: 156 pp
Spiral; illustrated; first edition $22.50

Betty Crocker's New Good and Easy Cookbook
Golden Press, NY, 1962: 192 pp
Spiral; illustrated; first edition $12.50

Betty Crocker's Picture Cook Book
McGraw Hill Book Co., NY, 1950: 449 pp, hc
Illustrated; first edition $48.00
1956: 472 pp, hc
Illustrated $35.00

Bible Cookbook, The
O'Brien, Marian Maeve
Bethany Press, St. Louis, MO, 1958: 350
pp, hc $15.00

Biblical Garden Cookery
Gaden, Eileen
Christian Herald Books, Chappaqua, NY,
1976: 214 pp, hc
Illustrated $22.50

Bibliography of American Cookery Books, 1742–1860
Lowenstein, Eleanor
American Antiquarian Society, Worcester,
MA, 1972: 132 pp, hc $50.00

Bless This Food
Bryant, Anita
Doubleday, Garden City, NY, 1975: 320 pp, hc
First edition $14.00

Blessings of Bread, The
Bailey, Adrian
Paddington Press, 1975: 287 pp, hc
Dust jacket; illustrated $22.50

Blue Hills and Shoofly Pie
Hark, Ann
Lippincott Company; NY, 1952: 284 pp,
hc $22.50

Blue Ribbon Recipes: County Fair Winners
Cookbook Collectors Library, Favorite Recipes
Press, 1968: 384 pp, hc $12.50

Blue Sea Cookbook
Alberson, Sarah
Hastings House, NY, 1968: 290 pp, hc $10.00

Blueberry Hill Kitchen Notebook
Masterton, Elsie
Thomas Crowell Company, NY, 1964: 258 pp,
hc
First printing $25.00

Blueberry Hill Menu Cookbook
Masterton, Elsie
Thomas Crowell Company, NY, 1963: 373 pp,
hc
First printing $25.00

Bon Vivant's Cookbook, A
Veach, William T.
Little, Brown, Boston, MA, 1965: 236 pp, hc
First edition $10.00

Book of Bread, The
Jones, Judith and Evan
Harper and Row, NY, 1982: 384 pp, hc
Dust jacket; fine condition $12.50

Book of Butter, The
Bailey, L.H.
Macmillan Company, New York, NY, 1918:
270 pp, hc
Illustrated $12.50

Book of Chowder, The
Hooker, Richard
Harvard Common Press, Harvard, MA, 1978:
136 pp, hc
Illustrated $12.50

Book of Entertainments and Frolics for All Occasions
Dawson, Mary, and Telford, Emma
David McKay, NY, 1911: 235 pp, hc
Illustrated $15.00

Book of Famous New Orleans Recipes
Peerless Printing Co., New Orleans, LA, ca.
1930: 57 pp
Spiral bound; illustrated $12.50

Book of Receipts and Helpful Information on Canning
Hazel-Atlas Glass Co., Wheeling, WV, 1926:
52 pp
Wraps; illustrated $6.00

Book of Recipes, A
Rudolph Wurlitzer Company; Tonawanda, NY,
1956: 172 pp, hc
Illustrated; mint condition; signed by company
president $25.00

Book of Unusual Soups, A
Chambers, Mary
Little, Brown and Company, Boston, MA,
1923: 162 pp, hc
Illustrated $12.50

Books and My Food
Cary, Elisabeth
Moffat, Yard and Co., NY, 1906: 235 pp,
hc $20.00

Boston Cooking School Cook Book, The
Farmer, Fannie Merritt
Little, Brown & Company, Boston, MA, 1906:
648 pp, hc
Illustrated $25.00

Bountiful Breakfasts
DeBaun, Stephen
Fireside Books, NY, 1970: 62 pp
Wraps $6.00

Boys' Cook Book, The
Brown, Helen and Philip
Doubleday, Garden City, NY, 1959: 285 pp, hc
First edition $25.00

Bratwurst Festival Cook Book
Bratwurst Festival, Bucyrus, OH, 1969:
unpaged
Spiral; signed recipes; first edition $9.00

Brazilian Cookery, Traditional and Modern
De Andrade, Margarette
A Casa Do Livro Eldorado, Rio de Janeiro,
Brazil, 1975: 349 pp
Wraps $12.00

Breads and Coffee Cakes with Homemade Starters, The
Roberts, Ada Lou
Hearthside Books, NY, 1967; 192 pp, hc
Illustrated $10.00

Brer Rabbit's New Book of Molasses Recipes
Penick & Ford, Ltd., 1937: 48 pp
Wraps; illustrated; molasses advertising
booklet $3.00

Brown Derby Cookbook
Doubleday Company, Garden City, NY, 1949:
272 pp, hc
Illustrated $30.00

Brown Gold: The Amazing Story of Coffee
Uribe, Andres
Random House, NY, 1954: 255 pp, hc
Illustrated $30.00

Bucks The Artist's County Cooks
Woman's Auxiliary of Trinity Chapel, Solebury,
PA, 1950: 238 pp
Spiral bound; first edition; signed and celebrity
recipes $20.00

Bull Cook and Authentic Historical Recipes and Practices
Herter, George
Self, Waseca, MN, 1969: 384 pp, hc
Illustrated $25.00

Bull Cook and Authentic Historical Recipes and Practices, Vol. 2
Herter, George
Self, Waseca, MN, 1967: 762 pp, hc
Illustrated $30.00

Busy People's Cookbook
Nemiro, Beverly
Random House, NY, 1971: 203 pp, hc
Dust jacket; first edition $9.00

Cake Cook Book, The
Rushing, Lilith, and Voss, Ruth
Chilton Books, NY, 1965: 200 pp, hc
First edition $15.00

Cakes and Characters
Henisch, Bridget
Prospect Books, London, 1984: 236 pp, hc
Illustrated $22.50

Cakes, Pastry and Dessert Dishes
Hill, Janet M.
Little, Brown and Co., Boston, MA, 1920: 276
pp, hc
Illustrated $22.50

Calendar of Dinners, A
Neil, Marion
Proctor and Gamble Co., Hamilton, Canada,
1923: 231 pp, hc
Illustrated $10.00

Calumet Cook Book
Calumet Baking Powder Co., Chicago: IL,
1910: 84 pp
Illustrated; advertising; Calumet Kid
character $9.00

Can-Opener Cookbook, The
Cannon, Poppy
Thomas Y. Crowell Company, NY, 1951: 281
pp, hc
Illustrated first edition $20.00

Candy Book, The
Sondheim, Claire
Culinary Arts Press, Reading, PA, 1938: 48 pp
Wooden cover; illustrated $12.50

Candy Hits
Pitts, ZaSu
Duell, Sloan and Pearce, NY, 1963: 93 pp
First edition; illustrations $17.50

Canning, Preserving and Jelly Making
Hill, Janet M.
Little, Brown and Company, MA, 1917: 197
pp
Wraps; illustrated $15.00

Cape Cod Cook Book
Gruver, Suzanne
Boston, 1936: 214 pp, hc $50.00

Cape Cod Kitchen Secrets
Yarmouth Branch Cape Cod Hospital Aid
Association, MA, 1949: 115 pp
Spiral; signed recipes; local ads $15.00

Caribbean Cookery
Grey, Winifred
Collins, London, 1971: 256 pp, hc $12.00

Carolina Housewife, The
Rutledge, Sarah
Babcock & Co., Charleston, SC, 1847:
hc $125.00

Carolina Housewife, The (1847) (Reprint)
Rutledge, Sarah
Univ. of S. Carolina Press, Columbia, SC,
1987: 236 pp
Wraps $12.00

Celebration of Cooking in America, A
Pet Incorporated, Elmsford, NY, 1984: 222 pp
Easel back, illustrated $9.00

Century Cook Book, The
Ronald, Mary
Appleton-Century Co., New York, NY, 1937:
635 pp, hc
Illustrated $12.50

**Chamberlain Sampler of American Cooking,
The**
Chamberlain, Narcisse
Hastings House, NY, 1961: 232 pp, hc
Dust jacket; illustrated $20.00

Charting Your Courses
St. George's Church, Newport, RI, 1948: 399
pp
First printing; spiral binding; local ads;
illustrated; signed recipes $20.00

Chef Paul Prudhomme's Louisiana Kitchen
Prudhomme, Paul
William Morrow and Co., NY, 1984: 351 pp,
hc
Illustrated $14.00

Child Life Cook Book
Judson, Claire Ingram
Rand McNally and Company, Chicago and
NY, 1926: 39 pp, hc
Illustrated $45.00

Children's Mission Cook Book, The
Children's Mission, Canton, OH 1937: 288
pp, hc
Fine condition $22.50

Chinese Cooking for American Kitchens
Lee, Calvin
G.P. Putnam's Sons, NY, 1958: 190 pp, hc
Dust jacket $14.00

Chocolate Bible, The
Marcus, Adrianne
G.P. Putnam's Sons, NY, 1979: 279 pp, hc
Illustrated $14.00

Chop Sticks
State Street Methodist Episcopal Church, Troy,
NY, 1883: 158 pp
Signed recipes; local ads $35.00

Christmas Memories with Recipes
Kitchen Arts and Letters, Farrar, Straus &
Giroux, NY, 1988: 315 pp, hc
First edition $15.00

**Chuckwagon Cooking from Marlboro
Country**
Phillip Morris, 1981: 28 pp
Wraps; illustrated $7.00

Church and Club Woman's Companion, The
Seranne, Ann, and Gaden, Eileen
Doubleday, Garden City, NY, 1964: 340 pp, hc
First edition $22.50

Civil War Cook Book, A
Smith, Myrtle Ellison
Lincoln Memorial University, Harrogate, TN,
1961: 268 pp, hc
Signed by author $25.00

**Closet of Sir Kenelme Digbie Opened, The
(1669) (Reprint)**
Mallinckrodt Chemical Works, St. Louis, MO,
1967: 312 pp
Wraps; slipcase $30.00

Coastal Carolina Cooking
Ocean View Memorial Hospital, Myrtle Beach,
SC, 1958: 328 pp
Spiral, signed recipes, local ads $15.00

Coffee Cookbook, The
Kaufmann, William
Doubleday, Garden City, NY, 1964: 191 pp,
hc $10.00

Collection Cookbook, The
Junior League of Austin; TX, 1976: 315 pp,
hc $15.00

Collection of Creole Recipes, A
Weiss, Caroline
Kiskatom Farm, New Orleans, LA, 1941: 47 pp
Spiral $9.00

Colonial Cook Book, The
Ladies Union, Flatbush Congretional Church,
Brooklyn, NY, 1911: 287 pp, hc
Signed recipes $20.00

**Colonial Kitchens, Their Furnishings and
Their Gardens**
Phipps, Frances
Hawthorn Books, New York, NY, 1972: 346
pp, hc
Illustrated $45.00

Come and Get It!
Martin, George
A.S. Barnes and Company, New York, NY,
1942: 1849 pp, hc $12.50

**Come and Get It: Montana Centennial
Cookbook**
Gallatin Canyon Women's Club, Gallatin, MO,
1964: 88 pp
Wraps $10.00

Come into the Kitchen
Lydia E. Pinkham, Company, Lynn, MA, 1930:
32 pp
Wraps, advertising booklet, very good
condition $4.00

Comfort Food
Garrison, Holly
Donald Fine, NY, 1988: 205 pp, hc $5.00

**Common Sense Cook Book of Tested
Recipes, The**
Ladies' Aid of Grace Evangelical Lutheran
Church, E. Stroudsburg, PA, ca. 1920: 100
pp
Wraps, local ads, signed recipes, fair
condition $8.00

Common Sense in the Household
Harland, Marion
Scribner, Armstrong & Co., NY, 1872: 556 pp,
hc $70.00

Common-place Book of Cookery
Grabhom, Robert
Northpoint Press, San Francisco, CA, 1985:
175 pp, hc $12.50

Compleat Housewife, The (1753) (Reprint)
Smith, Eliza
L.S. and P. London, 1973: 396 pp
Facsimile, wraps, folding plates $25.00

Compleat Housewife, The (Fifth edition)
Smith, Eliza
L.S. and P., London, 1732: 396 pp,
hc $650.00

Complete Book of Caribbean Cooking, The
Ortiz, Elisabeth
M. M. Evans, NY, 1973: 450 pp, hc $12.50

Complete Book of Outdoor Cookery, The
Brown, Helen, and Beard, James
Doubleday Co., Garden City, NY, 1955: 255
pp, hc $9.00

Complete Book of Table Settings, The
Hill, Amelia
Greystone Press, NY ca. 1940: 288 pp, hc
Illustrated $14.00

**Complete Guide to Preparing Baby Foods at
Home**
Castle, Sue
Doubleday Company, NY, 1973: 314 pp,
hc $7.00

Complete Holiday Cookbook, The
Favorite Recipes Press, Louisville, KY, 1964:
185 pp, hc
Illustrated $13.00

Complete Home Book of Baking
Seranne, Ann
Doubleday and Co., Garden City, NY, 1950:
386 pp, hc
Dust jacket $20.00

Complete Potato Cookbook
Bakalar, Ruth
Prentice Hall, Englewood Cliffs, NJ, 1969: 312
pp, hc $12.50

Complete Small Appliance Cookbook
Roberson, John and Marie
A.A. Wyn, NY, 1953: 299 pp, hc
Illustrated $12.50

Congressional Club Cook Book, The
The Congressional Club, Wash., DC, 1965:
510 pp
Signed by senator $30.00
1927: 799 pp, hc
First edition $75.00

Connecticut Cookbook, The
Woman's Club of Westport
Harper and Brothers, NY, 1944: 261 pp, hc
Illustrated $35.00

Cook Book
Baptist Church, Cape Neddick, ME, 1903: 94 pp
Wraps, local ads, signed recipes $25.00

Cook Book
King's Daughters of Grace Church, Ravenna,
OH, ca. 1930: 225 pp, hc
Signed recipes $18.50

Cook Book
United Daughters of the Confederacy,
Blackwater, MO, 1916: 165 pp
Wraps; signed recipes $15.00

Cook Book
Woman's Missionary Federation, Plentywood,
MT, 1942: 192 pp
Spiral, signed recipes $20.00

Cook Book and Business Directory
Blessed Sacrament Church, Albany, NY, ca.
1940: 48 pp
Local ads $6.00

Cook Book Decoder, The
Grosser, Arthur
Beaufort Books, NY, 1981: 203 pp, hc $10.00

Cook Book: Favorite Recipes
Sewing Circle; Belfast, ME, 1953: 104 pp
Spiral bound; local ads $10.00

Cook Book of the Woman's Educational Club
Woman's Educational Club, Toledo, OH,
1911: 256 pp, hc
Signed recipes, local ads $20.00

Cook Book: Tried and Tested Recipes
Houlton Country Club, Houlton, ME, 1929:
104 pp
Wraps, signed recipes, local ads $15.00

Cook Book: Twentieth Century Club
Oshkosh: WI, 1936: 144 pp
Wire spiral, signed recipes $15.00

Cook Book: Woman's Benevolent Society
First Baptist Church, New Haven, CT, 1920:
64 pp
Wraps; local ads $8.00

Cook with the Past Presidents
Rebekah Assembly, IOOF, 1931: 61 pp
Wraps; signed recipes $12.00

Cookbook
Girl's Friendly Society, Little Falls, NY, 1905:
68 pp
Wraps; signed recipes; local ads $14.00

Cookbook of the Seven Seas
Freuchen, Dagmar
M. Evans Co., NY, 1968: 256 pp, hc $10.00

Cookbook of the United Nations, The
Kraus, Barbara
Simon and Schuster, NY, 1970: 288 pp,
hc $12.50

Cooking a la Ritz
Diat, Louis
Lippencott, NY, 1941: 524 pp, hc
Illustrated $15.00

Cooking Bold and Fearless
Lane Books, Menlo Park, CA, 1967: 160 pp
Wraps $9.00

Cooking by the Calendar: A Family Weekly Cookbook
Hansen, Marilyn
Times Books, NY, 1978: 308 pp, hc $10.00

Cooking Legacy, A
Elverson, Virginia, and McLanahan, Mary Ann
Walker and Company, NY, 1975: 180 pp, hc
Illustrated; dust jacket; very good
condition $15.00

Cooking on a Ration
Mills, Marjorie
Houghton Mifflin Co., Boston, MA, 1943: 190
pp, hc $12.50

Cooking Out of Doors
Girl Scouts of the USA; NY 1960: 216 pp
Spiral; index tabs $11.00

Cooking Plain
Linsenmeyer, Helen Walker
Southern Illinois University Press, Carbondale,
IL, 1976: 275 pp, hc $12.50

Cooking the Jewish Way
Wald, Ann
Spring Books, London 1961: 207 pp, hc
Signed by author $12.50

Cooking with a Continental Flavor
Nationalities Service Center, Cleveland OH
1971: 341 pp
Spiral bound; signed recipes $12.50

Cooking with Cornelius: the Corning Cookbook
O'Donnell, Cornelius
Random House, NY 1982: 183 pp, hc
Illustrated $10.00

Cooking with Hougen
Hougen, Richard
Abingdon Press, Nashville, TN, 1960: 256 pp,
hc
Signed by author $12.50

Cooking with Love
Hall, Alice
International Atomic Energy Agency, for
Unicef Austria, 1972: 222 pp, hc
Illustrated; signed by author $15.00

Cooking with the Experts
Kaufman, William
Random House, NY, 1955: 248 pp, hc
Celebrity recipes and photographs $13.00

Cooking with Wholegrains
Orton, Helen and Vrest
Farrar, Straus and Young, NY, 1955: 64 pp,
  hc $6.00

Cook's Blessing, The
Taylor, Demetria
Random House, NY, 1965: 306 pp, hc
First printing $14.00

Cooks' Books
Coyle, L. Patrick
Facts on File, NY, 1985: 239 pp, hc
Illustrated $22.50

Cook's Choice: A Selection of Recipes
Rosenbach Museum & Library, Philadelphia,
  PA, 1982: 32 pp
Wraps $5.00

**Cooks, Gluttons and Gourmets: A History of
Cookery**
Wason, Betty
Doubleday, Garden City, NY, 1962: 381 pp, hc
First edition, illustrated $30.00

Cook's Guide, The
Francatelli, Charles Elmé
Richard Bentley and Son, London, 1877: 524
  pp, hc
Fair condition $60.00

Cook's Handbook, The
Blake, Mary
Carnation Company, Los Angeles, CA, 1951:
  95 pp
Spiral; illustrated $7.00

Cook's Oracle, The
Kitchener, William
Monroe and Francis, Boston, MA 1822: 380
  pp, hc
First American edition $175.00

Cook's Own Book, The
Lee, Mrs. N.K.M.
Oliver Felt, NY, 1865: 300 pp, hc $165.00

Cook's Own Book, The (1832) (Reprint)
Lee Mrs. N.K.M.
Arno Press, NY, 1972: 170 pp, hc $15.00

Cook's Tour of San Francisco
Muscatine, Doris
Charles Scribner's Sons, NY, 1963: 370 pp, hc
Dust jacket; illustrated $12.50

Cordon Bleu Cook Book, The
Lucas, Dione
Little Brown Company, Boston, MA, 1947:
  322 pp, hc $12.50

Corned Beef and Caviar
Hillis, Marjorie, and Foltz, Bertina
Bobbs-Merrill Company, NY, 1937: 196 pp, hc
First edition $22.50

Cosmopolitan Recipes
Woman's Improvement Club, St. Helena, CA,
  1905: 99 pp
Local ads $17.50

Country Gourmet Cookbook
Roth, Sherrill and Gil
Workman Publishing, NY 1981: 416 pp,
  hc $11.00

**Country Home Book of Kitchen Hints and
Selected Recipes**
Brewer, Lucile
GLF Flour and Co-op, 1951: 112 pp
Illustrated $8.00

Country Inns of America Cookbook
Reid, Robert
Holt, Rinehart and Winston, NY, 1982: 180 pp
Illustrated; first edition $22.50

Country Kitchen, The
Lutes, Della
Little, Brown & Co., Boston, MA, 1936: 264
  pp, hc
Dust jacket $25.00

Country Kitchen Cook Book
Webb Publishing Co., St. Paul, MN, 1924: 151
  pp
Wraps $8.00

Country Kitchen Cook Book, The
Heth, Edward Harris
Simon and Schuster, NY, 1968: 238 pp, hc
First printing $12.50

Court Dishes of China
Davis, Lucille
Charles E. Tuttle Co., Rutland, VT, 1966: 243
  pp, hc
Illustrated; first edition $20.00

Cracklin Bread and Asfidity
Solomon, J.
University of Alabama, AL, 1979: 215 pp,
  hc $17.50

**Craig Claiborne's Favorites from The New
York Times**
Claiborne, Craig
Bonanza Books, NY, 1972: 310 pp, hc $10.00

Creole Kitchen Cook Book
Cooper, Virginia
Naylor Company, San Antonio, TX, 1946: 248
  pp, hc $15.00

Cross Creek Cookery
Rawlings, Marjorie Kinnan
Charles Scribner's Sons, NY, 1942: 230 pp
Decorated hardcover $45.00

Cruising Cookbook, The
Jones, Russell, and Norton, C.
W.W. Norton and Co., NY 1949: 302 pp, hc
First edition $11.00

Cuisines of Mexico, The
Kennedy, Diana
Harper and Row, NY 1972: 378 pp, hc
Illustrated; first edition $17.50

Culinary American
Brown, Cora and Bob
Bobrich Library, NY, 1961: 417 pp, hc $50.00

Curries from the Sultan's Kitchen
Ady, Doris
Drake Publishers, NY 1973: 126 pp
Spiral $7.00

Cy Littlebee's Guide to Cooking Fish and Game
Nagel, Werner
Missouri Conservation Commission, MO,
    1960: 131 pp
Wraps; signed recipes; woods and
    foodlore $10.00

Daily Dessert Calendar, The
Wayne, Margaret
Bone Brothers Dallas, TX 1924: unpaged
Advertising booklet with daily recipes $6.00

Daily New Food, A
Ladies of St. Paul's Church; Morrisania, NY,
    1885: 128 pp, hc
Illustrated; signed recipes; local ads $45.00

Dainty Desserts for Dainty People
Chas. B. Knox Gelatine Co, Johnstown, NY
    1924: 41 pp
Wraps, Illustrated $6.00

Dallas Woman's Forum Cook Book
Dallas Woman's Forum, Dallas, TX, 1949: 129 pp
Spiral; illustrated; signed recipes; first
    edition $14.00

Dates
Hills Brothers Company; NY, 1923: 16 pp
Wraps; illustrated $5.00

DC Superheroes Super Healthy Cookbook
Saltzman, Garlan, Grodner
Warner Books, NY, 1981: 97 pp
Wraps; illustrated; first printing $12.50

Del Monte Kitchen Cookbook
Del Monte Corporation, San Francisco, CA,
    1972: 150 pp
Ring binder; illustrated; first edition $15.00

Delectable Past, The
Aresty, Esther
Simon and Schuster, New York, NY, 1964:
    254 pp, hc
Dust jacket $30.00

Delightful Food
Salter, Marjorie, and Whitney, Adrianne
Sidgwick and Jackson, London, 1957: 148 pp,
    hc
Illustrated; foreward by Noel Coward $15.00

Delineator Cook Book
Van Rensselaer, Flora and Martha
Butterick Publishing Company, NY 1928: 789
    pp, hc
Illustrated $15.00

Diamond Spectacle Recipes Book
Diamond Trademark Spectacles, NY, 1873: 49
    pp
Wraps; local advertisements; advertising
    booklet $8.00

Dictionary of American Food and Drink, The
Mariani, John
Ticknor and Fields, NY 1983: 477 pp, hc
Dust jacket $14.00

Diners Club Cookbook, The
Waldo, Myra
Gramercy Publishers, NY, 1959: 241 pp,
    hc $12.50

Dining In America
Grover, Kathryn
Univ. of Massachusetts Press, Amherst, MA,
    1987: 217 pp
Illustrated $12.50

Dinner Party Cookbook, The
Lane Books, Menlo Park, CA, 1967: 160 pp
Illustrated $9.00

Domestic Manners of the Americans (1832) (Reprint)
Trollope, Frances
Alfred A. Knopf, NY, 1949: 454 pp, hc
First edition $17.50

Down on the Farm Cook Book
Worth, Helen
Greenberg Publishers, NY 1943: 322 pp, hc
Dust jacket $20.00

Dr. Chase's Recipes
Chase, A.W.
R.A. Beal, Ann Arbor, MI, 1870: 384 pp
Illustrated, 6th edition $45.00

Dr. Miles Candy Book
Dr. Miles Medical Company, Elkhart, IN, ca.
    1912: 33 pp
Wraps; advertising leaflet for patent
    medicines; illustrated; $7.00

Ducks Unlimited Cookbooks
Favorite Recipes Press, Nashville, TN, 1982:
    200 pp
Spiral $8.00

Dunkard-Dutch Cook Book
Applied Arts Publishers, Lebanon, PA, 1975:
    42 pp
Wraps; illustrated $3.00

Early American Beverages
Brown, John Hull
Bonanza Books, New York, NY 1966: 171 pp, hc
Illustrated $12.50

Early American Cookbook, The
O'Connor, Hyla
Rutledge Books, NY, 1974: 160 pp, hc
Illustrated $15.00

Early American Herb Recipes
Brown, Alice Cooke
Charles E. Tuttle Co, VT, 1966: 152 pp, hc
Illustrated $20.00

Early American Inns and Taverns
Lathrop, Elise
Tudor Publishing Co., NY 1935: 365 pp, hc
Illustrated; first edition in slipcase $55.00

Early American Recipes
Frost, Heloise
Phillips Publishers, Newton, MA, 1953: 112 pp
Spiral; illustrated $12.50

Easter Idea Book
Adams, Charlotte
M. Barrows Publishing, NY, 1954: 192 pp, hc
Dust jacket; illustrated $11.00

Eat, Drink and Be Merry in Maryland
Stieff, Frederick P.
G.P. Putnam's Sons, NY, 1932: 326 pp, hc
Illustrated $40.00

Economical Cook Book, The
Paul, Sara
Greenhut-Siegel Cooper Co., NY, 1905: 338
    pp, hc
Illustrated $15.00

Edith Bunker's All in the Family Cookbook
Boe, Eugene, editor
Popular Library, NY 1971: 250 pp
Wraps; signed by author $5.00

Eggbeater Book, The
Thornton, Don
Arbor House, NY, 1983: 160 pp, hc
Illustrated $12.50

Eight Immortal Flavors
Kan, Johnny
Howell-North Books, Berkeley, CA, 1963: 246
    pp, hc
First edition $30.00

Electric Epicure's Cookbook, The
Cannon, Poppy
Thomas Y. Crowell, NY, 1961: 340 pp, hc
Illustrated; first edition $12.50

Electric Refrigerator Menus and Recipes
Bradley, Alice
General Electric Company, Cleveland, OH,
    1927: 144 pp
Illustrated $15.00

Elena's Favorite Foods California Style
Zelayeta, Elena
Prentice-Hall, Englewood Cliffs, NJ, 1967: 310
    pp, hc $10.00

*Elena's Famous Mexican and Spanish
Recipes*
Zelayeta, Elena
Self; San Francisco, CA, 1950: 127 pp
Spiral $8.00

Elinor Fettiplace's Receipt Book
Spurling, Hilary
Viking, NY, 1986: 250 pp, hc
Dust jacket $22.50

Elsie's Cook Book
Elsie the Cow
Wheelwright, 1952: 374 pp, hc
Illustrated; dust jacket; first edition $17.50

Emma Jane's Souvenir Cook Book
Moncure, Blanche
Self, 1937: 87 pp
Wraps $15.00

Encore: Favorite Dishes of Famous Musicians
Minnesota Home Economics Association,
    Minneapolis, MN, 1958: 308 pp, hc
Signed celebrity recipe; first edition $17.50

Encyclopedia of Practical Gastronomy
Ali-Bab (E. Benson, trans.)
McGraw Hill Book Company, NY, 1974: 471
    pp, hc
First American edition $40.00

English Bread and Yeast Cookery
David, Elizabeth
Viking, NY, 1979: 572 pp, hc
First edition $35.00

*English Country House Cooking: A Family
Cookery Book*
Stanley, Fortune
Pall Mall Press, London, 1972: 160 pp
Illustrated $14.00

Enterprising Housekeeper, The
Johnson, Helen Louise
Enterprise Manufacturing Company,
    Philadelphia, PA, 1906: 97 pp
Wraps; illustrated $10.00

Entree Cook Book, The
Epworth League; Laurens, NY, 1899: 38 pp
Local ads $12.00

Epicurean, The
Ranhofer, Charles
1894: 1183 pp
Lavishly illustrated; first edition $275.00

Epicurean, The
Ranhofer, Charles
John Wiley Publisher, Chicago, IL, 1920
edition $200.00

Epicure's Companion, The
Bunyard, Edward and Lorna
J.M. Dent, London 1937: 539 pp, hc $12.50

Episcopal Epicure, The
St. Mark's Episcopal Church, Mesa, AZ, 1961:
98 pp
Spiral $10.00

Ergatikan Cook Book, The
Ergatikan Circle of St. Paul's ME Church,
South, Fresno, CA, 1905: 195 pp
Wraps; local ads $17.50

Essay on Bread, An (1758) (Reprint)
Jackson, H.
Mallinckrodt Chemical Works, St. Louis, MO,
1966: 55 pp
Wraps; slipcase $25.00

Everybody's Cookbook
Lord, Isabel
Harcourt, Brace and Co., NY, 1937: 945 pp,
hc
Illustrated; dust jacket $15.00

Experienced English Housekeeper
Raffald, Elizabeth
London, 1776: 382 pp, hc
Illustrated $150.00

Fading Feast
Sokolov, Raymond
Farrar, Straus, Giroux, 1981: 276 pp, hc
Dust jacket; first edition $20.00

Fairs and Fetes
Benton, Caroline
Dana Estes and Company, Boston, MA, 1912:
168 pp
Illustrated $25.00

Famous American Recipes Cookbook, The
Roberson, John and Marie
Prentice-Hall, Englewood Cliffs, NJ, 1957: 258
pp, hc
First edition $15.00

Famous Chicken Recipes
National Chicken Cooking Contest, 1959:
unpaged
Wraps; signed; winning recipes $4.00

Famous Old Receipts
Smith, Jacqueline
John Winston Co., Philadelphia, PA, 1908:
383 pp, hc
Signed recipes; food lore $45.00

Famous Woodstock Cooks
Barile, M., and Michaels, J.
M. & J.
JMB Publications, 1985: 125 pp
First edition, signed by contributors $25.00

Fannie Farmer Junior Cook Book, The
Perkins, Wilma Lord
Little, Brown and Company, Boston, MA,
1942: 208 pp, hc
First edition $12.50

Farm and Household Cyclopaedia, The
F.M. Lupton, NY, 1885: 544 pp, hc
Illustrated $15.00

Farm Cook and Rule Book, The
Nichols, Nell
Harcourt Brace Jovanovich, NY, 1976: 303 pp,
hc $17.50

Farm Journal's Complete Pie Cookbook
Doubleday, Garden City, NY, 1965: 309 pp, hc
Illustrated $8.00

Farmhouse Cookbook, The
Tarr, Yvonne Young
Quadrangle, NY, 1973: 581 pp, hc $17.50

Farm Journal's Country Cookbook
Nichols, Nell
Doubleday and Co., Garden City, NY, 1959:
420 pp, hc
Illustrated $20.00

Fashions in Foods in Beverly Hills
Beverly Hills Woman's Club, CA, 1930: 223
pp, hc
Signed celebrity recipes; illustrated $40.00

Father Was A Gourmet
Truax, Carol
Doubleday, Garden City, NY, 1965: 160 pp, hc
Dust jacket; signed by author $15.00

Favorite Recipes
First Congregational Church: Kansas, MO,
1914: 64 pp
Wraps; local ads; signed recipes $12.50

Favorite Recipes
Woman's Club, Bayside, NY, 1919: 65 pp
Wraps; signed recipes; local ads $14.00

Favorite Recipes of California Winemakers
Hecker, Lee
Wine Advisory Board; San Francisco, CA,
1963: 128 pp
Spiral; signed recipes $15.00

Favorite Recipes of New York
Beirne, Rose
Favorite Recipes Press, Montgomery, AL,
1964: 188 pp
Spiral; signed recipes $10.00

Favorite Recipes of the Southwest
Favorite Recipes Press, Louisville, KY, 1965:
    184 pp
Spiral; illustrated $9.00

Feast: A Tribal Cookbook
True Light Beavers
Doubleday; New York, NY, 1972: 264 pp
Wraps; illustrated; commune cooking $12.50

Feast Day Cookbook
Burton, Katherine, and Ripperger, Helmut
David McKay Co., NY, 1951: 194 pp,
    hc $20.00

Feasts for All Seasons
deGroot, Roy
Alfred Knopf, NY, 1966: 763 pp, hc $14.00

Festival Cookbook, The
Good, Phyllis
Good Books, Lancaster, PA, 1983: 223 pp
Spiral; signed recipes $10.00

Festival of Frozen Food Recipes
National Frozen Food Association, Hershey,
    PA, 1973: 156 pp
Wraps; illustrated cut-out bookmarks $7.50

Few Cooking Suggestions, A
Stroud, Della
Proctor and Gamble Company, 1914: 16 pp
Wraps; illustrated $5.00

Fifteenth Century Cookry Boke, A
Anderson, John
Scribners; NY, 1962: 92 pp, hc
Illustrated $20.00

Fifty Years in a Maryland Kitchen
Howard, Mrs. B.C.
J.B. Lippencott, Philadelphia, PA, 1873: 230
    pp, hc $65.00

**Fifty Years in a Maryland Kitchen (1873)
(Reprint)**
Howard, Mrs. B.C.
Dover, Mineola, NY, 1986: 234 pp
Wraps $6.00

Fifty Years of Prairie Cooking
Szathmary, Louis
Arno Press, NY, 1973: 250 pp, hc $22.50

Fine Food, Wine and Pickled Pine
Cole, Ann
David McKay Company, NY, 1962: 212 pp,
    hc
Illustrated; first edition $20.00

Fine Old New England Recipes
Morrow, Kay
Culinary Arts Press, Reading, PA, 1936: 48
    pp
Wooden cover; ring binder $15.00

Finger Lickin Barbecue
Butel, Jane
Workman Publishing, NY, 1982: 96 pp,
    hc $10.00

Fire Island Cook Book
Hull, Georgiana
Cornerstone Library, NY, 1971: 127 pp
Wraps; local food lore $8.00

Fireside Cookbook, The
Beard, James
Simon and Schuster, NY, 1949: 322 pp, hc
Illustrated $30.00

First Church Congregational, Cook Book
First Church Congregational, Swampscott,
    MA, 1941: 82 pp
Spiral; signed recipes; local ads $12.50

First Dutch Reformed Cook Book
Pompton Plains, NJ, 1889: 119:
Wraps; local ads; signed recipes; fair
    condition $20.00

First Ladies Cook Book, The
Klapthor, Margaret
Parents' Magazine Press, NY, 1965: 228 pp, hc
Dust jacket; illustrated $22.50

Fish and Game Cook Book
Botsford, Harry
Cornell Maritime Press, NY, 1947: 290 pp, hc
First edition $12.50

500 Dakota Recipes
South Dakota Federated Woman's Clubs,
    Yankton, SD, 1961: 157 pp
Spiral $12.50

500 Recipes by Request
Hall, Jeanne and Ebner, Belle
Bramhall House: 1948, 318 pp, hc
Dust jacket; very good $15.00

**Five Star Recipes: Recipes from Friends of
Mamie and Ike**
Golden Press, NY, 1974: 272 pp, hc
Illustrated; signed celebrity recipes $25.00

Flavor Zone Electric Cookery
Westinghouse Electric Company, Mansfield,
    OH, ca. 1925: 70 pp
Illustrated $7.00

Flower City Cook Book
Leiter, Mrs. H.
Berith Kodesh Sisterhood, Rochester, NY,
    1925: 219 pp, hc
Signed recipes; first edition $18.00

Folk Medicine
Jarvis, D.C.
Henry Holt and Company, NY, 1958: 182 pp,
    hc
Food lore $8.00

Folk Wines, Cordials and Brandies
Jagendorf, J.A.
Vanguard Press, New York, NY, 1963: 414
pp, hc
Illustrated $15.00

**Folklore and Odysseys of Food and
Medicinal Plants**
Lehner, Ernst and Johanna
Noonday Press, NY, 1973: 128 pp
Wraps; illustrated $9.00

Fondue, Chafing Dish and Casserole Cookery
Murphy, Margaret
Hawthorne Books, NY, 1969: 290 pp,
hc $8.00

Food
Root, Waverly
Simon and Schuster, NY, 1980: 602 pp, hc
Illustrated $27.50

**Food and Cookery for the Sick and
Convalescent**
Farmer, Fannie Merritt
Little, Brown Co., Boston, MA, 1907: 289 pp,
hc $17.50
1917: 305 pp, hc
Illustrated; local ads $20.00

Food and Drink in Great Britain
Wilson, Anne
Harper and Row, NY, 1974: 472 pp, hc
Illustrated $15.00

Food and Drink of Mexico
Booth, George
Ward Ritchie Press, Los Angeles, CA, 1964:
190 pp, hc $15.00

Food and Finesse: The Bride's Bible
Charpentier, Henri
Self; Chicago, IL, 1945: 981 pp, hc
Signed and numbered by author $125.00

Food Editor's Favorite Recipes Cookbook
Ostmann, Barbara, and Baker, Jane
Weathervane Books, NY, 1986: 314 pp, hc
Dust jacket $8.00

Food for the Body, For the Soul
Youngren, Mrs. Frances
Moody Press Bible Institute, Chicago, IL, 1943:
128 pp
Spiral $12.50

Food from the Arab World
Khayat, Marie, and Keatinge, Margaret
Khayats, Beirut, Lebanon, 1959: 163 pp, hc
Illustrated $15.00

Food Garden, The
Blair, Laurence and Edna
Macmillan Company, NY 1942: 147 pp, hc
Illustrated; first edition $17.50

Food in Antiquity
Brothwell, Don and Patricia
Thames and Hudson, London, 1969: 248 pp,
hc
Illustrated $20.00

Food is a Four Letter Word
Elisofon, Eliot, and Lee, Gypsy Rose
Rinehart and Company, NY, 1948: 176 pp,
hc $12.50

Food Lover's Companion, The
Jones, Evan
Harper & Row, NY, 1979: 380 pp, hc
First edition $25.00

Food Processor Baking Magic
Hemingway, Mary, and de Lima, Suzanne
Hastings House, NY, 1978: 221 pp, hc
Illustrated $7.00

**Food That Really Schmecks; Mennonite
Country Cooking**
Staebler, Edna
Follett Publishing Co., Chicago, IL, 1968: 297
pp, hc
First edition $15.00

**Food Traditions of Jews from the Soviet
Union**
Sitomer, Marion
Federation of Jewish Philanthropies 1982: 78
pp
Wraps; illustrated $10.00

Foodbook, The
Trager, James
Grossman Publishers, NY, 1970: 578 pp, hc
Illustrated $22.50

Foods and Homemaking
Greer, Carlotta
Allyn and Bacon, NY, 1933: 635 pp, hc
Illustrated $12.50

Foods from Sunny Lands
Wallace, Lily
Hills Brothers Company, 1925, unpaged
Wraps; illustrated $8.00

Foods of Long Island
Katalinich, Peggy
Newsday, NY, 1985: 192 pp, hc
Illustrated $15.00

Foods of Old New England
Mosser, Marjorie
Doubleday, NY 1947: 428 pp, hc
Dust jacket $12.50

Ford Treasury of Favorite Recipes
Kennedy, Nancy
Simon and Schuster, NY, 1950: 252 pp
Illustrated; spiral bound; first edition in
series $15.00

Four Winds Cookbook, The
Baumann, Cyril, and Harris, Beulah
Thomas Crowell, NY 1954: 292 pp, hc $12.50

French Chef Cookbook
Child, Julia
Alfred Knopf, NY, 1968: 440 pp, hc $17.50

French Pastry Book, The
Crippen, Alice Hotchkiss
Brentano's, NY, 1926: 103 pp, hc
Illustrated; dust jacket $15.00

French's Never-A-Boring-Meal-Wheel
R.T. French Company, ca. 1976: 65 pp
Mechanical advertising booklet; menus
revolve $6.00

Fresh from the Garden State
NJ Cancer Society 1981: 189 pp
Spiral; signed recipes $10.00

From Famous Kitchens: Brand Names Cook Book
English, Marguerite editor
Dow Company, Midland, MI 1961: 384 pp, hc
Illustrated $8.00

From Sturbridge Kitchens
The Evening Women's Club, Sturbridge, MA,
1957: 192 pp
Spiral; signed recipes $15.00

Fun Food Cookbook, The
Davis, Adele
Self, 1975: 245 pp, hc $6.00

Fun with Food: for the Busy Maryland Housewife
Roeder, Virginia
Baltimore Evening Sun, MD, ca. 1960 96 pp
Wraps $10.00

Gala Day Luncheons
Burrell, Caroline B.
Dodd, Mead & Company, New York, NY,
1901: 221 pp, hc
Illustrated $35.00

Gasparilla Cookbook
Junior League of Tampa, FL, 1961: 326 pp
Spiral; signed recipes $20.00

Gastronomic Bibliography
Bitting, Katherine Golden
Holland Press: London, 1981: 718 pp, hc
Illustrated $90.00

Gastronomical Me
Fisher, M.F.K.
Duell, Sloane and Pearce, NY, 1943: 295 pp,
hc
First edition $40.00

Gem Chopper Cook Book
Sargent and Company, NY, 1902: unpaged
Illustrated; advertising; cloth cover $7.00

Gems of the Household
Northrop, Henry
A.B. Kuhlman and Co., Chicago, IL, 1893:
720 pp, hc
Illustrated $35.00

Gene Hovis's Uptown, Down Home Cookbook
Hovis, Gene
Little, Brown Co., Boston, MA, 1987: 235 pp,
hc
First edition $10.00

General Foods Cook Book
General Foods Corp., NY, 1932: 370 pp, hc
Illustrated $17.50

General Mills Short Course on Cake
General Mills, Minneapolis, MN, 1932: 174
pp, hc
Illustrated $30.00

General's Diary of Treasured Recipes, A
Dorn, Frank
Cookbook Collectors Library, 1963: 341 pp,
hc $20.00

Gentleman's Companion: Exotic Cookery and Drink
Baker, Charles
Crown Publishers, NY, 1946: hc $45.00

Gifts from Your Kitchen
Laklan, Carli, and Thomas, Frederick
M.M. Barrows, NY, 1955: 256 pp, hc
Illustrated $12.50

Girl's Life Eighty Years Ago, A
Bowne, Eliza
Charles Scribner's Sons, 1887: 239 pp, hc
Illustrated $25.00

Girl's Own Indoor Book
Peters, Charles
Lippincott Company, Philadelphia, PA, 1888:
548 pp, hc
Illustrated; very good condition $17.50

Guide to Good Things to Eat
Laurel Park Social Club, Northampton, MA,
1900: 64 pp
Wraps $12.50

Gladys Taber's Stillmeadow Cook Book
Taber, Gladys
J.B. Lippincott Company, NY, 1965: 335 pp,
hc $30.00

Glens Falls Cookery Book
Ladies' Aid Society, NY, 1923: 325 pp, hc
Local ads; signed recipes $20.00

Glow of Candlelight
Murphy, Patricia
Prentice-Hall, NJ, 1961: 260 pp, hc
Illustrated; dust jacket; $12.50

Glow of Candlelight: The Story of Patricia Murphy
Murphy, Patricia
Prentice Hall, 1961: 260 pp, hc
Illustrated; first edition $12.50

Gold Cook Book, The
De Gouy, Louis
Greenberg Publisher, 1947: 1098 pp
  hc $22.50

Gold Medal Home Service Recipes
Crocker, Betty
Washburn and Crosby Company, ca. 1925
Recipe cards in box $15.00

Golden Gate Gourmet
Robertson, R.
Golden Gate Gourmet Co., San Francisco, CA,
  1958: 177 pp, hc $12.50

Golden Gate Gourmet
Robertson, Roxana
Golden Gate Gourmet Co., San Francisco, CA,
  1958: 177 pp, hc
Dust jacket; signed celebrity recipes $12.50

Gone with the Wind Cook Book
Pebeco Toothpaste, ca. 1939: 48 pp
Wraps; illustrated $25.00

Good Egg, The
White, Loretta
Rand McNally & Co., NY, 1959: 192 pp
Spiral $12.50

Good Goodies
Dworkin, Stand and Floss
Rodale Press, Emmaus, PA, 1974: 280 pp,
  hc $11.00

Good Heart and a Light Hand
Gaskin, Ruth
Simon and Schuster, NY, 1968: 110 pp
Spiral; illustrated $15.00

Good Housekeeping Everyday Cook Book
Curtis, Isabel
Reilly and Britton Co., Chicago, IL, 1909: 320
  pp, hc
Illustrated $15.00

Good Maine Food
Mosser, Marjorie
Doubleday & Company, 1939: 424 pp, hc
Illustrated $25.00

Good Things To Eat and How To Prepare Them
Larkin Company, 1906: 80 pp
Wraps; illustrated $12.50

Good Things to Eat Made With Bread
Neil, Marion
The Fleischmanns Company, 1913: 32 pp
Wraps; illustrations; advertising booklet for
  Fleischmanns yeast $5.00

Goodholme's Domestic Cyclopaedia of Practical Information
Goodholme, Todd
Scribner's and Sons, NY, 1889: 652 pp, hc
Illustrated $35.00

Gourmet Cooking for Free
Angier, Bradford
Stackpole Books, Harrisburg, PA, 1970: 190
  pp, hc
First edition $11.00

Grace Harley's Southern Cookbook
Hartley, Grace
Galahad Books, NY, 1976: 300 pp, hc
Signed recipes $15.00

Graham Kerr Cookbook, The
Kerr, Graham
Doubleday and Company, Garden City, NY,
  1969: 284 pp, hc
First edition $14.00

Grand Union Cook Book
Compton, Margaret
Grand Union Tea Company 1902: 322 pp, hc
Illustrated $15.00

Grandma Rose's Book of Sinfully Delicious Cakes
Naftalin, Rose
Random House, NY, 1975: 255 pp, hc $15.00

Grandma Rose's Book of Sinfully Delicious Snacks
Naftalin, Rose
Random House, NY, 1978: 259 pp, hc $15.00

Grandma's Cooking (Reprint)
Keller, Alan
Gramercy Publishers, NY, 1955: 240 pp, hc
Dust jacket $8.00

Grandmother in the Kitchen
Adamson, Helen
Crown Publishers, NY, 1965: 308 pp, hc
Dust jacket $12.50

Grass Roots Cookbook, The
Anderson, Jean
Times Books, NY, 1977: 334 pp, hc
Illustrated $15.00

Great American Ice Cream Book, The
Dickson, Paul
Atheneum, NY, 1973: 206 pp, hc
Illustrated $12.50

Great British Cooking: A Well Kept Secret
Garmey, Jane
Random House, NY, 1981: 295 pp, hc $10.00

Great Classic Recipes of Europe
Lesberg, Sandy
Prentice Hall, Englewood Cliffs, NJ, 1972: 224
  pp, hc
Illustrated $14.00

Great Cooks and Their Recipes
Willan, Anne
McGraw Hill, NY, 1977: 199 pp, hc
Illustrated $22.50

Great Dinners from Life
Graves, Eleanor
Time-Life Books, NY, 1969: 239 pp, hc
Illustrated $35.00

Great Home Cooking in America
Doubleday, Garden City, NY, 1976: 213 pp, hc
Illustrated $12.00

Green Thumb Cookbook, The
Moyer, Anne
Rodale Press, Emmaus, PA, 1977: 316 pp, hc
Illustrated $12.00

Greenwich Village Cookbook
Kramer, Vivian
Fairchild Publications, NY, 1969: 511 pp, hc
Dust jacket $20.00

Greenwich Village Gourmet
Wheeler, Clementine
Bryan Publications, NY, 1949: 127 pp
Spiral; celebrity recipes $15.00

Greyston Bakery Cookbook, The
Glassman, Helen, and Postal, Susan
Shambhala, Boston, MA, 1986: 148 pp, hc
First edition $20.00

Guide to Distinctive Dining
Noble, Ruth
Berkshire Publishing Company, MA 1954: 132
  pp
Spiral; illustrated $8.00

Guild Cook Book and Birthday Calendar
Women's Guild, First Congregational Church,
  Ainsworth, NE, 1947: 96 pp
Wraps; local ads; signed recipes $12.50

Hadassah Cookery
Livingston Chapter, Livingston, NJ, 1976: 147
  pp, hc $9.00

Harvest Sale Cook Book
Ladies Aid of Malden Hospital, MA, 1916: 78
  pp
Charity $15.00

Hawaii Cookbook and Backyard Luau
Toupin, Elizabeth
1967: 216 pp, hc
Illustrated $15.00

Hawaii Cooks
Yardley, Maili
Charles E. Tuttle Company, Rutland, VT,
  1970: 112 pp, hc
Dust jacket $22.50

Hay Dieting Menus and Receipts
Boyer, Josephine, and Cowdin, Katherine
Charles Scribners Sons, NY, 1936: 404 pp,
  hc $17.50

Health Food Dictionary with Recipes, The
Carroll, Anstice, and Vona, Embree
Prentice-Hall, Englewood Cliffs, NJ, 1973: 200
  pp, hc
Illustrated $10.00

Hearthstone, The
Holloway, Laura
L.P. Miller, Philadelphia, PA, 1888: 560 pp
Very good condition; illustrated $45.00

*Helen Gurley Brown's Single Girl's
Cookbook*
Brown, Helen G.
Bernard Geis Associates, NY, 1969: 405 pp,
  hc $11.00

*Henry's Cook Book and Household
Companion*
John Henry and Co., New York, NY, 1883:
  unpaged
Wraps; illustrated; fine condition $8.00

Herbs for the Medieval Household
Freeman, Margaret
Metropolitan Museum of Art, NY, 1971: 48
  pp, hc
Illustrated $10.00

Herbs, Spices and Specialties
North Country Garden Club, Long Island, NY,
  ca. 1960: 163 pp
Spiral $6.00

Highlander's Cookbook
Cameron, Sheila
Ward Ritchie Press, Los Angeles, CA, 1966:
  113 pp, hc $12.50

History and Virtues of Cyder, The
French, R.R.
St. Martin's Press, NY, 1982: 200 pp,
Fine condition $15.00

History of a Mouthful of Bread
Mace, Jean
Harper & Brothers, NY, 1871: 398 pp,
  hc $65.00

Holiday Candy and Cookie Cook Book
DeGros, J.H.
Arco Publishing Co., NY, 1963: 144 pp, hc
Illustrated $12.50

Holiday Cook Book, The
Peter Pauper Press, Mt. Vernon, NY, 1950: 61
  pp, hc
Illustrated $12.50

Holiday Magazine Book of the World's Fine Food
Simon and Schuster, NY, 1960: 260 pp, hc
Illustrated $25.00

Hollywood Glamor Cook Book
Mariposa
Glamor Publications, Miami, FL, 1941: 427
pp, hc $25.00

Home Book of Scottish Cookery
King, Aileen and Dunnett, Fiona
Faber and Faber, London, 1967: 124 pp,
hc $12.50

Home Canning for Victory
Pierce, Anne
M. Barrows and Co., NY, 1942: 106 pp, hc
Illustrated $15.00

Home Comfort Cook Book
Wrought Iron Range Company, 1924: 211
pp
Wraps; illustrated $8.00

Home Cooking
Colwin, Laurie
Alfred Knopf, NY, 1988, 193 pp, hc
First edition $17.00

Home Grown
Lutes, Della
Little, Brown and Co., Boston, MA, 1937: 272
pp, hc
Signed by author $20.00

Home Helps
Rorer, Sarah Tyson
N.K. Fairbank Company, Chicago, IL, 1900:
70 pp
Local ads; wraps $12.50

Home Helps: A Pure Food Cook Book
N.K. Fairbank Company, 1910: 80 pp
Wraps; illustrated $9.00

Home Maker Magazine, Vol. 1, The
Hardland, Marion, editor
NY, 1888–89: 490 pp, hc
Illustrated $45.00

Homemade Bread
Food Editors of Farm Journal
Doubleday & Co., NY, 1969: 152 pp, hc
Dust jacket $9.00

Homemade Ice Cream and Cake
Manning, Elise
Doubleday, Garden City, NY, 1976: 228 pp,
hc
Illustrated $12.00

Homemade is Better
Tupperware Home Parties, 1981: 144 pp, hc
Illustrated $9.00

Homestyle Korean Cooking in Pictures
Ok, Cho Joong
Japan Publications, Tokyo, 1981: 96 pp, hc
Illustrated $10.00

Honey of A Cookbook
Nickerson Farms, MO, 1972: 58 pp
Spiral $8.00

Honor Among Cooks
Spahr, Mary
William A. Church, Co., Ithaca, NY, 1939: 106
pp
Spiral; signed recipes $12.50

Horizon Cookbook
Hale, William
American Heritage Publishing Co., PA, 1968:
768 pp, hc
Illustrated $35.00

Horn of Plenty, The
Harvey, Peggy
Atlantic, Little Brown, Boston, MA, 1964: 264
pp, hc
Celebrity recipes $12.50

Hotel St Francis Cook Book, The
Hirtzler, Victor
Hotel Monthly Press, 1919: 432 pp
Illustrated; recipes for a year of restaurant
service $100.00

House at Hyde Park, The
Steeholm, Clara and Hardy
Viking, NY, 1950: 277 pp, hc
Fine condition; dust jacket $25.00

House Servant's Directory
Robert, Roberts
Self, Boston, MA, 1827: 180 pp, hc $1,200.00

Household Companion
Flick, Lawrence, and others
Lawrence
Uplift Publishing Co., Philadelphia, PA, 1909:
357 pp, hc
Illustrated $35.00

Household Searchlight Recipe Book
Migliaro, Titus, et al
Household Magazine, Topeka, KA, 1939: 328
pp, hc
Thumb tabs; revised edition; $12.50

Housekeeper's Apple Book, The
MacKay, Gertrude
Little, Brown and Company, Boston, MA,
1917: 122 pp, hc $12.50

Housekeeping in Old Virginia (1879) (Reprint)
Tyree, Marion Cabell
Cookbook Collectors Library; Louisville, KY,
1965: 528 pp
Facsimile reprint $22.50

Housewifery
Balderston, Lydia
Lippincott Co., NY, 1936: 352 pp, hc
Illustrated $20.00

How I Cook It
McDonald, Virginia
Frank Glenn Publishing Co, Kansas City, MO,
1949: 256 pp, hc $17.50

How I Feed My Family of Five on $135 a Month
Gaffin, Jean
Creation House, Carol Stream, IL, 1973: 90
pp, hc $8.00

How It Is Done
McDonald, Virginia
McDonald Tea Room, Gallatin, MO, 1937: 36 pp
Wraps; illustrated $15.00

How Not to Miss the Cocktail Hour Cookbook
Lowman, Edward
The Barn, Garrison, NY, 1964: 159 pp
Spiral $6.00

How to Begin and Conduct the Canning Business Successfully
Warford, C.O.
Self; Newburgh, NY, 1902: 26 pp
Wraps; illustrated $8.00

How to Cook Reagan's Goose
Woman's National Democratic Club;
Washington, DC, 1984: 115 pp
Spiral; signed celebrity recipes $12.50

How to Freeze Foods
International Harvester Company, 1951: 83 pp
Spiral; illustrated $6.00

How to Keep Him After You've Caught Him
Kragen, Jinx, and Perry, Judy
Doubleday and Company, Garden City, NY,
1968: 228 pp, hc
Dust jacket $12.00

How to Serve Davis Delicacies
Frank E. Davis Co., Gloucester, MA, ca. 1930:
40 pp
Wraps; advertising booklet $4.00

How to Take a Trick a Day with Bisquick
Crocker, Betty
General Mills, 1935: 41 pp
Wraps; illustrated; movie star photos $15.00

Hundred Menu Chicken Cookbook
Ackart, Robert
Grosset and Dunlap, New York, 1971: 180
pp, hc $7.00

Hung, Strung and Potted: A History of Eating Habits
Booth, Sally
Clarkson Potter, NY, 1971: 238 pp, hc
First edition; illustrated $22.50

Hungarian Cookbook, The
Derecskey, Susan
Harper and Rowe, NY, 1972: 265 pp,
hc $10.00

Hungarian Cookery
Deeley, Lilla
Hale, Cushman and Flint, Boston, MA, 1938:
88 pp, hc $15.00

Hunters Cook Book
Claire, Mabel
Greenburg, Publisher, NY, 1932: 416 pp, hc
Illustrated $17.50

Huntsville Heritage Cookbook
Junior League of Huntsville, AL, 1984: 387 pp,
hc
Signed recipes $12.50

Hyde Park Cook Book
New Congregational Church; Hyde Park VT,
1912: 152 pp
Illustrated; local ads; fine condition; signed
recipes $15.00

I Hate to Cook Book, The
Bracken, Peg
Harcourt, Brace and Co., NY, 1961: 176 pp, hc
First edition $15.00

I Hate to Cook Book Almanack, The
Bracken, Peg
Harcourt, Brace, Jovanovich, NY, 1976: 283
pp, hc
First edition $12.50

I Hear America Cooking
Fussell, Betty
Viking, NY, 1986: 516 pp, hc
Illustrated $18.00

Ice Cream Cook Book
Goldman, Earl
Nitty Gritty Productions, Concord, CA, 1970:
142 pp
Wraps $5.00

Ice Cream Desserts
DeGouy, Louis
Greenberg Publishers, NY, 1948: 281 pp, hc
Dust jacket $20.00

Illustrated Lark Rise to Candleford
Thompson, Flora
Crown Publications, NY, 1983: 224 pp, hc
Illustrated; first edition $15.00

Inglenook Cook Book (1911 edition) (Reprint)
Brethren Press, Elgin, IL, 1970: 416 pp
Color imprinted cover $15.00

Inn Cookbook, The
Kropotkin, Igor and Marjorie
Castle, Secaucus, NJ, 1983: 336 pp, hc $9.00

Inside History of the White House
Willets, Gilson
Christian Herald, NY, 1908: 492 pp, hc
Illustrations; kitchen lore $20.00

Institute Cook Book, The
Cramp, Helen
International Institute, Philadelphia, PA, 1913:
508 pp, hc
Illustrated $16.00

International Cook, The
Campbell Soup Company, Camden, NJ, 1980:
303 pp, hc
Illustrated, advertising $9.00

International Institute Cook Book
International Institute; Lawrence, MA, 1938:
146 pp
Spiral; signed recipes $12.50

Invitation to Better Living from Deepfreeze, An
Deepfreeze Division, Motor Products Inc.,
North Chicago, IL, 1947: 66 pp
Wraps; illustrated $4.00

Irish Countryhouse Cooking
Tinne, Rosie
Gill and Macmillan, Dublin, 1974: 222 pp,
hc
Illustrated; celebrity recipes $14.00

Iroquois Foods and Food Preparation (1916 edition) (Reprint)
Waugh, F.W.
National Museums of Canada 1973: 235 pp
Wraps; illustrated $12.50

Isabella and Sam: The Story of Mrs. Beeton
Freeman, Sarah
Coward, McCann and Geoghegan, NY, 1971:
336 pp, hc
Illustrated $15.00

Island Cookery
Country Store, Deer Isle, ME, 1955: 176 pp
Spiral; signed recipes $15.00

James Beard's American Cookery
Beard, James
Little, Brown and Co., Boston, MA, 1972: 877
pp, hc
Dust jacket; first edition $35.00

James Beard's Theory & Practice of Good Cooking
Beard, James
Knopf, NY, 1977: 465 pp, hc
Illustrated $20.00

Jane Grigson's British Cookery
Grigson, Jane
Atheneum, NY, 1984: 231 pp, hc
Illustrated; first American edition $25.00

Jell-O Gelatin Salad Selector, The
General Foods Corporation, 1980: unpaged
Mechanical book; revolving recipe
cards $12.50

Jersey Shore Cooks and Artists
Point Pleasant Hospital Giuld, Point Pleasant,
NJ, 1958: 230 pp
Spiral; illustrated; first printing $15.00

Jesse's Book of Creole and Deep South Recipes (Reprint)
Watts, Edith and John
Weathervane Books, NY, 1954: 184 pp,
hc $8.00

Jessie Marie Deboth's Cook Book
DeBoth, Jessie
Whitman Publishing Co., Racine, WI, 1940:
192 pp
Spiral $10.00

Jolie Gabor's Family Cookbook
Kaufman, Ted and Jean
Thomas Crowell Co., NY, 1962: 271 pp, hc
Dust jacket $12.50

Josephine Cook Book
Fitzhugh, Josie M.
Josephine Circle, Memphis, TN, 1936: 186 pp,
hc
Signed recipes $20.00

Josie McCarthy's Favorite TV Recipes
McCarthy, Josie
Prentice Hall, Englewood Cliffs, NJ, 1958: 250
pp, hc $12.50

Joy of Cooking, The
Rombauer, Irma
Bobbs Merrill, NY, 1941: 628 pp, hc $35.00

Joy of Cooking, The
Rombauer, Irma
St. Louis, MO, 1931: 395 pp
First edition $1,000.00

Joy of Eating Natural Foods, The
Toms, Agnes
Devin Adair Co, CT, 1962: 384 pp, hc $12.00

Joys of Cooking, The
Armstrong, Alison
Station Hill Press, Barrytown, NY, 1986: 252
pp, hc
Dust jacket; first edition $22.50

Julia Child and Company
Child, Julia
Alfred Knopf, NY, 1979: 243 pp, hc
Illustrated $15.00

Julia Child and More Company
Child, Julia
Alfred Knopf; NY, 1979: 243 pp, hc
Illustrated $15.00

Junk Food Cookbook
Saiger, Lydia
Jove Books, NY, 1979: 256 pp
Wraps $4.00

Kate Smith's Favorite Recipes
General Foods Corporation, 1939: 47 pp
Wraps; illustrated; celebrity recipes $15.00

Kelvinator Book of Kitchen Tested Recipes, The
Kelvinator Corporation, 1930s: 64 pp
Wraps; illustrated; recipes for use with
     range $5.00

Key West Cook Book
Woman's Club, Key West, FL, 1949: 298 pp
Spiral; signed recipes; first edition $15.00

Kings in the Kitchen
Booth, Gertrude
Barnes and Co., NY, 1961: 204 pp, hc
Signed celebrity recipes $19.00

Kitchen Kinks
McEvoy, James
Massachusetts Mutual Life Insurance Co.,
     1956: unpaged
Spiral bound $7.00

Kitchen Klinic
Women's Club of St. Vincent Charity Hospital,
     Cleveland, OH, 1936: 220 pp
Spiral; signed recipes $15.00

Kitchen Safari: Gourmet's Tour of Africa
Hachten, H.
Atheneum, NY, 1970: 274 pp, hc $12.50

Kitchen Wisdom
Arkin, Frieda
Holt, Rinehart & Winston, NY, 1977: 260 pp,
     hc
First edition $9.00

Kitchens Near and Far
Smith, Herman
M Barrows, NY, 1945: 277 pp, hc $12.50

Knox Gelatine: Dainty Desserts, Candies, Salads
Charles Knox Gelatine Company, Inc., 1930:
     47 pp
Wraps; illustrated $5.00

Knox On-Camera Recipes
Knox Gelatine, Inc., 1962: 48 pp
Wraps; illustrated; in form of television
     production boards. $6.00

La Crosse Cook Book, The
Ladies' Society, Presbyterian Church, La
     Crosse, WI, 1923: 308 pp, hc
Signed recipes $22.50

La Cuisine Creole
Hearn, Lafcadio
F.F. Hansell and Brother, 1885: 268 pp, hc
Second edition $35.00

La Technique
Pepin, Jacques
Times Books, NY, 1976: 470 pp, hc
Illustrated $17.50

Ladies Aid Cookbook
Vaughan, Beatrice
Stephen Greene Press, Brattleboro, VT, 1971:
     186 pp, hc
Dust jacket; illustrated $12.50

Ladies' Book of New Cookery
Hale, Sarah J.
H. Long and Brother, NY, 1852: 474 pp, hc
Illustrated $65.00

Ladies' Home Journal Adventures in Cooking
Ladies' Home Journal, NY, 1968: 384 pp, hc
Illustrated $15.00

Ladies' Home Journal Dessert Cookbook
Truax, Carol
Doubleday, Garden City, NY, 1964: 280 pp, hc
Illustrated $15.00

Ladies Who Lunch
Redd, Ann, and Pfaltz, Marilyn
Charles Scribner's Sons, NY, 1972: 174 pp, hc
Dust jacket $8.00

Lafayette Presbyterian Church Cook Book
Robertson Bible Class, Buffalo, NY, 1925: 200
     pp, hc
Local ads; signed recipes $20.00

Larkin Housewives' Cook Book
Larkin Co., Buffalo, NY, 1915: 139 pp, hc
Local ads $12.50

Larousse Gastronomique
Montagne, Prosper
Crown Publishers, New York, NY, 1961: 1098
     pp, hc
First American edition $40.00

LBJ Barbecue Cook Book
Jetton, Walter
Pocket Books, NY, 1965: 80 pp
Signed by author $9.00

Lebanon Valley Cookery
Church of Our Saviour, Lebanon Springs, NY,
     1926: 133 pp
Signed recipes; photos of Shaker
     communities $25.00

LeJon Cook Book, The
Owen, Jeanne
National Distillers Products Corp., NY, 1947:
     63 pp
Wraps $6.00

Leone's Italian Cookbook
Leone, Gene
Harper and Row, NY, 1967: 244 pp, hc
Dust jacket $15.00

Let's Start to Cook
Nichols, Nell
Doubleday and Company, Garden City, NY,
    1966: 254 pp, hc $20.00

Let's Talk Turkey
Dietz, F. Meredith
Dietz Press, Richmond, VA, 1948: 340 pp, hc
Dust jacket, illustrated $12.50

Let's Talk Turkey
Dietz, Mabel
Dietz Press, Richmond, VA, 1948: 340 pp, hc
Illustrated; first edition $15.00

Little Acorn: Joy of Cooking, the First Fifty Years
Becker, Marion Rombauer
Bobbs-Merrill Co., NY, 1981: unpaged
Wraps; illustrated $10.00

Little House Cookbook, The
Walker, Barbara
Harper and Row; NY, 1979: 240 pp, hc
First edition; illustrated; dust jacket $15.00

Little Preserving Book for a Little Girl, A
Waterman, Amy
Page Company, Boston, MA, 1920: 197 pp
Wraps; illustrated $12.50

Lively Lemon Recipes
Crumal, Joyce
Howell-North Books, Berkeley, CA, 1967: 128
    pp, hc $10.00

Living Off The Land: A Handbook for Living in the Subtropics
Van Atta, Marian
Self, 1973: 56 pp
Spiral $10.00

Loaves and Fishes Cookbook, The
Pump, Anna
Macmillan Publishing Co., NY, 1985: 258 pp
First edition $20.00

Logistics of Good Eating
G-4 Ladies Military Group, 1955: 72 pp
Wraps; signed recipes $8.00

Long Island Favorites
Oyster Bay Visiting Nurse Association, NY,
    1935: 126 pp
Ring binder; celebrity recipes $15.00

Look and Cook Cook Book
Lanseth-Christensen, Lillian
Brown and Bigelow, St. Paul, MN, 1956:
    unpaged
Ring binder $17.50

Lost Country Life
Hartley, Dorothy
Pantheon Books, NY, 1979: 374 pp, hc
Illustrated $20.00

Lowbush Moose
Nelson, G.
Self; AK, 1978: 198 pp
Wraps $8.00

Lowney's Cook Book
Howard, Maria
Walter M. Lowney Company; Boston, MA,
    1907: 367 pp
Illustrated $20.00

Luchow's German Cookbook
Mitchell, Leonard
Doubleday Company, Garden City, NY, 1952:
    178 pp, hc
Dust jacket; first edition $20.00

Ma Cuisine
Ratto, Mario
Home Lines; Trieste, Italy, 1970: 275 pp, hc
Illustrated $17.50

Macy's Salad, Dessert Book
Claire, Mabel
Greenberg Publishers, 1933: 304 pp, hc
Illustrated $12.50
Same $16.00

Magic and Husbandry
Burdick, Lewis Dayton
Otseningo Publishing Co., Binghamton, NY,
    1905: 315 pp, hc $35.00

Magic Chef Cooking
Shank, Dorothy
American Stove Company, St. Louis, MO,
    1924: 204 pp
Advertising cookbook $6.00

Magic! The Most Amazing Short-Cuts in Cooking
The Borden Company, 1920s: 37 pp
Wraps; illustrated; recipes for sweetened
    condensed milk $12.00

Maine Coastal Cooking
Courier-Gazette, Inc. Rockland, ME, 1964: 86
    pp
Spiral; food lore and local history $8.00

Make Your Own Groceries
Harwig, Daphne
Bobbs-Merrill Co., New York, 1979: 256 pp,
    hc $11.00

Making Your Own Liqueurs
Van Doom, Joyce
Prism Press, London, 1980: 117 pp
Wraps $12.50

Manna: Foods of the Frontier
Harris, Gertrude
101 Productions, San Francisco, CA, 1972:
192 pp
Wraps $10.00

Manners and Social Usages
Sherwood, Mrs. J.
Harper and Brothers, Franklin Square, NY,
1887: 487 pp, hc $30.00

Manual for Army Cooks
War Department
Military Publishing Co., 1916: 270 pp, hc
Fold-out charts $25.00

Manuscript Cookbook
Anonymous
ca. 1880: 80 pp
Food and medical recipes; hardcover
    notebook; fair $25.00
1883: 100 pp
Handwritten; hardcover notebook; contains
    recipes and medical suggestions $45.00

Maple Sugar Book, The
Nearing, Helen and Scott
John Day Co., NY, 1950: 271 pp, hc $12.50

Margaret Rudkin Pepperidge Farm Cookbook, The
Rudkin, Margaret
Atheneum, NY, 1963: 440 pp
First edition $35.00

Margaretta Acworth's Georgian Cookery Book
Prochaska, Alice and France
Pavilion Books, London, 1987: 159 pp, hc
Illustrated $22.00

Mariechen's Saxon Cook Book
Crooks, Elva
Central Verband der Siebenbuerger Sachsen,
    Cleveland, OH, 1955: 70 pp
Spiral; signed recipes $12.50

Marion Cook Book
Royal Oak Missionary Society, Pulaski, VA,
    1921: 110 pp
Wraps; yarn-bound; signed recipes $15.00

Marion Harland's Cookery for Beginners
Harland, Marion
D. Lothrop Company, Boston, MA, 1893: 214
    pp, hc
Illustrated $75.00

Martha Deane's Cooking for Compliments
Taylor, Marion Young
M. Barrows Co., NY, 1954, 312 pp, hc
Dust jacket $12.50

Martha Washington's Booke of Cookery
Hess, Karen
Columbia University Press, NY, 1981: 518 pp,
    hc $35.00

Martha's Vineyard Cook Book
King, Louise, and Wexler, Jean
Harper and Row, New York, NY, 1971: 305
    pp, hc
Illustrated $15.00

Mary and Martha Fellowship Cookbook
First Baptist Church, Rhinebeck, NY, 1979: 98
    pp
Spiral; signed recipes $8.00

Mary Cullen's Northwest Cook Book
Laughton, Catherine
Binfords and Mort, Portland, OR, 1946: 340
    pp, hc
Dust jacket; first edition $17.50

Mary Margaret McBride's Harvest of American Cooking
McBridge, Mary Margaret
G. Putnam's Sons, New York, NY, 1957: 453
    pp, hc
Dust jacket; fine condition $20.00

Maryland's Way
Hammond-Harwood House Association,
    Annapolis, MD
1963, 1966: 372 pp, hc
Bicentennial edition; illustrated $15.00

Matter of Taste, A
Humphrey, Sylvia
Macmillan Company, New York, 1965: 370
    pp, hc
Dust jacket $16.00

Maxwell House Coffee Cookbook
Townsend, Doris M.
Ridge Press Book, NY, 1964: 274 pp, hc
Dust jacket $9.00

McCall's Book of Wonderful One-Dish Meals
Sullivan, Kay
Saturday Review Press, NY, 1972: 212 pp,
    hc $6.00

Meals Tested, Tasted and Approved
Good Housekeeping Institute, NY, 1930: 256
    pp, hc
First edition $12.00

Memoirs of An American Lady
Grant, Anne
Dodd, Mead and Co., NY, 1909: 300 pp, hc
Illustrated $35.00

Mennonite Community Cookbook
Showalter, Mary Emma
Herald Press, Scottdale, PA, 1957: 494 pp, hc
Dust jacket; illustrated $20.00

Meta Given's Modern Encyclopedia of Cooking
Givens, Meta
J. G. Ferguson and Associates, Chicago, IL,
    1954: 1702 pp, hc
Illustrated; one volume $22.50

Midwestern Home Cookery
Szathmary, Louis
Arno Press, NY, 1973: 400 pp, hc $22.50

Milwaukee Cook Book, The
Magie, Mrs.
Wisconsin Training School for Nurses, WI,
   1894: 380 pp, hc
Local ads $30.00

Minute Cook Book
Minute Tapioca Co., Orange, MA, 1915: 32 pp
Wraps; illustrated; advertising booklet $5.00

Miss Beecher's Domestic Receipt Book
Beecher, Catharine
Harper & Bros., NY, 1864: 306 pp, hc
Illustrated $80.00
1856, third edition $250.00

**Miss Dine About Town Marvelous Meals
with Minute Tapioca**
General Foods Corporation, 1928: 23 pp
Wraps; illustrated $6.00

Miss Leslie's New Cookery Book
Leslie, Eliza
T.B. Peterson and Brothers, 1857: 662 pp, hc
Fair condition $200.00

Mixer, Hand Mixer and Blender Cookbook
Deproft, Melanie
Spencer Press, Chicago, IL, 1954: 256 pp, hc
Illustrated $12.50

Modern Cookery in All Its Branches
Acton, Eliza
Longman, Brown, Green, et al, London, 1849:
   608 pp, hc
Illustrated $275.00

Modern Herbal, A
Stevenson, Violet
Crescent Books, NY, 1974: 144 pp, hc
Dust jacket; illustrated $12.50

Molly Goldberg Jewish Cookbook, The
Berg, Gertrude, and Waldo, Myra
Doubleday and Company, Garden City, NY,
   1955: 320 pp
Fine condition; dust jacket $15.00

Moonshine: Its History and Folklore
Kellner, Esther
Weathervane Books, NY, 1971: 235 pp,
   hc $10.00

Mountain Relics
Thompson, Frances
A.S. Barnes and Co., Cranbury, NJ, 1977: 188
   pp, hc
Illustrated $17.50

Mrs. Appleyard's Kitchen
Kent, Louise
Houghton Mifflin Company, Boston, MA,
   1942: 319 pp $12.50

**Mrs. Bridges' Upstairs, Downstairs Cookery
Book**
Bailey, Adrian, editor
Simon and Schuster, NY, 1974: 193 pp, hc
Dust jacket $12.50

**Mrs. Harding's Twentieth Century Cook
Book**
Geographical Publishing Co., Chicago, IL,
   1921. 182 pp, hc
Illustrated $22.50

Mrs. Lincoln's Boston Cook Book
Lincoln, Mrs. D.A.
Roberts Brothers, Boston, MA, 1884: 536 pp,
   hc
First edition $200.00
1891: 527 pp, hc $85.00

Mrs. Rorer's Philadelphia Cook Book
Rorer, Sarah Tyson
Arnold and Company, Philadelphia, PA, 1886:
   581 pp, hc
Illustrated $65.00

Much Depends on Dinner
Robotti, Peter
Fountainhead Publishers, NY, 1961: 306 pp,
   hc $15.00

Mushroom Feast, The
Grigson, Jane
Alfred A. Knopf, NY, 1975: 305 pp, hc $12.50

My Better Homes and Gardens Cook Book
Meredith Publishing Co., Des Moines, IA, 1930
Three ring binder; first edition $35.00

My Cookery Books
Pennell, Elizabeth Robins
Holland Press Limited; London, 1983: 171 pp,
   hc
Illustrated; one of a numbered series $95.00

My One Best Recipe
Hunter, Fred
Steamer Hose Co., Cooperstown, NY, 1908:
   unpaged
Wraps; illustrated; local ads; signed
   recipes $15.00

Myrtle Reed Cook Book, The
Reed, Myrtle
G.P. Putnam's Sons, NY, 1916: 552 pp,
   hc $20.00

Mystery Chef's Own Cook Book
MacPherson, John
Longmans, NY, 1940: 366 pp
Dust jacket; signed by Mystery Chef $37.50

Mystic Seaport Cookbook
Langseth-Christensen, Lillian
Marine Historical Association, Mystic, CT,
   1970: 267 pp, hc $15.00

Nantucket and other New England Cooking
Hawkins, Nancy, and Kavemeyer, Mary
Hastings House, NY, 1976: 212 pp, hc $14.00

Nantucket Island Cook Book
Old People's Home Association, Nantucket,
MA, ca. 1940: 95 pp
Spiral bound; local ads; signed recipes $15.00

National Cook Book, The
Harland, Marion
Charles Scribner's Sons, NY, 1896: 550 pp,
hc $45.00

National Cook Book, The
Hibben, Sheila
Harper & Bros., NY, 1932: 452 pp, hc $25.00

National Treasury of Cookery, A
Bullock, Helen Duprey
Heirloom Publishing Company, 1967: 365 pp, hc
Slipcase; illustrated $25.00
1967: hc
5 vols. in slipcase; illustrated by Charles
   Wysocki $25.00

Native American Cookbook
Henry, Edna
Julian Messner, NY, 1983: 91 pp, hc $10.00

Native Harvests
Kavasch, Barrie
Random House, NY, 1977: 202 pp, hc
Illustrated; first edition $25.00

Native Seafood Cookery
Oyster Museum, Chincoteague, VA, 1972:
   unpaged
Wraps $6.00

**Natural Sweet Tooth Breakfast, Dessert and
Candy Cookbook**
Hobart, Billie
Straight Arrow Books, San Francisco, CA,
   1974: 76 pp
Wraps $7.00

Nero Wolfe Cook Book, The
Stout, Rex
Viking Press, NY, 1973: 203 pp, hc
First edition $25.00

New Almond Cookery
Schmidt, M.
Simon and Schuster, NY, undated, 193 pp, hc
Illustrated $15.00

**New Book of Favorite Breads from Rose
Lane Farm, The**
Roberts, Ada Lou
Hearthside Books, NY, 1970: 192 pp, hc
Illustrated $10.00

New Connecticut Cookbook, The
Woman's Club of Westport, CT,
Harper and Brothers, NY, 1947: 338 pp
Illustrated; first edition; dust jacket $20.00

New England Butt'ry Shelf Cookbook, The
Campbell, Mary, and Tudor, Tasha
World Publishing Company, Cleveland, OH,
   1969: 192 pp, hc
Dust jacket $15.00

New England Cook Book
Harland, et al
Charles Brown Publishing, Boston, MA, 1906:
   286 pp
Illustrated; local ads $45.00

New England Cook Book, The
Morrow, Kay
Culinary Arts Press, 1936: 48 pp
Wooden covers; illustrated $12.50

New England Yankee Cookbook, The
Wolcott, Imogene
Coward-McCann, NY, 1939: 398 pp,
   hc $30.00
Cookbook Collector's Library, reprint: 398 pp,
   hc $17.50

New Home Cook Book, The
Illinois State Register, IL, 1923: 128 pp
Wraps; from local ladies' societies $12.00

New Household Receipt Book, The
Hale, Sarah Josepha
H. Long and Brother, NY,
1853: 394 pp, hc
Fair condition $65.00

New Milwaukee Cook Book, The
Visiting Nurse Association, WI, 1938: 320 pp
Spiral bound; illustrated; local ads $17.50

New Orleans Cook Book
Richard, Lena
Houghton Mifflin Company, Boston, MA,
   1940: 146 pp, hc $15.00

New Orleans Creole Recipes
Bremer, Mary Moore
Dorothea Thompson, New Orleans, LA, 1958:
   86 pp
Spiral $15.00

New Perfection Cook Book
Perfection Stove Company, 1912: 96 pp
Wraps; illustrated $6.00

New Pillsbury Family Cookbook
Pillsbury Co., Minneapolis, MN, 1973: 408 pp
Ring binder; illustrated; index tabs $17.50

New York Cookbook
LoPinto, Maria
A.A. Wyn, NY, 1952: 250 pp, hc
Signed by author $12.50

New York Evening Telegram Cook Book
Telford, Emma
Cupples and Leon Company, NY, 1908: 254
   pp $12.50

New York Times Cook Book, The
Claiborne, Craig
Harper & Row, NY, 1961: 717 pp, hc
Dust jacket $15.00

New York Times Correspondent's Choice
Foster, Lee
New York Times Book Company, NY, 1974:
300 pp, hc
Signed celebrity recipes $15.00

New York Woman's Exchange Dining for Moderns
Hackney, Mrs. G.
NY Exchange for Woman's Work, NY, 1940:
72 pp
Wraps; illustrated; local ads $15.00

NFRW Republican Woman's Cookbook: Desserts
National Federation of Republican Women:
Montgomery, AL, 1970: 382 pp
Spiral; illustrated; signed, celebrity
recipes $15.00

NFRW Republican Woman's Cookbook: Meats
National Federation of Republican Women,
Montgomery, AL, 1969: 382 pp
Spiral; illustrated; signed, celebrity
recipes $15.00

Norman Table, The
Frumkin, Paul, and Guermont, Claude
Charles Scribner's Sons, NY, 1985: 297 pp,
hc $11.00

North Carolina and Old Salem Cookery
Sparks, Elizabeth
Elizabeth Sparks, Kernersville, NC, 1955: 226
pp, hc
Illustrated; fine condition; first edition $35.00

Northern Lites Tasty Bites Cook Book
First Presbyterian Church, Fairbanks, AK,
1976: 111 pp
Spiral; signed ads $10.00

Not in Front of the Servants
Dawes, Frank
Taplinger Publishing Co., NY, 1973: 160 pp, hc
Illustrated $15.00

Notes from a Country Kitchen
Innes, Jocasta
William Morrow and Co., NY, 1979: 248 pp, hc
Illustrated $19.00

Nothing Whatever To Do
Masterton, Elsie and John
Crown Publishers, NY, 1956: 277 pp $20.00

Nut Cookbook
Kaufman, William
Doubleday, Garden City, NY, 1964: 310 pp,
hc $8.00

Old American Kitchenware: 1725–1925
Lantz, Louise
Thomas Nelson, NY, 1970: 290 pp, hc
Illustrated $22.50

Old and New British Recipes
Owen, Adelaide
British War Relief Association of Northern
California, CA, 1940: 125 pp
Spiral bound $10.00

Old Cook Books
Quayle, Eric
Brandywine Press Books, EP Dutton, NY,
1978: 256 pp, hc
Illustrated; first edition $35.00

Old Tamarack's Collection
Hammond Book Company, Hammond, IN,
1941: 200 pp,
Illustrated $12.50

Old Timey Recipes
Connor, Phyllis
Self, Bluefield, WV, 1970: 65 pp
Wraps $6.00

Omelets, Crepes and Other Recipes
Stanish, Rudolph
Harbor Press, NY, 1970: 70 pp, hc
Dust jacket $7.00

One Hundred Delights: Dates
Hills Brothers Company 1922: 31 pp
Wraps; illustrations $5.00

150 New Ways to Serve Ice Cream
Moody, Sue
Sealtest System, 1936: 62 pp
Wraps; illustrated; advertising booklet $10.00

101 Prize Recipes
Postum Cereal Company, Battle Creek, MI,
1924: 40 pp
Wraps; contest winning recipes $4.00

121 Tested Recipes
Mason, Mary
Chr. Hansen's Laboratory, Inc., NY, 1940: 31
pp
Wraps; illustrated; World's Fair edition $10.00

1001 Questions Answered About Food
Adams, Charlotte
Dodd, Mead & Co., NY, 1961: 230 pp,
hc $9.00

One Thousand Salads
Green, Olive
G.P. Putnam's Sons, NY, 1909: 415 pp
Very good condition; printed color
cover $12.50

Orange Judd Cookbook, The
Goessling, Adeline
Orange Judd Company, NY, 1914: 276 pp, hc
Illustrated $12.50

Organic Grow It, Cook It, Preserve It Cookbook
Fenten, Barbara
Grosset and Dunlap, NY, 1972: 164 pp, hc
Dust jacket $12.50

Original Picayune Creole Cook Book
Times-Picayune Publishing Co., New Orleans, LA, 1954: 446 pp
Illustrated; classic Creole recipes $22.50

Other Half of the Egg, The
McCully, Helen, and Pepin, Jacques
M. Barrows and Co., NY, 1967: 240 pp, hc $14.00

Our Daily Bread
Bruton Parish Church, Williamsburg, VA, 1978: 136 pp
Spiral; signed recipes $9.00

Our Daily Bread
Standard, Stella
Bonanza Books, NY, 1970: 280 pp, hc
Dust jacket $9.00

Our Deportment
Young, John
F.B. Dickerson and Company, Detroit, MI, 1882: 424 pp
Illustrated; fine condition $35.00

Our Dining Car Recipes
Southern Pacific Railroad, 1935: 24 pp
Advertising booklet $12.00

Our Favorite Recipes
St. John's Guild, West Bend, WI, 1949: 408 pp
Spiral; signed recipes; local ads $14.00

Our Favorites
Congretional Ladies Aid Society, Hayward, WI, 1933: 148 pp
Wraps; local ads $12.50

Our Favorites
Trinity Church, Lime Rock, CT, ca. 1960: 134 pp
Spiral; signed recipes $10.00

Out of Alaska's Kitchens
Easter Seal Society, Anchorage, AK, 1961: 253 pp
Spiral; signed recipes $15.00

Out of Vermont Kitchens
Trinity Mission of Trinity Church, Rutland, VT, 1939: 400 pp
Spiral, illustrated, first edition, local ads; signed recipes $17.50

Outdoor Cooking
Brown, Cora, Rose, and Bob
Greystone Press, NY, 1940: 506 pp, hc
Dust jacket $20.00

Oven Magic
Alabama College, Birmingham, AL, 1940: 268 pp
Spiral; illustrated; signed recipes; local ads $17.50

Overbrook Town Shop Recipes
McCurdy, Ruth, and Coan, Flora
Self, Scranton, PA, ca. 1936: 209 pp, hc
Illustrated $15.00

Painesville Cook Book
Alumnae Association of Lake Erie College, OH, ca. 1914: 191 pp, hc
Local ads $17.50

Palatists Book of Cookery
Assistance League of S. Calif, Hollywood, CA, 1933: 230 pp, hc $25.00

Palmer House Cook Book, The
Amiet, Ernest
Hotel Monthly Press, Chicago, IL, 1940: 317 pp, hc
Dust jacket; illustrated $25.00

Pan-Pacific Cook Book
McLaren, L.L.
Blair-Murdock Company, San Francisco, CA, 1915: 170 pp
Illustrated; from Panama-Pacific Exposition $65.00

Park's Success with Herbs
Foster, Gertrude, and Louden, Rosemary
Geo. W. Park Seed Co., Greenwood, SC, 1980: 182 pp, hc
Illustrated $14.00

Paul Richard's Pastry Book
Richard, Paul
Hotel Monthly Press, Chicago, IL, 1907: 172 pp, hc
Illustrated $25.00

Peacemeal
Greenwich Village Peace Center, 1973: 142 pp
Spiral; signed recipes $10.00

Pear Culture for Profit
Quinn, P.T.
Tribune Association, NY, 1869: 136 pp, hc
Illustrated $25.00

Pease Porridge Hot
Hart, Katherine
Encino Press, Austin, TX, 1967: 55 pp, hc
Illustrated $22.50

Penn Family Recipes
Benson, Evelyn
George Shumway, York, PA, 1966: 213 pp, hc
Dust jacket $25.00

Pennsylvania Dutch Cook Book of Fine Old Recipes
Culinary Arts Press, Reading, PA, 1936: 48 pp
Wraps; illustrated $6.00

Pennsylvania Dutch Cookbook
Lestz, Gerald
Grosset and Dunlap, NY, 1970: 88 pp, hc
Amish signed recipes $10.00

Pennsylvania Grange Cook Book
Pennsylvania State Grange Committee,
Harrisburg, PA, 1925: 168 pp, hc
Signed recipes $40.00

People and Shopping
Harrison, Molly
Rowman and Littlefield, Totowa, NJ, 1975:
143 pp, hc
Illustrated $12.50

Perfect Hostess Cook Book, The
Knopf, Mildred
Alfred A. Knopf, NY, 1964: 499 pp, hc
Dust jacket $12.50

Pet Recipes
Pet Milk Company, St. Louis, MO, 1931: 84 pp
Ring binder; illustrated; advertising $10.00

Peter Hunt's Cape Cod Cookbook
Hunt, Peter
New York, 1954: 181 pp, hc
Dust jacket $20.00

Physiology of Taste
Brillat-Savarin, Jean Anthelme
Horace Liverogjt, 1926: 360 pp, hc $15.00

Picnic Book, The
Hazelton, Nika
Atheneum, NY, 1969: 265 pp, hc
First edition $17.50

Pie Book, The
De Gouy, Louis
Greenberg Publishers, NY, 1949: 380 pp, hc
Dust jacket $25.00

Pie Marches On
Strause, Monroe
Ahrens Publishing Co., NY, 1951: 328 pp, hc
Illustrated $16.00

Pilgrim Service Guild Gourmet
First Congretional Church, Ottawa, IL, 1949:
unpaged
Spiral; signed recipes $12.50

Pillsbury Bake-Off Booklet #1
Pillsbury Co., Minneapolis, MN, 1950
Wraps; illustrated $75.00

Pillsbury Bake-Off Booklets
Pillsbury Co., Minneapolis, MN, 1951 on
Wraps; illustrated $9.00 each

Pillsbury Family Cookbook
Pillsbury Co., Minneapolis, MN, 1963: 575 pp,
hc
Illustrated $17.50

Pillsbury's Best 1000 Recipes, Best of the Bake Off
Pillsbury, editor, Ann
Consolidated Book Publishers, Chicago, IL,
1959: 608 pp, hc
Illustrated $25.00

Pillsbury's Cook Book
Pillsbury Flour Mills Company, 1923: 78 pp
Illustrated $15.00

Pine Valley Springs Trout Cookbook
Erdmenger, Betty and Bill
Pine Valley Springs, Viola, WI, 1978: 146 pp
Spiral; illustrated $12.50

Pioneer Potluck: Stories and Recipes of Early Colorado
State Historical Society of Colorado, CO,
1963: 110 pp
Spiral; signed recipes $12.50

Placid Eating
Wikoff, Climena
Tuttle Publishing Company, Rutland, VT,
1948: 109 pp, hc $20.00

Plan-A-Meal
Oxford Filing Supply, Brooklyn, NY, 1937
440 recipe cards in wooden box with
revolving index cards $20.00

Plantation Cookbook
Junior League of New Orleans, LA, 1972: 223
pp, hc
Illustrated $12.50

Plantation Recipes
Bowers, Lessie
Robert Speller and Sons, NY, 1959: 194 pp, hc
Dust jacket $25.00

Pleasures of Colonial Cooking
Miller Cory House Museum, NJ Historical
Society, NJ, 1982: 173 pp
Wraps; illustrated $10.00

Plimoth Colony Cook Book, The
Bruce and Jones
Plymouth Antiquarian Society, 1957: 88 pp, hc
Wraps; signed recipes $12.50

Plum Crazy: A Book About Beach Plums
Mirel, Elizabeth
Clarkson N. Potter, Inc., NY, 1973: 144 pp, hc
First edition $15.00

Pocumtuc Housewife, The
Deerfield Academy, Deerfield, MA, 1906: 66 pp
Rare edition $45.00

Pomfret Cookery
Church Beautification Committee, Pomfret,
CT, 1887: 68 pp $25.00

Pomperaug Plantation
Southbury Newcomers Club, CT, 1980: 212 pp
Spiral; illustrated $9.00

Pooh Cook Book
Ellison, Virginia
E.P. Dutton, NY, 1969: 120 pp, hc $12.50

Pot Shots from a Grosse Ile Kitchen
Corbett, Lucy and Sidney
Harper and Brothers, NY, 1947: 213 pp, hc
First edition $20.00

Pot Stirred Round the World, The
Roberts and Williams
1975: 120 pp
Illustrated; spiral bound; Bicentennial
    collectible $9.00

Practical Cooking and Dinner Giving
Henderson, Mary F.
Harper & Bros., NY, 1878: 376 pp, hc
Illustrated $70.00

Practical Housekeeping
Buckeye Publishing Company, Minneapolis,
MN, 1883: 688 pp
Illustrated; Revised edition of Buckeye
    Cookery $45.00

*Practical Italian Recipes for American
Kitchens*
Cuniberti, Julia
Self 1918: 32 pp
Wraps $10.00

Praise for the Cook
Proctor and Gamble, Co., Cincinatti, OH,
1959: 120 pp
Spiral; illustrated $5.00

Presbyterian Cook Book
First Presbyterian Church, Dayton, OH, 1877:
178 pp
Wraps; illustrated; local ads $45.00

Presbyterian Ever-Ready Cook Book
First Presbyterian Church, Chateaugay, NY,
1931: 108 pp
Wraps; signed recipes; local ads; very
    good $15.00

President's Cookbook, The
Cannon, Poppy, and Brooks, Patricia
Funk and Wagnalls, 1968: 545 pp, hc
Insert for additional recipes $22.00

Princess Cook Book
Akerstrom, Jenny
Albert Bonnier Publishing House, NY, 1936:
315 pp, hc
Illustrated; first edition $45.00

Prudence Penny's Cookbook
Penny, Prudence
Prentice Hall, Englewood Cliffs, NJ, 1941: 385
pp, hc $12.50

Puerto Rican Dishes
Cabanillas, Berta, and Ginorio, Carmen
Waverly Press, Baltimore, MD, 1956: 151 pp,
hc
Dust jacket $15.00

Putting Food By
Hertzberg, R., Vaughn, B., and Greene, J.
Stephen Greene Press, Brattleboro, VT, 1973:
360 pp
Wraps; illustrated $9.00

Pyrex Experts Book on Better Cooking
Bradley, Alice
Corning Glass Works, Corning, NY, 1925: 28
pp
Advertising; illustrated $4.00

Queen of Hearts Cook Book
Peter Pauper Press, Mt. Vernon, NY, 1955: 64
pp, hc
Dust jacket $9.00

Queen of the Household
Elssworth and Brey, Detroit, MI, 1905: 755
pp, hc
Illustrated $22.50

Quick and Easy Cooking with Tupperware
Meredith Corp., Des Moines, IA, 1986: 156
pp, hc
Illustrated $10.00

Quick Trick Cookery
American Can Company, 1940s; 48 pp
Wraps; illustrated $6.00

Ransom's Family Receipt Book
D. Ransom and Son, Buffalo, NY, 1914: 30 pp
Wraps; advertising $6.00

Rare Recipes Old and New
Veltin School, New York, NY, 1923: 268 pp,
hc
Limited edition $25.00

Ration By-Pass
Garden Club of Halifax Country, Daytona
Beach, FL, 1944: 36 pp
Wraps; signed recipes $12.50

Reader's Digest Secrets of Better Cooking
Reader's Digest, Pleasantville, NY, 1973: 761
pp, hc
Illustrated $11.00

Receiptfully Yours
Merriam Park Chapter, OES, St. Paul, MN,
1955: 200 pp
Spiral; illustrated; signed recipes $12.50

Recipe Book for Club Aluminum Ware, The
Club Aluminum Company, Chicago, IL, 1927:
35 pp
Wraps; illustrated $8.00

Recipes from a Cape Cod Kitchen
McCue, Doris
James Westaway McCue, MA, 1946: 72 pp,
hc $15.00

Recipes from Historic Long Island
Nassau County YWCA, 1940: 416 pp
Spiral; signed ads; first edition $15.00

Recipes from Old Hundred
Brown, Nellie
M. Barrows and Company, NY, 1939: 255 pp,
hc $17.50

Recipes of All Nations
Morphy, Countess
William Wise and Company, NY, 1935: 821
pp, hc
Thumb tabs $22.50

Recipes You'll Enjoy!
Wright, Julia Lee
Safeway Stores, Oakland, CA, 1930: unpaged
Ring binder $17.50

Rector's Naughty 90s Cook Book
Kirkland, Alexander
Doubleday, Garden City, NY, 1949: 247 pp, hc
Illustrated $15.00

**Rediscovering German Cookery in Adams
County**
Brickman, Mrs. K.
Quincy, IL, 1976: 121 pp
Wraps $10.00

Republican Cookbook, The
Brownstone Press, Barrington, IL, 1969: 200
pp, hc
Illustrated; fine condition $17.50

Rice and Spice
Jervey, Phyllis
Charles E. Tuttle Co., Rutland, VT, 1958: 200
pp, hc $15.00

Rice, Spice and Bitter Oranges
Perl, Liula
World Publishing Co., Cleveland, OH, 1967:
272 pp, hc
Dust jacket $17.50

River Road Recipes
Junior League of Baton Rouge, LA, 1959: 262
pp
Spiral; signed recipes; first edition $20.00
1962: 262 pp
Spiral; signed recipes; fifth printing $10.50

Rokeach Cookbook
I. Rokeach & Sons, Inc., 1933: 100 pp
Wraps; text appears in English and
Hebrew $8.00

Roundup of Beef Cookery
Taylor, Demetria, editor
Bonanza Books, NY, 1960: 198 pp, hc
Dust jacket $10.00

Roundup Recipes
Peplow, Bonnie and Ed
World, 1951: 278
First edition; signed recipes; dust
jacket $17.50

Royal Baker and Pastry Cook
Royal Baking Powder Company, NY, 1906: 44
pp
Illustrated; advertising $6.00

Royal Cook Book
Royal Baking Powder Company, NY, 1925: 50
pp
Wraps; illustrated $5.00

Rumford Complete Cook Book, The
Wallace, Lily H.
Rumford Co., Providence, RI, 1918: 241 pp,
hc $8.00

Russian Cook Book for American Homes
Maddox, Gaynor
Russian War Relief, NY, 1942: 92 pp
Spiral bound; signed recipes $10.00

Russwin Cook Book, The
Russell and Erwin Mfg. Co., New Britain, CT,
1910: 31 pp
Illustrated; guide to using food cutter $5.00

**Ruth Wakefield's Toll House Tried and True
Recipes**
Wakefield, Ruth
M. Barrows and Co., NY, 1945: 273 pp
Illustrated; signed by author $25.00

Ryzon Baking Book
Neil, Marion Harris
General Chemical Company, 1916. 81 pp
Wraps; illustrated $6.00

Salute to American Cooking, A
Longstreet, Stephen and Ethel
Hawthorn Books, NY, 1968: 308 pp,
hc $22.00

Salute to the Great American Chefs
Benjamin Co., Elmsford, NY, 1988: 222 pp
Spiral $10.00

Sand Country Cooking
Howard United Methodist Charge, Howard,
GA, 1978: 440 pp
Spiral; signed recipes; local ads $12.50

Saratoga Favorite, The
Young Women's Mission Circle, Saratoga
    Springs, NY, 1882: 167 pp, hc
Signed recipes; local ads; fine
    condition $85.00

SAS World-Wide Restaurant Cookbook
Adams, Charlotte
Random House, NY, 1960: 398 pp, hc
Dust jacket; signed by author $12.50

Savannah Cook Book, The
Colquitt, Harriet Ross
1933: 186 pp, hc
Illustrated; first edition $40.00

Savory Suppers and Fashionable Feasts
Williams, Susan
Pantheon Books, NY, 1985: 335 pp, hc
Illustrated $20.00

Say Good-by to Hand-Beating!
Fitzgerald Manufacturing Company, 1933: 31
    pp
Wraps; illustrated instruction booklet for using
    Magic Maid mixer $4.00

Scentuous Cookery
Johnston, Jane, and Jedlicka, Phyllis
Piper Co., Blue Earth, MN, 1971: 233 pp, hc
First edition $12.50

Scots Kitchen, The
McNeill, F. Marian
Blackie and Son Ltd., London, 1940: 259 pp,
    hc $17.50

Seasonal Hearth, The
Hechtlinger, Adelaide
Overlook Press, Woodstock, NY, 1986: 256 pp
Illustrated $20.00

Seasonal Kitchen, The
Meyers, Perla
Holt, Rinehard & Winston, NY, 1973: 421 pp, hc
First edition $20.00

Second Church Cook Book
Second Church, West Newton, MA, 1938:
    184 pp
Spiral bound; signed recipes $17.50

Secrets of the Jam Cupboard
Certo Corporation, 1930: 23 pp
Wraps; illustrated; recipes call for Certo $3.00

Secrets of the Still
Firth, Grace
EPM Publications, McLean, VA, 1983: 286 pp,
    hc
Illustrated $25.00

Selected Recipes and Menus
Parker, Marian Jane
Calumet Baking Powder Company, 1931: 40
    pp
Wraps; illustrated $5.00

Sensible Cook, The
Rose, Peter
Syracuse University Press, NY, 1989: 142 pp, hc
Fine $22.50

Sensible Etiquette
Ward, Mrs. H.O.
Porter and Coates, Philadelphia, PA, 1878:
    567 pp, hc $22.50

Serv-U-Well Swedish Cook Book
First Lutheran Church, 1941: 149 pp
Spiral bound; signed recipes; ethnic
    recipes $12.50

Serve It and Sing: Sell's Liver Pate
Platt, June
Alfred A. Knopf, NY, 1945: 70 pp, hc
First edition $16.00

Serve It Buffet
Brobeck, Florence
M. Barrows and Co., NY, 1944: 288 pp, hc
First edition $9.00

Service Cook Book, The
Allen, Ida Bailey
F.W. Woolworth Co., NY, 1935: unpaged
Spiral; illustrations; local ads $11.00

Settlement Cook Book, The
Kander, Mrs. Simon
Settlement Cook Book Company, Milwaukee,
    WI, 1931 edition, 624 pp, hc
Illustrated $35.00

**Settlement Cook Book, The (Facsimile
edition)**
Kander, Mrs. Simon
Scribner Book Company, NY, 1984: 182 pp, hc
Illustrated $15.00

Seven Hundred Years of English Cooking
McKendry, Maxime
Treasure Press, London, 1983: 240 pp, hc
Illustrated $15.00

Seventeen Cookbook, The
MacMillan Company, NY, 1964: 430 pp, hc
First printing $14.00

Shafer Study Club Cook Book
Shafer, MN, 1953: 168 pp
Wire spiral; local ads; signed recipes $12.50

Shaker Cook Book: Not By Bread Alone, The
Piercy, Caroline
Crown, NY, 1977: 282 pp, hc $12.50

Shaker Recipes for Cooks and Homemakers
Lassiter, William
Greenwich Books, NY, 1959: 302 pp, hc
First edition; signed by author $22.50

Shakespeare Club Cook Book
Pasadena, CA, ca. 1930: 153 pp, hc
Signed by editor $20.00

Shellfish Heritage Cookbook
Robinson, Robert
Shellfish Digest, Georgetown, DE, 1981: 72 pp
Spiral; illustrated $6.00

Short-title Catalogue of Household and Cookery Books, A
Maclean, Virginia
Prospect Books, London, 1981: 197 pp,
    hc $95.00

Shower Parties for All Occasions
Wade, Carlson
A.S. Barnes Co., Cranbury, NJ, 1973: 143 pp, hc
Illustrated $8.00

Signature Recipes
Elm Grove Woman's Club, WI, 1962: 176 pp
Spiral; illustrated; signed recipes $12.50

Silent Hostess Treasure Book, The
General Electric Refrigeration Department,
    1931: 104 pp
Wraps; illustrated $5.00

Silver Sheaf Cook Book
McClintock, Sara
Westfield District Nursing Association,
    Westfield, NJ, ca. 1914: 69 pp $15.00

Simple Hawaiian Cookery
Beilenson, Edna
Peter Pauper Press, 1964: 62 pp, hc
Illustrated; dust jacket $8.00

Single Chef's Cookbook
Lesberg, Sandy
Prentice Hall, NY, 1970: 281 pp, hc
Dust jacket $10.00

Sinkin' Spells, Hot Flashes, Fits and Cravings
Mickler, Ernest
Ten Speed Press, Berkeley, CA, 1988: 158 pp
Spiral; illustrated; first printing $15.00

Six Hundred Dollars A Year
anon.
Ticknor and Fields, Boston, MA, 1867: 183
    pp, hc $40.00

Six Hundred Receipts Worth Their Weight in Gold
Marquart, John
John E. Potter and Company, Philadelphia,
    PA, 1867: 311 pp, hc
Very good condition $30.00

Sixpence in Her Shoe
McGinley, Phyllis
Macmillan, NY, 1964: 281 pp, hc
First printing $15.00

Ski Country Cook Book
Stillman, Ellen
Houghton Mifflin Co., Boston, MA, 1971: 144
    pp, hc
Dust jacket; first edition $12.50

Slade's Cooking School Recipes
By 25 Cooking School Teachers
D and L Slade Company, Boston, MA, 1909:
    76 pp
Wraps; illustrated $7.00

Sloan's Handy Hints and Up to Date Cookbook
Dr. Earl Sloan, Boston, MA, 1901: 48 pp
Wraps; advertising $6.00

Small Family Cook Book, The
Davenport, Laura
Reilly and Britton Company, Chicago, IL,
    1910: 256 pp
Very good condition; hardcover;
    illustrated $15.00

Smokey Mountain Wines and How to Make Them
Mahan, P.
Arco Books, NY, 1973: 114 pp, hc $15.00

Snow Country Cookbook
Christian Education Committee, Deerfield, CT,
    ca. 1970: 62 pp
Wraps $10.00

Social History of Bourbon, The
Carson, Gerald
Dodd, Mead & Co., NY, 1963: 280 pp, hc
Illustrated; first edition $14.00

Social Life in New Orleans
Ripley, Eliza
Appleton and Company, NY, 1912: 331 pp, hc
Illustrated $30.00

Social Servings
Social Service League of La Jolla, CA, ca.
    1950: 192 pp
Spiral; local ads $15.00

Solving the High Cost of Eating
Allen, Ida Bailey
Farrar, Straus and Young, NY, 1952: 545 pp,
    hc $9.00

Something Different
First Unitarian Church, Buffalo, NY, 1919: 125
    pp, hc
Signed recipes; local ads $22.50

Sons of Norway Cookbook
Vennelag #513, Mt. Horeb, WI 1981: 104 pp,
    hc
Spiral; signed recipes $12.00

Soup Book, The
DeGouy, Louis
Greenberg Publisher, NY, 1949: 414 pp, hc
Dust jacket $20.00

Southern Christmas Book, The
Kane, Harnett
Bonanza Books, NY, 1978: 337 pp, hc $10.00

Southern Cook Book, The
Brown, Marion
Univ. of North Carolina Press, Chapel Hill, NC,
    1951: 371 pp, hc
Signed recipes $17.50

Southern Cooking
Dull, Henrietta
Grosset and Dunlap, NY, 1941: 384 pp, hc
Illustrated; dust jacket $22.50

Southern Living Cooking Across the South
Marshall, Lillian
Oxmoor House, Birmingham, AL, 1980: 272
    pp, hc
Illustrated $17.50

**Southern Living Southern Country
Cookbook**
Sturges, Lena, editor
Oxmoor House, Birmingham, AL, 1975: 409
    pp, hc
Illustrated $15.00

**Southern Living Southern Heritage Breads
Cookbook**
Oxmoor House, Birmingham, AL, 1983: 143
    pp, hc
Illustrated $12.00

**Southern Living Southern Heritage
Company Cookbook**
Oxmoor House, Birmingham, AL, 1983: 143
    pp, hc
Illustrated $12.00

Southfork Ranch Cookbook, The
Terry, Bea
William Morrow, NY, 1982: 270 pp, hc
Dust jacket; first edition $15.00

Soyer's Paperbag Cookery
Soyer, Nicolas
Sturgis and Walton Co., NY, 1911: 130 pp, hc
Illustrated; first edition $20.00

Sparton Recipes
Sparks Withington Co., Jackson, MI, 1937: 24
    pp
Wraps $6.00

Specialites de la Maison
American Friends of France, NY, 1940: 111 pp
Fabric cover; signed celebrity recipes $30.00

Specialty Cookbooks
Ostroff, Harriet, and Nichols, Tom
Garland Publishing, NY, 1992: 659 pp,
    hc $90.00

Spice Cookbook, The
Day, Avanelle, and Stuckey, Lillie
David White Co., NY, 1964: 623 pp, hc
First printing $22.50

Spice Islands Cook Book, The
Lane Book Company, Menlo Park, CA, 1961:
    208 pp, hc
Dust jacket; first edition $20.00

Stag at Ease
Squire, Marian
Caxton Printers Ltd., Caldwell ID, 1938: 164
    pp $45.00

Standard Paper Bag Cookery
Telford, E.
Cupples and Leon Co., 1912: 156 pp, hc
Illustrated $15.00

State Fair Blue Ribbon Cook Book, The
Hurley, Lois, and Groetzinger, Isabelle
Frederick Fell Publishers; New York, NY, 1950:
    256 pp, hc
Dust jacket; very good condition $12.50

Stillroom Cookery
Firth, Grace
EPM Publications, McLean, VA, 1977: 278 pp,
    hc
Illustrated $25.00

Stockton Community Cook Book, The
Ladies of Temple Israel, Stockton, CA, 1924:
    205 pp, hc
Signed recipes; local ads $22.50

Store Cookbook, The
Greene, Bart, and Vaughan, Denis
Henry Regnery Company, Chicago, IL, 1974:
    272 pp, hc
Dust jacket $17.50

**Story of the White House and Its Home Life,
The**
Longworth, Alice Roosevelt
Swinell-Wright Company, Boston, MA, 1937:
    62 pp
Illustrated; advertising $9.00

Storybook Cookbook, The
MacGregor, Carol
Doubleday, Garden City, NY, 1967: 96 pp, hc
Illustrated $12.50

Sugar-Bush Antiques
Vidler, Virginia
A.S. Barnes and Co., NY, 1979: pp, hc 119
Illustrated; dust jacket $22.50

Sumptuous Dining in Gaslight San Francisco
Berger, Frances, and Custis, John
Doubleday, Garden City, NY, 1985: 230 pp, hc
Illustrated; first edition $17.50

Sunday News Cook Book
Petersen, Alice, and Elvin, Ella
Rowman and Littlefield, NY, 1962: 319 pp, hc
Illustrated $20.00

Sunset All-Western Foods Cook Book
Callahan, Genevieve
Lane Publishing, San Francisco, CA, 1947: 284
pp, hc
Illustrated $15.00

Sunset Cook Book of Breads, The
Lane Books, Menlo Park, CA, 1966: 96 pp
Wraps; illustrated $9.00

Sunshine Book, The
Allen, Ida Bailey
Sunshine Bakery
ca. 1920: 32 pp
Wraps; illustrated $5.00

Super Market Cook Book
Barber, Edith
Super Market Publishing Co., NY, 1955: 528
pp, hc $15.00

Suppers and Midnight Snacks
Bradshaw, George
David McKay Company, NY, 1969: 184 pp,
hc $8.00

Table Service
Allen, Lucy G.
Little, Brown Company, Boston, MA, 1915:
128 pp, hc
Illustrated $25.00

Table Settings and Service
Ufford, Helen
Delineator Institute, 1928: 64 pp
Illustrated $4.00

**Table Settings, Entertaining and Etiquette:
History and Guide**
Roberts, Patricia
Viking Press, NY, 1967: 271 pp, hc
Illustrated $16.00

Talisman Italian Cook Book
Boni, Ada
Crown Publishers, NY, 1950: 268 pp, hc
Dust jacket $7.00

Taste of America, The
Hess, Karen and John
Viking, NY, 1977: 384 pp, hc $17.50

Taste of Texas, A
Trahey, Jane
Random House, NY, 1949: 303 pp, hc
Dust jacket; compiled for Neiman-
Marcus $15.00

Tastes of Liberty
Chateau Ste. Michelle, Woodinville, WA,
1985: 256 pp, hc
Illustrated; Statue of Liberty Centennial
book $25.00

**Teakettle: A Collection of Recipes for
Cooking, The**
Fairfield Hall Association, Fairfield, ME, 1889:
58 pp
Wraps $22.50

Tested Receipts
Ladies of the First Baptist Church, New
Bedford, MA, 1913: 141 pp, hc
Signed recipes $40.00

Tested Recipes
New Century Club, Kennett Square, PA,
1925: 104 pp
Wraps; signed recipes; local ads $12.50

**Tested Recipes for the Westinghouse
Refrigerator**
Westinghouse Company, PA, 1930: 34 pp
Wraps; illustrated: guide to using
refrigeration $8.00

Texas Wild Game Cookbook
Morehead, Judith and Richard
Encino Press, Austin, TX, 1972: 81 pp, hc
Dust jacket; first edition $15.00

**Thatched Kitchen Harvest and Holiday
Cookbook, The**
Tested Recipe Publishers, Chicago, IL, 1972:
78 pp, hc
Illustrated $10.00

**The Table: How to Buy Food, How to Cook
It and How to Serve It**
Filippini, Alessandro
Charles L. Webster, NY, 1891: 432 pp, hc
Illustrated $35.00

Things Mother Used To Make
Gurney, Lydia Maria
The Suburban Press, 1912: 110 pp, hc
First edition $15.00

**Things You Always Wanted To Know About
Food & Drink**
McCully, Helen
Holt, Rinehart, Winston; NY, 1972: 248 pp,
hc $12.50

Thoughts for Festive Foods
Institute Publishing Co.
Houghton Mifflin Co., Boston, MA, 1964: 687
pp, hc $12.50

Thousand Ways to Please A Husband, A
Weaver, Louise, and LeCron, Helen
A.L. Burt Company, 1917: 463 pp
Illustrated $35.00

Three Hundred Games and Pastimes
Lucas, E.
Macmillan, NY, 1903: 390 pp, hc
Illustrated $45.00

300 Years of Carolina Cooking
Junior League of Greenville, SC, 1970: 319
pp, hc
First edition $15.00

Thrift Shop Cook Book
Williams, Mrs. John
The Thrift Shop, Washington, DC, 1932:
unpaged
Fabric cover; ring binder $15.00

Time-Life Holiday Cookbook
Time-Life Books, NY, 1976: 315 pp, hc
Illustrated $22.50

To A King's Taste
National Society of the Colonial Dames, New
Orleans, LA, 1952: 191 pp
Spiral; signed recipes $17.50

To Set Before A Queen
McKee, Alice
Simon and Schuster, NY, 1963: 112 pp,
hc $10.00

To The King's Taste
Sass, Lorna
Metropolitan Museum of Art, NY, 1975: 144
pp, hc
Illustrated; first edition $12.50

To Think of Tea!
Repplier, Agnes
Houghton Mifflin Co., Boston, MA, 1932: 208
pp, hc $12.50

Trader Vic's Pacific Island Cookbook
Bergeron, Vic
Doubleday and Company, Garden City, NY,
1968: 287 pp, hc $15.00

Transcendental Boiled Dinner, The
Pullen, John
Lippincott Co., Philadelphia, PA, 1972: 92 pp,
hc
First edition $20.00

Treadway Inns Cook Book
Robbins, Ann Roe
Little, Brown & Co., Boston, MA, 1958: 397
pp, hc
First edition $12.50

**Treasury of Household Hints To Help You
Beat the High Cost, A**
Gore, Michael
Handibook Library, 1948: 128 pp
Wraps; local ads $5.00

**Treatise on Adulterations of Food, A (1820)
(Reprint)**
Accum, Fredrick
Mallinckrodt Chemical Works, St. Louis, MO,
1966: 269 pp
Wraps; slipcase $25.00

Treatise on Baking, A
Wihlfahrt, Julius
Fleischmanns Company, NY, 1928: 364 pp, hc
Illustrated $70.00

Treatise on Cake Making, A
Standard Brands Inc., Fleischmanns Div., NY,
1948: 468 pp, hc
Illustrated $30.00

Treatise on Domestic Economy, A
Beecher, Catharine
Marsh, Capen, Lyon and Webb; Boston, MA,
1841: 441 pp, hc
Illustrated; first edition $80.00

Tried and True from Paint Pot Kitchens
St. Andrews Memorial Episcopal Church,
Yonkers, NY, 1947: 384 pp
Illustrated; spiral bound $15.00

Trinity Treats
Trinity Episcopal Church, Baton Rouge, LA,
1960: 177 pp
Wraps; local ads; signed recipes $10.00

Tullie's Receipts
Atlanta Historical Society, Atlanta, GA, 1976:
232 pp
Wraps; illustrated $10.00

Twentieth Century Book for the Baker
Gienandt, F.L.
Self; Boston, MA, 1927: 268 pp, hc
Illustrated $35.00

**Twentieth Century Cook Book and Practical
Housekeeping**
Smiley Publishing Company; Chicago, IL,
1900: 816 pp, hc
Illustrated $22.50

275 Tested Recipes Cook Book
Ladies of Centre Bennington, Bennington, VT,
1888: 60 pp, hc
Signed recipes $35.00

200 Years of Charleston Cooking
Rhett & Gay
Cape and Smith, NY, 1931: 289 pp, hc
Illustrated $45.00

Two Loaf Givers
Beck, Leonard
Library of Congress, 1984: 223 pp, hc
Illustrated $25.00

Unabridged Vegetable Cookbook
Hazelton, Nika
M. Evans and Co., NY, 1976: 381 pp,
hc $12.50

Uncommon Cook Book, The
Mellinkoff, Ruth
Ward Ritchie Press, Los Angeles, CA, 1968:
277 pp, hc $11.00

Uncooked Foods
Christian, Eugene
Health/Culture Co., New York, 1924: 246 pp,
hc $12.50

Une Affaire de Gout
Harrison, Pegram
Lilly Library; Indiana University, 1983: 110 pp
Wraps; illustrated $5.00

Unitarian Cook Book
Ladies of the Unitarian Society, Saco, ME,
1912: 49 pp $9.00

United States Regional Cook Book, The
Berolzheimer, Ruth
Culinary Arts Press, Chicago, IL, 1947: 752
pp, hc
Illustrated; thumb tabs $25.00

Universal Cook Book, The
1900: 54 pp
Wraps; advertising booklet $4.00

Up to Date Waitress, The
Hill, Janet McKenzie
Little, Brown, and Company, Boston, MA,
1929: 184 pp, hc
Illustrated; very good $40.00

Venus in the Kitchen
Bey, Pilaff
Viking Press, 1953: 192 pp, hc $17.50

Victory Vitamin Cook Book
Harris, Florence
Wm. Penn Publishing Corp., NY, 1943: 185
pp, hc $11.00

Village Cook Book, The
Village Improvement Society, Yarmouth, ME,
1956: 202 pp
Spiral; illustrated; signed recipes $12.50

Virginia City Cook Book, The
Brown, Helen Evans
Ward Ritchie Press, Los Angeles, CA,
148 pp, hc $12.50

Virginia Cookery Book
Virginia League of Women Voters, Richmond,
VA, 1921: 122 pp, hc
Local ads; signed recipes $25.00

Virginia Housekeeper, The (1860) (Reprint)
Randolph, Mary
Avenel Books, NY, ca. 1970: 180 pp,
hc $15.00

Visions of Sugarplums
Sheraton, Mimi
Random House, NY, 1968: 205 pp, hc $12.50

Waldorf Astoria Cookbook, The
James, James, and Cole, Rosalind
Bramhall House, NY, 1981: 274 pp, hc
Illustrated; fiftieth anniversary edition $17.50

Waldorf in the Catskills
Taub, Harold
Sterling Publishing Co., NY, 1952: 248 pp,
hc $15.00

Warren Cook Book
Young Ladies' Missionary Society, Warren, PA,
1903: 272 pc, hc
Signed recipes; advertisements $20.00

Wartime Cooking Guide
Voellmig, Gertrude
Reilly and Lee, Chicago, IL, 1943: 128 pp
Wraps $15.00

Wartime Suggestions
Frigidaire Division of General Motors, Dayton,
OH, 1943: 32 pp
Wraps; advertising booklet $3.00

Watkins Cook Book
J. R. Watkins Co., Winona, MN, 1938: 288 pp
Spiral $49.00

We Gather Together
Humphrey, Theodore and Lin
UMI Research Press, Ann Arbor, MI, 1988:
289 pp
Wraps; illustrated $20.00

Well-Dressed Dessert, The
General Foods Corporation, White Plains, NY,
1969: unpaged
Easel-back binding; illustrated $8.00

Western Barbecue Cookbook
Magee, Ed, and Ainsworth, Clyde
Murray and Gee, Culver City, CA, 1949: 225
pp, hc
First edition $18.00

Western Cooking: Hearty Food for Hungry Folk
McBride, Lois
David McKay Co., NY, 1975: 272 pp,
hc $14.00

Westminster Prebyterian Church Cook Book
Madison, WI, 1936: 57 pp
Wraps $12.50

What Can One Do With A Chafing Dish?
Sawtelle, H.L.
Stilwell and Co., NY, 1889: 76 pp, hc
Local ads; fair condition $35.00

What Cooks in Suburbia
Perl, Lila
E.P. Dutton, NY,
1961: 305 pp
Dust jacket; first edition $15.00

What Salem Dames Cooked in 1700, 1800 & 1900
Esther Mack Industrial School, Salem, MA,
1910: 40 pp
Very good condition $65.00

What's Cooking
Bailey, Jack
World Publishing, NY, 1949: 187 pp, hc
First edition; dust jacket $15.00

What's Cooking in Bermuda
Ross, Betsy
Bermuda Press, Hamilton, Bermuda, 1957: 94
pp
Spiral; local ads; first edition $12.50

What's Cooking on Grosse Ile
St. Anne's Guild; Wyandotte, MI, 1949: 151
pp
Spiral; signed recipes $12.50

When Meals Were Meals
Dickinson, Maude
Thomas Crowell Co., NY, 1967: 185 pp, hc
First edition $15.00

Whistler's Mothers's Cook Book
MacDonald, Margaret
G.P. Putnam's, NY, 1979: 144 pp, hc
Illustrated $22.50

White House Chef Cookbook, The
Verdon, Rene
Doubleday, NY, 1967: 287 pp, hc
Illustrated $15.00

White House Cook Book, The
Ziemann, Hugo, and Gillette, Mrs. F.
The Werner Company, Chicago, IL, 1897: 570
pp, hc
Illustrated $35.00

Who Says We Can't Cook!
Women's National Press Club, Washington,
DC, 1955: 176 pp
Spiral $12.50

Wide, Wide World of Texas Cooking, The
Clark, Morton Gill
Funk & Wagnalls, NY, 1970: 372 pp, hc
Dust jacket $12.50

Williamsburg Art of Cookery, The
Bullock, Helen
Colonial Williamsburg, VA, 1938: 276 pp, hc
Illustrated; signed by author $17.50

Williamsburg Cookbook, The
Colonial Williamsburg Foundation, VA, 1971:
168 pp, hc
Dust jacket; illustrated $15.00

Wine Cook Book, The
Brown, Cora, Rose and Bob
Little, Brown Co., Boston, MA, 1946: 462 pp,
hc $15.00

Wisconsin Country Cookbook and Journal
Heth, Edward
Tamarack Press, Madison, WI, 1979: 238 pp
Wraps $11.00

Wise Encyclopedia of Cookery
William H. Wise & Co., NY, 1978: 1329 pp, hc
Illustrated $17.50

With Bold Knife and Fork
Fisher, M.F.K.
G.P. Putnam's Sons, NY, 1969: 318 pp,
hc $35.00

Wiki Wiki Kau Kau
Kay, Tutu
Watkins Printery, Ltd., Honolulu, HW, 1953:
77 pp
Wraps $12.50

**Wolf and Dessauer Tried and Proved OK
Recipe Book**
Keller, E.F.
E.F. Keller; Fort Wayne, IN, 1914: 448 pp, hc
Illustrated; signed recipes $25.00

Woman's Day Encyclopedia of Cookery
Tighe, Eileen
Woman's Day, NY, 1965: 12 vols., hc
Illustrated $75.00

Woman's Day Old-Fashioned Desserts
Myers, Barbara
Lippincott Company, Philadelphia, PA, 1978:
239 pp, hc
Illustrated; first edition $12.50

**Woman's Evening Club Cook Book: Don't
Diet, Try It**
Woman's Evening Club, Brattleboro, VT,
1964: 100 pp
Spiral; signed recipes $9.00

Woman's Exchange of Memphis Cook Book
Woman's Exchange, Memphis, TN, 1964: 247
pp
Spiral; first edition $12.50

**Woman's Exchange Recipes: Fifty Years of
Good Cooking**
Hough, Stella
Arnold Powers, Detroit, MI, 1946: 189 pp,
hc $15.00

Woman's Home Missionary Society
Woman's Home Missionary Society, Mt.
Carmel, PA, 1905: 116 pp
Local ads; signed recipes $20.00

Woman's World Cook Book
Wallace, Lily Haxworth
Reilly and Lee Co., Chicago, IL, 1931: 468 pp,
hc
Illustrated $25.00

Women's Institute Library of Cookery
Women's Institute of Domestic Arts and
Sciences, PA, 1925: 5 vols., hc
Illustrated $45.00

Wonderful, Wonderful Danish Cooking
Jensen, Ingeborg
Simon and Schuster, NY, 1965: 335 pp,
hc $12.50

Woodstock Cook Book
Buell, Alice S.
Woodstock Historical Society, VT, 1946: 119
pp, hc
Signed recipes $16.00

Working Wives Cook Book, The
Zavin and Stuart
Crown, NY, 1963: 162 pp, hc $8.00

World of Good Eating, A
Frost, Heloise
Phillips Publishers, Newton, MA, 1951: 128
pp
Spiral; illustrated $12.50

Wright County Journal-Press Cook Book
Wright County Journal-Press, Buffalo, MN,
1942: unpaged
Local ads $8.00

Writer's Favorite Recipes
Vincent, Gillian
St. Martin's Press, NY, 1975: 175 pp, hc
Celebrity recipes $17.50

Yankee Hill Country Cooking
Vaughan, Beatrice
Stephen Greene Press, Brattleboro, VT, 1973:
202 pp, hc $11.00

Year Book, Cook Book, and Directory
Raleigh Court Methodist Church, Roanoke,
VA, 1927: 48 pp
Wraps; local ads $8.00

Year-Round Holiday Cookbook, The
Huntley, Suzanne
Atheneum, NY, 1969: 214 pp, hc $7.00

You Can Cook If You Can Read
Fitzsimmons, Muriel and Cortland
Viking Press, NY, 1946: 364 pp, hc
Dust jacket $12.50

Young Housekeeper's Friend, The
Cornelius, Mrs.
Taggard and Thompson, Boston, MA, 1864:
254 pp, hc $55.00

**Young People's Library of Entertainment
and Amusements**
Meek, Thomas
W.E. Schull, 1903: 444 pp, hc
Illustrated $25.00

Your Community Cook Book
Appleton-Century Crofts, 1949: 595 pp, hc
Illustrated; local ads $15.00

Your Kitchen and You
Wyse, Lois
Hoosier Manufacturing Co., Newcastel, IN,
1925: 32 pp
Wraps; illustrated; advertising booklet $12.50

Zabar's Deli Book
Katz, Susan
Hawthorne Books, NY, 1979: 190 pp, hc
Illustrated $12.50

Zane Grey Cookbook
Reiger, Barbara and George
Prentice-Hall, Englewood Cliffs, NJ, 1976: 239
pp, hc
Illustrated $25.00

Zenith Assorted, Gummed Canning Labels
Eureka Specialties; Scranton, PA, 1912: 10 pp
Colorful labels $5.00

Zucchini: the Zucchini Cookbook
Simmons, Paula
Pacific Search, Seattle, WA, 1974: 127 pp
Wraps; signed by author $6.00

Last Ingredients

Cookbook Time Line

It would be impossible to list all the cookbooks that had an effect on cooks, society, and everyday life in general. The following books were milestones in their way; although thousands of cookbooks appeared after 1972 and dozens of new food trends debuted, it seemed appropriate to stop the line at the new *American Cookery* (that is, *James Beard's American Cookery*) and come full circle in the history of American cookbooks. Collectors should never forget, however, that cookbooks that appeared in the bookstore only yesterday will eventually become sought-after additions to a library of cookbook collectibles.

First Century A.D.   *De Re Coquinaria* (The Art of Cooking) appeared, the first known extant cookbook from the Western world. The author, Marcus Apicius, is still something of a mystery; his work was added to and reprinted for nearly 1,700 years.

ca. 1375   Guillaume Tirel (also called Taillevent) wrote *Le Viandier de Guillaume dit Taillevent*, the first cookbook of the medieval period.

ca. 1390   *The Forme of Cury* (The Art of Cooking) appears at the English court of King Richard II. It is the first cookbook written in English.

1475   *De Honesta Voluptate* (Of Honest Indulgence) was written by a Vatican librarian, Platina, using the recipes of Martino, a court cook. This book provides a philosophical look at food in the early Renaissance.

1667	*De Verstandige Kock* (The Sensible Cook) is published in the Netherlands. The book was one of the most popular Dutch cookbooks and influenced cooking in the New World.
ca. 1725	Englishwoman Mary Kettilby publishes *A Collection of Above Three Hundred Receipts in Cookery* . . . , one of the earliest examples of contributed recipe cookbooks and a best-seller of the time. Kettilby advocated simple, plain cooking and encouraged women to be proud of their domestic skills.
1727	Eliza Smith writes *The Compleat Housewife,* an early best-seller in England and the first cookbook to be printed in America (1742).
1747	English cook Hannah Glasse writes and publishes *The Art of Cookery Made Plain and Easy,* a book that would become a popular kitchen manual for nearly fifty years.
1769	*The Experienced English House-Keeper,* by Elizabeth Raffald, a well-known confectioner and baker, is issued; it becomes popular in the colonies even though the recipes are not adapted for use in American kitchens.
1796	*American Cookery,* by Amelia Simmons, is published. It is a "first" on three counts: the first American cookbook, the first American cookbook written by a woman, and the first self-published American cookbook.
1824	*The Virginia House-Wife,* by Mrs. Mary Randolph, offers an early collection of southern specialties.
1827	Robert Roberts' *The House Servant's Directory* is published, the first household book by an African American.
1828	Eliza Leslie's *Seventy-Five Receipts for Pastry, Cakes and Sweetmeats* is published, one of the earliest American cookbooks to list the ingredients separately from the cooking directions.
1829	Lydia Maria Francis Child authors *The American Frugal Housewife* and becomes well-known for her emphasis on common sense and frugality in the home.
1841	Catharine Beecher, sister of Harriet Beecher Stowe, takes up the cause of domestic science in *A Treatise on Domestic Economy.*
1859	*Beeton's Book of Household Management,* by Isabella Beeton of England, becomes one of the most famous and well-used cookbooks to be published. Editions are still appearing under her name.
1864	*A Poetical Cook Book,* by Maria J. Moss, becomes the first cookbook used to raise funds for a charity.
1872	Marion Harland writes *Common Sense in the Household,* a popular cookbook filled with the personal observations and suggestions of a well-known teacher.
1876	Juliet Carson writes *Fifteen Cent Dinners for Workingmen's Families,* an early booklet aimed at cooks on limited budgets.

1877	Charles Francatelli offers his reading public *The Cook's Guide and Housekeeper's & Butler's Assistant,* which is a best-seller both in Europe and America but has little emphasis on American kitchens.
1883	*Mrs. Lincoln's Boston Cook Book,* by Mary Lincoln, brings cooking-school techniques and science to the home kitchen.
1889	*The Epicurean,* by Charles Ranhofer, shows the stylization of American food as chefs continued to copy recipes and service from European kitchens.
1896	Fannie Farmer's *The Boston Cooking-School Cook Book* makes its first appearance; the book, in revised edition, is still popular today.
1901	*The Settlement Cook Book—The Way to a Man's Heart* is used as a way to raise funds for the Settlement house in Milwaukee.
1930	*Two Hundred Years of Charleston Cooking* offers an unusual glimpse into regional kitchens of the past. The book was a popular one in the continuing line of fine southern cookbooks.
1930	*The Better Homes and Gardens New Cook Book* begins selling the first of its eventual 20 million books in print.
1931	*The Joy of Cooking* is formally published (earlier editions were self-published) and becomes a best-seller, with more than 10 million copies sold.
1941	*Army Food and Messing,* a service cookbook, helps to codify cooking for large groups of people under trying circumstances.
1949	*A Date with a Dish,* by Freda DeKnight, food editor for *Ebony* magazine, begins to explore African-American foods and traditions.
1949	The first Pillsbury baking contest occurs (the contest is eventually renamed the "Pillsbury Bake-Off"). The cookbooks that are issued after each contest are popular collector's items.
1950	*Charleston Receipts,* the earliest and one of the best-selling Junior League cookbooks, is published in South Carolina.
1952	Poppy Cannon writes *The Can Opener Cookbook,* which glorifies the ease and convenience of canned foods. The book went through several versions, ending with *The New New Can Opener Cookbook.*
1955	*The Super Market Cook Book* celebrates a quarter century of grocery shopping.
1961	*What Cooks in Suburbia* offers recipes for a typical housewife's menu.
1961	*Mastering the Art of French Cooking,* by Simone Beck, Louisette Bertholle, and Julia Child, helps to convince American cooks that sophisticated European food is within their reach.

1961	The *I Hate to Cook Book,* by Peg Bracken, becomes a best-seller, as some people finally admit to disliking spending time in the kitchen.
1968	Time-Life Books begins its series about foods of the world; twelve volumes focus on American regional foods.
1972	*James Beard's American Cookery* helps focus new interest on the traditional and newer foods of this country.

Measurements from Old Cookbooks

Sometimes when it comes to "translating" older recipes, the cook is stumped by a reference to a vague or incomprehensible measurement: butter the size of an egg, a peck of tomatoes, a wineglass of milk. In the past, ingredients were often weighed on scales or poured out in pewter measures. Even the old cooks couldn't agree: a teaspoon is variously described in old cookbooks as being between 25 and 45 drops. The following list has been compiled from many antique sources (when a discrepancy occurred, the average measurement was used) and may be of help to someone who is trying to make an antique "receipt" work.

pinch	1⁄16 teaspoon
few grains	less than 1⁄8 teaspoon
1 nutmeg grated	1 tablespoon
1 lemon	1 teaspoon strained juice
25 drops	1 teaspoon
2 coffee spoons	1 teaspoon
2 teaspoons	1 dessert spoon
2 dessert spoons	1 tablespoon
2 salt spoons	1 coffee spoon
3 teaspoons (dry)	1 tablespoon
4 teaspoons (liquid)	1 tablespoon
2 tablespoons	1 ounce
shot or jigger	1 ounce
jar	3 ounces
1 dram	1⁄8 ounce or 3 scruples
16 drams	1 ounce
butter the size of an egg	2 ounces
butter the size of a walnut	1 tablespoon
butter the size of a hazelnut	1 teaspoon
anything the size of a half-crown	1 teaspoon
16 ounces	1 pound
1 wineglass	1⁄4 cup
1⁄2 gill	4 tablespoons
1 gill	1⁄2 cup

Information in this section courtesy of Heritage Publications, *Just Cookbooks;* used by permission.

1 teacup	¾ cup
1 coffee cup	1 cup
1 tumbler	1 cup or 2 gills
1 sherry glass	½ gill
1–2 wineglasses	1 gill
5 sherry or whiskey bottles	1 gallon
4 gills	1 pint
1 pint	2 cups
1 quart	4 cups
1 peck	2 gallons, dry
1 cake (8 squares) chocolate	½ pound
1 pint (2 cups) chopped meat	1 pound
2⅓ cups Crisco	1 pound
2 cups finely chopped suet	1 pound
10 eggs without shells	1 pound
8 medium-size eggs with shells	1 pound
1 pint milk or water	1 pound
2 cups butter, solid	1 pound
5 cups of sifted flour	1 pound
4 cups whole wheat flour	1 pound
3 cups, scant, corn meal	1 pound
2⅔ cups oatmeal	1 pound
6 cups rolled oats	1 pound
4⅓ cups rye meal	1 pound
1⅞ cups rice	1 pound
2⅔ cups brown sugar	1 pound
3 cups sugar	1 pound
1 cup raisins or currants	1 pound
4 cups shelled walnuts	1 pound
2 tablespoons ground spice	1 ounce
penny roll	2″–3″ hard roll
emptin cakes	hard yeast cakes or equivalent
isinglass or hartshorn	unflavored gelatin
saleratus	baking soda

TABLE OF PROPORTIONS

1 cup liquid to 3 cups flour for bread	¼ teaspoon salt to 4 cups custard
1 cup liquid to 2 cups flour for muffins	2 teaspoons salt to 4 cups water
1 cup liquid to 1 cup flour for batters	¼ teaspoon salt to 1 cup white sauce
1 teaspoon soda to 1 pint sour milk	⅛ teaspoon pepper to 1 cup white sauce
1 teaspoon soda to 1 cup molasses	

OVEN TEMPERATURES

very slow oven	225°F–250°F	hot oven	350°F–400°F
slack or slow oven	250°F–300°F	quick oven	400°F–450°F
moderate oven	300°F–350°F	very hot oven	450°F–500°F

CAN SIZES

Information in parentheses indicates alternate name for cans.

No. ½ flat	1 cup	No. 303	2 cups
No. 8Z Tall (8 oz.)	1 cup	No. 2	2½ cups
No. 300	1¾ cups	No. 2½	3½ cups
No. 1 (picnic)	1¼ cups	No. 3 cylinder (46 oz.)	5¾ cups
No. 1 Tall	2 cups	No. 10	12 cups
No. 300	1¾ cups		

Sources

SOURCES FOR COOKBOOKS AND EPHEMERA

The following dealers, shops, and auctions are sources for out-of-print and rare cookbooks and ephemera. Many charge a fee for their catalogs and booklists, so write for information.

AB Bookman's Weekly, PO Box AB, Clifton, NJ 07015. Weekly magazine for the book collecting world; offers a special cookbook issue once a year. Excellent guide to out-of-print and rare books.

Astor House Books, Box 1701, Williamsburg, VA 23187. Issues catalogs and does book searches.

Books for Cooks, 4 Blenheim Crescent, London W11 1NN. Comprehensive source for out-of-print cookbooks, including American, United Kingdom, and European books.

Bookseller, PO Box 8183, Ann Arbor, MI 48107. Published twenty-four times a year, this oversized newsletter is filled with the names of book searchers, dealers, and collectors in search of specific books.

Buy Books Where, Sell Books Where. An annual directory listing people who sell and buy specialties, including cookbooks. For information write to Ruth E. Robinson Books, Rt. 7, Box 162A, Morgantown, WV 26505.

The Cookbook Collectors' Exchange, PO Box 32369, San Jose, CA 95152-2369. Publishes a newsletter for cookbook collectors; includes many buyers and sellers.

Cook Book, PO Box 88, Steuben ME 04680. A newsletter subtitled "The Food Book Review for Cooks Who Read." An outstanding source about cookbooks. Write for subscription information.

Cooks Books, 34 Marine Drive, Rottingdean, Sussex, BN27HQ, England. Offers a detailed catalog of both European and American cookbooks. Fine source.

The Cook's Library, 8373 W. Third St., Los Angeles, CA 90048. Issues cookbook catalogs.

Cornucopia, RD Box 2108, Edge Road, Syosset, NY 11791. The owner specializes in food and etiquette books; catalogs are issued.

Editions, Route 28, Boiceville, NY 12414. Offers catalogs containing dozens of out-of-print cookbooks—mostly mid- to late twentieth century, but also some unusual items.

Steve Finer, Box 758, Greenfield, MA 01302. Offers catalogs that include cookery and domestic subjects.

Barbara Gelink, 4756 Terrace Drive, San Diego, CA 92116. Offers search service and catalogs of out-of-print cookbooks.

Marian L. Gore, Bookseller, PO Box 433, San Gabriel, CA 91778. Offers excellent catalogs on food and beverages.

Hoppin' John's, 30 Pinckney St., Charleston, SC 29401. (803) 577-6932. Both southern cookbooks and other regional specialties are found here.

Household Words, PO Box 7231, Berkeley, CA 94747. Cookery and beverage books, ephemera, and cookbook-related publications are found in the occasional catalogs from this company.

Kay's Treasured Kookbook Kollection, Box 17, Kenilworth, IL 60043. Offers searches for out-of-print books.

Kitchen Arts and Letters, 1435 Lexington Avenue, New York, NY 10128. This unusual shop stocks a wide range of cookbooks and food-related art and issues booklists for mail order; there is also a search service.

MCL Associates, PO Box 26, McLean, VA 22101-0026. Issues catalogs.

Much Ado, Seven Pleasant Street, Marblehead, MA 01945. (617) 639-0400. Publishes delightful catalogs and a newsletter, usually with many culinary selections.

Oinonen Book Auctions, PO Box 470, 9 School Street, Sunderland, MA 01375. Offers some mail auctions that contain rare, unusual cookbooks; issues auction catalogs.

Oxford Books, 2395 Peachtree Road, Atlanta, GA 30305. Issues booklists; one of the largest out-of-print bookstores in the south.

Dick Perier Books, PO Box 1, Vancouver, WA 98666. Issues booklists of cookbooks and culinary publications.

Powell's Books for Cooks, 3739 SE Hawthorne Blvd., Portland, OR 97202. (503) 235-3802. Excellent source for cookbooks; offers catalogs.

Rainy Day Books, Box 775, Fitzwilliam, NH 03447. Offers catalog containing cookbook and ephemera collectibles.

Charlotte Safir, 1349 Lexington Avenue, #9B, New York, NY 10128. Specializes in cookbook searches for books from the eighteenth century to the present; write to ask for particular cookbooks.

Second Life Books, Inc., PO Box 242, 55 Quarry Road, Lanesborough, MA 01237. Catalogs are issued in several fields, including agriculture, horticulture, and women's issues; offers books and ephemera.

Barbara E. Smith, Books, PO Box 1185, Northampton, MA 01061. Issues catalogs of out-of-print and unusual cookbooks.

Swann Galleries, 104 East 25th Street, New York, NY 10010. One of the largest book auctioneers in the country, they allow mail bids at their auctions, which sometimes include rare cookbooks and ephemera. Write and ask to receive the company's free newsletter about upcoming sales, and the brochure "Selling and Buying at Swann Auctions."

The Wine and Food Library, 1207 West Madison, Ann Arbor, MI 48103. Issues excellent catalogs about food, wine, and the gastronomic arts. Also offers a search service. One of the outstanding cookbook sources in the world.

SOURCES FOR ARCHIVAL AND RECORD-KEEPING MATERIALS

These companies can fulfill the archival and record-keeping needs of individual collectors, as well as libraries. Write or call for catalogs and list prices.

Brodart, PO Box 3037, 1609 Memorial Avenue, Williamsport, PA 17705. 1-800-233-8959. Offers a comprehensive catalog of library and archival products, from acid-free folders to open shelving systems.

Conservation Materials, 1165 Marietta Way, Sparks, NV 89431. (702) 331-0582. Offers a catalog for conservation professionals that may also be purchased by collectors.

Heritage Publications, PO Box 335, Arkville, NY 12406. (914) 586-3810. Publishes a cookbook registry with detailed forms on which to record collection information.

Talas, 213 West 35th Street, New York, NY 10001. (212) 736-7744. Offers an extensive catalog of archival materials; issues price lists.

University Products Inc., 517 Main Street, PO Box 101, Holyoke, MA 01041-0101. 1-800-628-1912 (outside MA); 1-800-336-4847 (in MA). Offers catalog listing hundreds of items needed for conservation of books and ephemera, including acid-free paper and boxes, book covers, cleaning and storage materials, and conservation guides.

American Cookbook Libraries

So what does a cookbook collector do if she or he wants to enjoy a glimpse of a rare edition of *American Cookery* or the first issue of *The Joy of Cooking?* Head to the library. Of course, not just any library, but one of the dozens across the United States that have extensive cookbook holdings, from the rare to the mundane. Some of these libraries require permission for use, while others welcome browsers and readers of all types, so it is best to call ahead and ask about individual library policies. In addition to the libraries listed here, many others have excellent cookbook sections, including university and college libraries, historical associations, and state libraries, some of which have less stringent use requirements; a check of local sources may surprise you with what is available for reading and research on your own collection.

EAST

The American Antiquarian Society (185 Salisbury Street, Worcester, MA 01609, 508-755-5221) has more than 1,000 cookbooks from the Waldo Lincoln collection. Many of the volumes predate the 1870s; books in the collection span the seventeenth to the nineteenth centuries. The Schlesinger Library at Radcliffe College (Ten Garden Street, Cambridge, MA 02138, 617-495-8647) is the repository of thousands of cookbooks and manuscript materials (9,000 volumes) including many charity cookbooks. At the Millbank Memorial Library (Teachers College, Columbia University, 525 West 120th Street, NY 10027, 212-768-3031) over 1,000 rare volumes, including European and American cookbooks and culinaria, are available for research. Hotel and restaurant management are the focus of the Hotel Administration Library (Statler Hall, Cornell University, Ithaca, NY 14835, 607-255-3673), with more than 18,000 volumes and manuscripts on food and food preparation. they also maintain an extensive collection of menus from the nineteenth and twentieth centuries. The Culinary Institute of America (Katherine Angell Library), Route 9, Hyde Park, NY 12538, 914-452-9600) has a large cookbook collection, containing many hard-to-find modern cookbooks and videos. An unusual source for rare cookbooks and ephemera is the New York Academy of Medicine Rare Book Room (2 East 103 Street, New York, NY 10029, 212-876-8200), where volumes cover everything from nutrition to cooking, including many pre-nineteenth-century examples. One of the largest sources of cookbooks is found at the New York Public Library Science and Technology Research Center (Fifth Avenue at 42nd St., Room 121, 212-930-0573), where nearly 15,000 cookbooks and 25,000 pieces of culinary ephemera are available for perusal. The collection's heart is the Helen Hay Whitney Collection of cookbooks. Ephemera collectors with an interest in menus should try to visit the New York Historical Society (170 Central Park West, New York, NY 10024-5194, 212-873-3400), which has examples from eighteenth, nineteenth, and twentieth centuries.

SOUTH

The Rare Books and Special Collections Division of the Library of Congress (First and Independence Avenues SE, Washington, DC 20540, 202-707-5435) houses the Katherine Bitting and Elizabeth Pennel collections of gastronomy and culinary publications. Included in the collections are a "musical" cookbook, in which the recipes may be sung, and cookbooks from the Italian Renaissance. Many cookbooks of the eighteenth century, including American examples, are located at the Hugh M. Morris Library of the University of Delaware (South College Avenue, Newark, DE 19711, 302-831-2965). In North Carolina, volumes on southern cooking may be found at the Jackson Library (University of North Carolina, 1000 Spring Garden Street, Greensboro, NC 27412).

MIDWEST

At the Home Economics Library of Ohio State University (Campbell Hall, 1787 Neil Avenue, Columbus, OH 43210), a wide selection of cookbooks, old and new, are available for reading and research. Louis Szathmary, a chef and dedicated cookbook collector, donated his library of more than 20,000 historic books and selections of ephemera to the University of Iowa Library (Iowa City, IA, 319-335-3500), where the new Szathmary Collection of Culinary Arts is now housed for researchers and cookbook readers alike. In Michigan, two libraries have excellent culinary collections: the Detroit Public Library, Rare Books Division (5201 Woodward Avenue, Detroit, MI 48202) and the Michigan State University Library (East Lansing, MI 48824, 517-355-2344) include selections from early English and American cookery books. The Lilly Library (Indiana University, Bloomington, IN 47405, 821-855-2452) is home to the Gernon Collection, with more than 1,200 books and pamphlets on cooking from the fifteenth century on, with an emphasis on European food. In Milwaukee, the Milwaukee Public Library (814 West Wisconsin Avenue, Milwaukee WI 53233) has a large collection of regional American cookery books.

SOUTHWEST AND WEST

For lovers of charity cookbooks, Bralley Memorial Library (Texas Woman's University, Box 23715, TWU Station, Denton, TX 76294) has the Margaret Cook and the Mrs. Thomas M. Scruggs Collections, along with culinary ephemera (over 19,000 pieces). Historic cookbooks, pamphlets, and menus and an unusual selection of culinary magazines of the nineteenth and twentieth centuries form the core collection at the Alice Statler Library (Hotel and Restaurant Department, City College of San Francisco, 50 Phelan Avenue, San Francisco, CA 94112, 415-239-3460).

Bibliography

The following books were consulted in the preparation of *Cookbooks Worth Collecting;* only those cookbooks not identified in the text are listed here. This bibliography also provides an excellent reading list for anyone interested in learning more about cookbook and culinary history.

American Heritage Cookbook and Illustrated History of American Eating and Drinking. 2 vols. New York: American Heritage, 1964.

Aresty, Esther. *The Delectable Past.* New York: Simon and Schuster, 1964.

Barile, Mary. *Just Cookbooks: A Directory to the World of American Cookbooks.* New York: Heritage Publications, 1991.

Beck, Leonard. *Two Loaf Givers.* Washington, D.C.: Library of Congress, 1984.

Better Homes and Gardens. *Better Homes and Gardens Heritage Cookbook.* 1975.

Brown, Eleanor and Bob. *Culinary Americana: Cookbooks published in the cities and towns of the United States of America during the years from 1860 through 1960.* New York: Roving Eye Press, 1961.

Bullock, Helen. *The Williamsburg Art of Cookery.* Williamsburg, Va.: Colonial Williamsburg Foundation, 1938.

Camp, Charles. *American Foodways: What, When, Why and How We Eat in America.* Arkansas: August House, 1989.

Carson, Jane. *Colonial Virginia Cooking.* Williamsburg, Va.: 1985

Carter, John. *ABC for Book Collectors.* New York: Alfred A. Knopf, 1981.

Cook, Margaret. *America's Charitable Cooks: A Bibliography of Fund-Raising Cook Books Published in the United States, 1861–1915.* Ohio: Cookery Bibliography, 1971.

Coyle, Patrick. *Cooks' Books: An Affectionate Guide to the Literature of Food and Cooking.* New York: Facts on File Publications, 1985.

Dee, Ann Patterson, ed. *The Four Star American Community Cookbook,* Pa.: Running Press, 1988.

Driver, Elizabeth. *A Bibliography of Cookery Books Published in Britain 1875–1914.* London and New York: Prospect Books, 1989.

Egerton, John. *Southern Food: At Home, On the Road, In History.* New York: Alfred A. Knopf, 1987.

Fennelly, Catherine, ed. *Food, Drink and Recipes of Early New England.* Old Sturbridge Village, Mass.: 1963.

Freeman, Sarah. *Isabella and Sam: The Story of Mrs. Beeton.* New York: Coward, 1978.

Gourley, James. *Regional American Cookery 1881–1934.* New York: New York Public Library, 1936.

Grover, Kathryn, ed. *Dining in America 1850–1900.* Amherst, Mass.: University of Massachusetts Press, and Rochester, N.Y.: The Margaret Woodbury Strong Museum, 1987.

Haller, Margaret. *The Book Collector's Fact Book.* New York: Arco Publishing Company, 1976.

Harrison, Molly. *The Kitchen in History.* New York: Charles Scribner's, 1972.

Harrison, Pegram. *Une Affaire de Gout: A Selection of Cookbooks: 1475 to 1873.* Indiana University, Ind.: Lilly Library, 1983.

Hess, Karen. *Martha Washington's Booke of Cookery.* New York: Columbia University Press, 1982.

Hess, Karen and John. *The Taste of America.* New York: Viking, 1977.

Hibben, Sheila. *American Regional Cookery.* Boston: Little, Brown & Co., 1946.

———. *The National Cookbook.* New York: Harper & Bros., 1932.

Internal Revenue Service. *Determining the Value of Donated Property.* Publication 561. 1991.

Jones, Evans. *American Food: The Gastronomic Story.* NY, 1975.

Longone, Janice and Daniel. *American Cookbooks and Wine Books, 1797–1950.* Ann Arbor, Mich.: University of Michigan, 1984.

Lowenstein, Eleanor. *Bibliography of American Cookery Books, 1742–1860.,* Mass.: American Antiquarian Society, 1972.

Lowry, Marcia Duncan. *Preservation and Conservation in the Small Library.* Chicago, Ill.: American Library Association, 1989.

Maclean, Virginia. *A Short-title Catalogue of Household and Cookery Books Published in the English Tongue 1701–1800.* London: Prospect Books, 1981.

Mariani, John. *The Dictionary of American Food and Drink.:* Ticknor & Fields, 1983.

Montagne, Prosper. *Larousse Gastronomique.* New York: Crown, 1961.

Quayle, Eric. *Old Cook Books.* New York: 1978.

Roberts, Robert. *Roberts' Guide for Butlers and Other Household Staff.* New York: Charles S. Francis, 1827. Reprinted by Applewood Books, 1989.

Rose, Peter. *The Sensible Cook: Dutch Foodways in the Old and the New World.* Syracuse, N.Y.: Syracuse University Press, 1989.

Rudkin, Margaret. *The Margaret Rudkin Pepperidge Farm Cookbook.* New York: Atheneum, 1963.

Shapiro, Laura. *Perfection Salad: Women and Cooking at the Turn of the Century.* New York: Henry Holt, 1986.

Simmons, Amelia. *The First American Cookbook: A Facsimile of American Cookery, 1796.* New York: Dover, 1984 reprint.

Spurling, Hilary. *Elinor Fettiplace's Receipt Book: Elizabethan Country House Cooking.* New York: Viking, 1986.

Stryker-Rodda, Harriet. *Understanding Colonial Handwriting,* Md.: Genealogical Publishing Co., 1986.

Vaughan, Beatrice. *The Ladies Aid Cookbook.* Burlington, Vt.: Stephen Greene Press, 1971.

Vehling, Joseph, ed. *Apicius: Cookery and Dining in Imperial Rome.* New York: Dover, 1977 reprint.

Visser, Margaret. *The Rituals of Dinner.* New York: Grove Weidenfeld, 1991.

Wason, Betty. *Cooks, Gluttons & Gourmets: A History of Cookery.* New York: Doubleday, 1962.

Weaver, William Woys. *America Eats—Forms of Edible Folk Art.* New York: Harper and Row, 1989.

Willan, Anne. *Great Cooks and Their Recipes: From Taillevent to Escoffier.* New York: McGraw-Hill, 1977.

Williams, Susan. *Savory Suppers and Fashionable Feasts: Dining in Victorian America.* New York: Pantheon, 1985.

Index